ACHIEVING EXCELLENCE IN HIGH PERFORMANCE SPORT

£1

ACHIEVING EXCELLENCE IN HIGH PERFORMANCE SPORT

THE EXPERIENCES AND SKILLS BEHIND THE MEDALS

TIM KYNDT AND SARAH ROWELL

BLOOMSBURY

Note

While every effort has been made to ensure that the content of this book is as technically accurate and as sound as possible, neither the authors nor the publishers can accept responsibility for any injury or loss sustained as a result of the use of this material.

Published by Bloomsbury Publishing Plc
50 Bedford Square
London WC1B 3DP
www.bloomsbury.com

First edition 2012

Copyright © 2012 Tim Kyndt and Sarah Rowell

ISBN (print): 978-1-4081-7210-0
ISBN (e-pub): 978-1-4081-8215-4
ISBN (e-pdf): 978-1-4081-8214-7

Acknowledgements
Cover photographs: front © Getty; back © Shutterstock
Inside photographs: © Shutterstock, except pp. 1 and 6 © Jared Deacon; pp. 18, 22 and 27 © **sport**scotland institute of sport; pp. 35 and 40 © Sander van der Borch/Artemis Racing; pp. 55, 67 (left), 93, 98, 146, 151 and 180 © English Insitute of Sport; p. 61 © Paul Brice; p. 67 (right) © Nova International, photo by Dan Vernon; pp. 74 and 81 © Sarah Rowell and Tim Kyndt; p. 110 © Nigel Mitchell; pp. 127 and 132 © Deirdre Angella; pp. 163 and 167 © Jurg Gotz; p. 186 © Getty; pp. 198 and 203 © EHB/Ady Kerry. Illustrations for pp. x, 11, 52, 125, 194, by Dave Gardner.
Commissioned by Kirsty Schaper
Edited by Nick Ascroft

This book is produced using paper that is made from wood grown in managed, sustainable forests. It is natural, renewable and recyclable. The logging and manufacturing processes conform to the environmental regulations of the country of origin.

Typeset in 10pt Minion by Saxon Graphics Ltd., Derby

Printed and bound by CPI Group (UK) Ltd, Croydon, CR0 4YY

CONTENTS

FOREWORD

Over the years of competing internationally, I've had the privilege of getting to know a large number of athletes from a wide range of sports. They are a group of inspiring, driven individuals and as diverse in their characters as they are in their sports. There are, however, a few things that unite them. One of these is that no matter how confident, how experienced, how successful, how ambitious they are, none of them claim to have succeeded on their own. Credit is always given to the people behind the scenes: the wider team, the people who don't often get the public recognition or share the limelight. Without their support the medals, the awards, the successes of the athletes would be a lot tougher to come by and in many cases might never have been achieved.

I have worked closely throughout my career with that wider team of support staff, and as the expectation of my performance has increased, so has my expectation of the people I work with. It might seem an unfair expectation, but as a world-class athlete I want to work with a world-class team to push me, support me, challenge me and inspire me. I consider myself incredibly lucky that in this country we have a vast wealth of talent in fields such as psychology, strength and conditioning, physiotherapy, nutrition, and biomechanics. There is clear pride in being a valuable part of a successful team. It is not only athletes who want to lead the way in their sport. Support teams too are often leaders in their own field and have as much drive, determination and ambition to push the barriers as the athletes have. I have been repeatedly impressed with the passion, the excellence, the performance, the honesty, the genuine care, the values and the communication skills of those I work with. Athletes respect individuals who have clear values of their own, who can build trusting relationships, who are strong but not unyielding and, crucially, who have the ability to see the athlete as a whole person, not just a sportsperson.

These skills are not always easily acquired. One of the toughest things to handle is the transition from a learning situation to the practical application of what has been learned. Practitioners can learn the theory of their job in the classroom, but it is far more difficult to learn how to work in a high-performing team with multiple interrelated parts with often apparently competing interests, all under enormous stress in high-pressure situations. How, for example, do you balance the needs of overtired athletes with the demands of determined coaches when they conflict and you are the person caught in the middle?

There are hundreds of practitioners working in sport who have the right level of theoretical and practical technical knowledge of their discipline, whether it is coaching, science or medicine, but as Tim and Sarah explain in this book, it is how you apply these skills, how you work with other people, and having a strong understanding of self that makes a truly great practitioner. I have had the pleasure of seeing the work that Tim and Sarah do in developing practitioners at the start of their high-performance career, and this book is a great adjunct to that.

I would recommend that anyone who wants to work in high-performance sport reads it not only to get a better understanding of the wonderful but hard world they want to enter, but most importantly to get a true understanding of the skills you need to be successful in it.

For people already working in this area, I urge you to keep trying for more: never to feel that you have done enough or achieved sufficient. Keep improving, keep learning. There's always more that can be done. For those starting out in this field, I would say you are at the start of a fantastic journey, and how that journey unfolds and where it leads is up to you. Use the skills you have been taught and listen to the voices in this book while asking yourself what you would do in each situation. Get to know yourself, challenge yourself and set no limits on yourself. Everything that has gone before can be bettered and this is your opportunity to make that difference.

Katherine Grainger: multiple Olympic medallist, Rowing

INTRODUCTION

Achieving excellence as a coach, sports science or sports medicine practitioner or other member of the support team in high-performance sport requires you to have excellent technical or discipline-specific skills. But those skills alone are not enough. Under the intense pressures of elite sport, certain coaches and applied practitioners are able to thrive and deliver outstanding support that helps those athletes they work alongside to reach the podium. However, many others with equal technical prowess, falter and fail. The difference between these successes and failures is often laid at the door of so-called non-technical skills, as though these skills were a separate discipline to the technical ones. The reality is quite different. This book is therefore for anyone interested in, or currently developing a career in, high-performance sport.

Technical and non-technical skills are two sides of the same coin: together – and only together – they deliver the excellence that remains beyond reach if the two were dissociated. The market knows this and that is why employers are looking for people who have not only the technical skills, but also the skills to best deliver them. Performance directors, institutes of sport and national governing bodies all want coaches and applied practitioners who have more to offer than just their technical excellence. They place greater value on those with the skills that enable them to deliver their technical services in a way that supports and ultimately helps to enhance the athletes' performances.

WHAT THIS BOOK COVERS

Aspiring practitioners and coaches need to be able quickly to gain the trust, confidence and collaboration of the athlete as well as the rest of the support team. That requires excellence in interpersonal skills and those with that level of expertise tend to rise to the top in high-performance sport.

Interpersonal skills are best viewed as the scaffolding that supports, indeed enhances the delivery of our technical skills. They are the people skills: how we relate to others and how we build effective working relationships with them, as well as how we as individuals cope with factors like additional pressure and stress. These skills develop from an understanding of our own personality, our values, our motivations, our emotions and our behaviours. This self-awareness enables us to raise our technical game in many areas, such as communicating, influencing, teamwork, managing conflict, performing under pressure, inspiring, managing change and leading others. However, the truth is that for many technical people, these interpersonal techniques can be hard to master. Like any technique, some people appear to be more naturally gifted, but everyone can develop them to the level of a skill. Those that do, have a clear source of advantage in reaching the highest positions working with Olympic, Paralympic and professional sports.

Achieving Excellence in High-Performance Sport is the manual to help you understand and develop your interpersonal skills to enable you to deliver your technical skills with distinction. It is designed to help ensure that you have the non-technical skills required to enable you to optimise the delivery of your technical ones. The book provides a way to explore how these skills can advance your career through a combination of case studies, interpersonal techniques and practical exercises. The case studies are based on interviews with 12 coaches and applied practitioners from across the UK's high-performance system, all of whom have already demonstrated their expertise working 'behind the medals'. The interpersonal techniques and practical exercises are informed by our experience of working with numerous applied practitioners, coaches, managers and performance directors across Olympic, Paralympic and professional sport. They are a distillation of our experience of designing and delivering successful training courses to hundreds of applied practitioners, coaches, administrators and directors since 2004. This has given us a unique and privileged insight into the key skills that help people advance and succeed in this competitive environment.

HOW THIS BOOK IS STRUCTURED

The structure of this book enables you to dip in and out wherever you choose. However, the skills are covered in a progressive manner: those skills that are describedtowards the end of the book are best acquired and practised with an understanding of the underpinning techniques covered at the beginning of the book (as illustrated opposite). This system of deconstructing complex and advanced skills into their component interpersonal techniques has helped many of the people whose development we have supported within the high-performance system.

OUR INTERVIEWEES

Our interviewees are drawn from a range of sports practitioner disciplines across the Olympic and Paralympic sports. They also bring a perspective from their experience in professional sport as well as in high-performance systems in other countries. All the interviewees generously agreed to be part of this book and they sought neither recognition nor recompense. They were merely content to share their story, on the understanding that it may be of use to those earlier on in their careers. The 12 people interviewed for this book are all distinct individuals: they have trodden different paths to excellence and made diverse contributions to the success of some of the world's most successful athletes and teams. They have an impressive range of skills, yet they also display some qualities in common. For one, they all remain determined

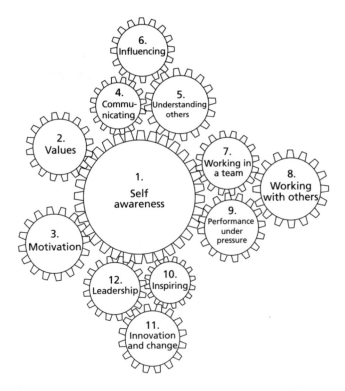

FIG. 0.1 Skills covered in later chapters build on techniques covered in earlier chapters

to the pursuit of excellence in their careers, to which they often dedicate their energy at considerable personal cost to their private lives. For another, none of them is self-seeking in their endeavours and their humility is evident.

Humility should not be mistaken for false modesty. All of our interviewees have a legitimate confidence based on their knowledge that they are world-aspiring if not already world-leading in their chosen field, as is evidenced by the quotations about them in the book from others. Yet they are not complacent, as they all continue to develop their skills to an even higher level, particularly the very ones covered in this book. They realise that high-performance sport is a global enterprise and that nations seek competitive advantage from whatever intervention offers the marginal gain that gets their athletes on the podium. There is an increasing line of evidence that as the medal quest of elite sport accelerates and intensifies across the world, the advance of interpersonal skills provides a source of competitive advantage that has yet to be fully mined.

We hope that this book both enthuses and supports you in your own quest for excellence, as well as giving you the practical tools and the confidence to make your impact in the world of high-performance sport.

CASE STUDY: KNOWING YOURSELF

JARED DEACON

Central Lead for Strength and Conditioning, English Institute of Sport

FIG. 1.1 Jared Deacon

In the build-up to the London 2012 Olympic and Paralympic Games, there was a phrase that worked its way through the world of elite sport: 'podium athletes need podium coaches + podium support staff'.

In other words, for athletes to get their hands on those coveted London 2012 medals, they needed coaches and support staff that were the best in the world at what they did. If there were podia for both coaches and support staff, then the people contributing to the athletes' success would rightly be invited to step onto them.

One person in the GB system has a rare perspective on all three of these provinces from first-hand experience. He has certainly earned a place on at least one of those podia and is a contender for the other two. He is Jared Deacon, a Commonwealth and European 400m athletics gold medallist, an English Institute of Sport (EIS) strength and conditioning coach and, until recently, UK Athletics development coach (sprints and hurdles). We apologise now to Jared for highlighting his ability to transition across his careers first as an athlete, then as a sport scientist, then as a coach and now as sports scientist again – he probably won't thank us for labelling him in that way. He stated quite categorically in his interview with us: 'I just want to be known as "Jared the person", not "Jared the half-decent ex-athlete" or "Jared the coach".'

It is not just a humility that is behind that statement; there is also Jared's belief that there is a more important consistency in everything he does, or as he puts it: 'Drive, determination, motivation, pride, living and breathing it, never accepting that good was good enough.' So that is why we make the point about his multiple careers. For whether he was an athlete, strength and conditioning coach or an athletics coach, these have been and remain the qualities and values that drive the man. In whatever he does.

And this is what makes Jared such an interesting and fitting start to *Achieving Excellence in High-Performance Sport*. Any high-performance journey that has even half a chance of succeeding, must start with the desire and courage to develop high self-awareness – the ability to develop a clear understanding of your values, personality, emotions and motives. If you really understand what drives you, what makes you tick, you are far more likely to be able to summon the drive from within, the 'true grit' that you will undoubtedly need during the hard times. As a coach, this is now something that Jared works hard to instil in his athletes – but that is jumping too far ahead in the story.

Jared Deacon started his quest to stand on the podium at a later age than most, training in earnest only at the age of 15. By then he was familiar with the athletics track, as his Dad and brothers were all runners, training at the same time as such luminaries as Steve Cram and David Sharpe. While some of Jared's earliest memories are of being around an athletics track, Jared says that there was no 'ignition'[1] moment that spurred him on to the next level of dedication to his training. He just enjoyed the camaraderie of being around the track. He didn't need to be motivated by anyone or anything:

It was a self-motivational thing. I got support in what I was doing, but it was always down to me. I never felt any pressure from my parents at all. When I was competing, I never felt that I was competing for anyone else other than myself.

FIRST-HAND VIEW

What makes Jared a world-class practitioner? He has a constant thirst for knowledge and is not afraid to ask around in order to obtain this. Unlike many coaches who believe that they possess 'secrets' that no one else is allowed to know, Jared is more than happy to share anything he does with anyone. He's one of the most genuine people I know and you appreciate the time he puts into coaching you so much more.

David Riley
Athlete

Even so, Jared acknowledges the substantial coaching support of his brother Dave, 11 years older than him:

> He was always there. He took me [as my coach] from 60 seconds to 45 seconds.

There was still that unambiguous core drive, which Jared recalls from those early days at the track:

> It was very much about being there. I just purely enjoyed running fast. Just being at a track on a hot balmy night and running free. I even wrote a little poem about that: that feeling when you're running down the back straight, when you're feeling healthy, everything's going right, the smell of the track – the whole feeling of the atmosphere, running fast, feeling free. That's what sets you up ready to race.

The recall of these powerful and evocative emotions provides some insight into a man who still seeks to both feel and deploy that same level of passion in whatever he does. That translates into a conviction and a sharply focused sense of purpose in everything he does for his athletes and for himself.

Where does this all come from? Well, maybe it has something to do with being the second youngest of eight children. Or maybe growing up as one of four brothers fosters a determination and competitive instinct. In any case, it appears that the flame was kindled fairly early on:

> As a young lad everything was about that little bit of competition. When you grow up with four brothers in the house, everything is about competition. It was everyone's dream to make the Olympics. Everything was about making the most of a training opportunity: down a bank at the side of the supermarket Asda in South Shields there were these three metal barriers about 12 or 13 strides apart, similar to the 400m hurdles. So when I was in town I'd get to the top of that hill and I would run those hurdles every time. When the 1992 Olympics were on, some guy saw me do that and said: 'I bet that they want you in Olympics!' As I jogged away, I said to myself: 'Yeah, some day, some day.'

Jared recalled that promise to himself eight years later at the Sydney Olympic Games, as he sat at the starting block as the lead-off member of the Team GB 4 x 400m relay squad. On this occasion the podium was two seconds out of reach, with Team GB placing sixth. In less than two years, Jared stepped to the top of the podium at two major international games. Firstly as a member of the England 4 x 400m relay gold medal team at the Manchester Commonwealth Games and then in the same event competing for Great Britain at the European Athletics Championships in the Munich Olympic stadium. It was also in that year, at the age of 26, that Jared recorded his 400m personal best of 45.57 seconds.

Reflecting back on this time, Jared comments on what he believes led to these performances:

I didn't have a huge amount of talent, but I felt that I was able to get more out of myself than my contemporaries: I was the one still flat on his back 40 minutes after a race and they weren't. Why was that? Well, I think that I was able to take myself to a place that they were possibly prepared not to go. I needed to get every single bit of performance out of myself and that extra little bit of drive was important.

But did this lead to Jared pushing himself too hard?

Yes. Several times. The biggest one was in February/March 2003. I'd had a good winter up to that point and a successful year the year before [winning Commonwealth and European gold medals]. But I finished a few sessions and I knew that it wasn't the right sort of pain. My Dad had just died and the stress came out physically, my training fell apart. Jonathan Edwards came over to me and said: 'What's the matter with you? You look like you've lost 10 kilos.' But I never felt ill, I just felt as though I didn't have that extra little bit. It wasn't clicking together.

So what did Jared do about this?

Well, I did ease off a bit, but it wasn't until the end of the year that I realised how rundown I was.

It is an interesting example not only of how far someone is prepared to push themselves, but also how our self-awareness can dip when we are under pressure. But such setbacks go hand-in-hand with an elite athlete's career. On a wider perspective, how does Jared deal with setbacks in general?

If something has gone wrong, rather than back down from it I'll try and attack it. I'll do everything possible to make my goals and I'll give as much as I can.

FIRST-HAND VIEW

One of the fundamental aspects to Jared's approach is to instil core values in the athletes he coaches. He believes it is vital that athletes develop a performance attitude and become self-managers. This is established through athletes taking responsibility for time management, organisation, preparation and communication. Jared is the ultimate role model in all of these areas, which is why I believe his athletes respond.

Jo Suddes
Athlete, now assistant coach

While competing, Jared also completed a sports science degree followed by a PGCE teaching qualification. For a few years he taught part-time and lectured while still competing. He then joined the EIS as a strength and conditioning coach. By this time Jared was also married and a father, but he still managed to start to do some athletics coaching in what little spare time he had.

How did he manage the transition from athlete to support scientist and coach? In exploring this, we talked about the challenge for athletes of managing their ego when they stop being the focus of attention and take on a *behind the scenes* role as an applied practitioner or coach:

> As an athlete, you have to have an ego and that level of selfishness. But as a sports scientist or coach, you are doing it for someone else. I'm not sure that every sports scientist or coach thinks like that, as some are more interested in it in terms of what is in it for them. The way I view it is that with my training group, that selfishness that I had as an athlete, I transfer to the group and try and get the best for them, in the same way as I tried to get the best for myself as an athlete.

This appears a smart way to recognise that having an ego is important in whatever we do, but it is the way that it is subsumed into the benefit of the athlete and the group that works particularly well. In any case, Jared just enjoys the process of coaching and finds enough reward and expression for his ego anyway:

> Although my ego can be fed from a 'thanks' every now and then, the majority is self-fed, which I think is the same for the majority of athletes. I take more pleasure from the signs of an athlete's progress. When I see an athlete doing a lift and six months ago they'd never touched a bar and I've got them to that point where they are competent and confident in what they are doing, then that's fantastic. I just love that, and that feeds my ego.
>
> An athlete once said to me, 'You just love teaching people from scratch, don't you?' And he is right, because you're seeing something develop from nothing in front of your own eyes, that's fantastic!

Does this extend to a coaching philosophy for Jared?

> Well, one of my phrases is 'stop messing around'. In other words, stop doing this, that and the other when you should be focusing on your practice. Also as a coach I'm always trying harder to do something that little bit better or smarter. I believe that athletes need to try and do that. Some athletes will try harder by making it hurt more. But what they actually need to do is to focus more on their technique and relaxation, and then they'll get more out of it. So I would say that my overall philosophy is to try and get the athlete to think about the quality of what they are doing versus run-of-the-mill just getting out there and hurting themselves.[2]

Have there been any role models that have influenced Jared's coaching philosophy?

> Virtually everyone: tiny little pieces from lots and lots of people. I've certainly learned a lot from Malcolm Arnold in my chats to him. I would add Tony Lester to that. But it's anyone, it's coaches, it's scientists and it's athletes themselves.
>
> I would also include my brother Dave along with Jeremy Moody [at the time lead strength and conditioning coach in north east region EIS] and Terry Lomax, who was UK Athletics performance manager for the north east region for some time.

While Jared certainly remains open to outside influence, it is striking how well-grounded his practice is in his own values. With that proposition, we are back to the principles that Jared stated at the beginning of this interview:

> Drive, determination, motivation, pride, living and breathing it, never accepting that good was good enough.

They are as consistent now that Jared is an elite coach as they were when Jared was an aspiring athlete. They are grounded in a strong self-awareness that appears not to have wavered over the years. There is not a hint of complacency or arrogance about this; rather, this position is possible with someone who is at ease with himself, knows what he is good at and has a hunger for learning more and improving whenever possible. These values manifest in the working relationships that Jared cultivates:

FIG. 1.2 Jared coaching

I tend to work well with people who have egos that don't need boosting. They're comfortable with what they're doing and prepared to put themselves out for the good of someone else. The likes of 'Bricey' [Paul Brice, pages 55–64] are a good example of that. He is very intelligent, very good at his job and he genuinely does have athletes' interests at heart.

But how does Jared take that one step further, from just working well with someone to actually influencing him or her?

I find it easier to influence the ones who believe in you and what you're doing. I try to take them [the athlete] beyond just me telling them what to do. But if I know that is what they are like, then I try to work with that. It's sussing out people as you go along, the different personality types. I think I'm OK at that, but I'm getting better at it. My wife's great at it!

It's about constantly maintaining relationships, I try to make sure that I spend some time with every athlete in every session in order to build that understanding.

Working with athletes is one challenge, but as an elite coach surely Jared has to operate on a broader basis and influence other coaches, colleagues and managers within UK Athletics?

It's less about me piping up in meetings and making my opinions heard, it is more about the work that I'm doing. I think that the way I present is important in terms of demonstrating the process I work through, the organisation I have and the sense I make of things. That delivery gets fed back and people come and ask me questions because they see what I have to offer.

So Jared's influence comes more from his actions than his words. He acknowledges that this approach may not be the most progressive way to influence *the system*. However, it has the hallmark of Jared's self-awareness and values: using his strengths to focus on developing his athletes' performance.

Yet while Jared may not be the most vociferous coach, he will certainly stand up for what he believes in. And he believes passionately about the potential of those of his athletes who are prepared to train hard and to train smart. But when does Jared know when it's right to make a stand?

I do a lot of reflection and questioning of myself and if I keep coming back to the same answers, if I've investigated the issue from every single point possible and I still come back to 'this is the thing to do', then that gives me more confidence to take it on.

As an example, Jared talks about when he publicly stood up for preserving athlete services in the North East and found himself squared up against his then employer, the EIS, which was implementing changes required by UK Sport. The incident happened after the 2008 Beijing Olympic Games, when there were structural changes made to the way the EIS delivered its services to national governing bodies of sport. As a consequence, the services delivered to athletes in the North East region were in jeopardy of being seriously depleted. This was a moment of truth for Jared. He felt strongly that the athletes were being let down and that elite sport in the region was in danger of being adversely affected. Believing that the athletes and local people needed to know what was happening, he was prepared to put himself in a very difficult position. He spoke out and found himself quoted on the front page of the local paper, in contravention of his employment terms with the EIS. As a result, he ended up in front of a disciplinary hearing.

> Ultimately some athletes are still getting the support in the area, so for me it was worth it. For me, it came down to loyalty, to the athletes, to the team and to the region. I felt that I was standing up for something that was right. Maybe it is [the] influence from what my Dad would have done, but I don't want to be a yes man. Even now, I would still do the same thing again. But I'll always back it up with the facts when I can.

FIRST-HAND VIEW

Jared asked me once who had inspired me in my career ... After working with Jared for over four years, I can honestly put my hand on my heart and say it was him. He not only has an excellent knowledge base, but it is the other attributes that distinguish Jared from others. Jared is one of the most conscientious coaches I know. What I believe took Jared to the next level of coaching was the improvement in his leadership and management skills; he was able to have difficult conversations, negotiate to his advantage, and communicate on all levels.

Julie Twaddle
Strength and conditioning coach

These moments of truth are career-defining for those in any high-performance environment who have the courage to rise to them. For many, they are also life-defining, as such times can act as the catalyst for emboldened action and self-belief. However, there are considerable career risks, so how to you put yourself on as sure a foot as possible? In this example, Jared's determination to fight for the benefit of the athletes is clear in the emotion that permeates his recall of that time. However, all through the interview another of Jared's qualities leaps out: his strong preference for analysis. This characteristic is key to Jared's approach at all times, as indicated earlier when he talked about reflecting and questioning himself. Jared seeks, absorbs and lives for data. People say he has 'a constant thirst for knowledge and he is not afraid to ask around to obtain it' and that Jared is 'meticulous in his planning and organisation'. For him, it is all in the detail and the analysis. And yet none of this stifles Jared's passion one iota. Throughout it all, almost like a background mantra, is

Jared's motif: 'Drive, determination, motivation, pride, living and breathing it, never accepting that good was good enough.'

True to this belief, by 2009, when he moved to the role of UK Athletics development coach (sprints and hurdles), Jared had also completed his MSc part-time. Nothing has changed about him from the athlete to the coach, via the sports scientist. It is almost as though Jared wrote it himself:

podium athletes need podium coaches + podium support staff.

(Since the time of the interview, Jared has been appointed as lead for strength and conditioning for the EIS central region).

CHAPTER 1

KNOWING YOURSELF

How well do you know yourself? Do you know yourself inside out or do you sometimes wonder what it is that really makes you tick? Perhaps many of us would answer confidently that actually we do know ourselves pretty well, thank you very much. But it is worth pausing for thought about this for a while, because if you want to succeed in elite sport, or indeed any high-performance environment, knowing yourself is a critical skill, and one that shouldn't be taken for granted. You only have to scan the interviews in this book to see that the one theme that comes up time and time again is *self-awareness*. Some of our interviewees refer to it directly and others indicate that it is the development of their own self-awareness that has contributed significantly to their progress. For example, Jared Deacon displayed strong self-awareness about his identity and how he wishes to be seen by others when he said: 'I just want to be known as "Jared the person", not "Jared the half-decent ex-athlete" or "Jared the coach".'

Jared had clearly given some thought about how he saw himself and how he wanted his actions and behaviours to be consistent with that appraisal. He would also like others to see him as 'Jared the person', so he behaves and responds to others in a way that enables others to see him in that way. When we asked Jared, 'What makes you tick?', he answered: 'Drive, determination, motivation, pride, living and breathing it, never accepting that good was good enough.' It didn't matter whether he was referring to 'Jared the athlete' or 'Jared the sports scientist' or 'Jared the coach', the answer was consistent and he didn't hesitate in giving it. Jared's self-awareness helps to create the impression he wants to give, one that is constant and authentic to his values and personality.

This chapter looks at what self-awareness is and why it is so important in the high-performance arena. We then cover a few techniques that can help to enhance your self-awareness.

SELF-AWARENESS

Self-awareness is the ability to develop a clear understanding of your values, personality, emotions and motives. More than that, it is the capacity to reconcile the private you with the public you, enabling others to see you as authentic and trustworthy. High self-awareness enables individuals to act in accordance with their values, as well as to manage their emotions and behaviours. Just as importantly, increased self-awareness helps us to understand other people better – i.e. to build empathy with them. The more we understand our own values, personality, emotions and motives, the more open we are to understanding the emotions and motives of

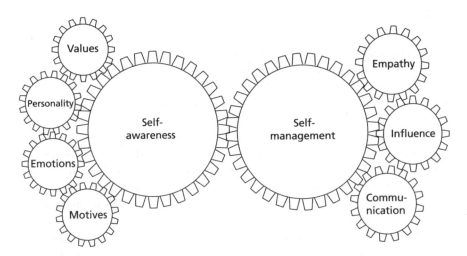

FIG. 1.3 Self-awareness: understanding more about yourself so that you can work better with others

others. This helps us to communicate more effectively and therefore build better relationships. Low self-awareness can lead to an obvious discrepancy between what someone says and what he or she actually does. More importantly, low self-awareness can lead to a difference between how you see yourself and how others see you. This can result in a low level of trust from other people.

Self-awareness at work is important because it leads to higher performance in a range of skills from communication to influencing and leadership.[3] Increasing the accuracy of your self-awareness helps you to be more objective about your assessment of your strengths and weaknesses.[4] Self-awareness is also the principal component of *Emotional Intelligence (EI)*,[5] the ability to recognise, monitor and manage your own emotions as well as respond to others' emotions. The self-awareness element of EI delivers higher performance in the workplace because it helps improve communication and relationships.[6]

WHY SELF-AWARENESS MATTERS

Self-awareness matters because it helps you understand and manage yourself, so that you are more in control of being the person you want to be. It may be an uncomfortable exercise, but really understanding your core values and motivations enables you to make sure that you behave in a way that is consistent with them. We may not always be in control of our emotions and behaviour (or, indeed, want to be on some occasions), but if we know what is causing them and how our behaviour changes, we at least have the option. It is when we are running on autopilot, and not aware of our emotional state and consequent behaviour, that problems can arise. This can be even more challenging when we are under stress and our emotions and behaviours may be out of our conscious control.[7] This is particularly evident in the camps and Games environment, as many of our interviewees mentioned. You will find a more in-depth perspective of the importance of self-awareness in this situation in the interview with Deirdre Angella (see page 130).

One key proviso to increasing self-awareness is that it is not about changing your personality; it is more about understanding your personality, being comfortable with it and adapting your behaviour to be more consistent with your underlying values and motivations. We'll look at values and motivations in more depth in Chapters 2 and 3.

Self-awareness also matters because it enables you to make a more objective assessment of your strengths and those areas you need to develop. When we have low self-awareness, we are at risk of not knowing what we don't know or not realising how we come across to others. Low self-awareness can lead to us thinking that we have all the answers, when in fact we may not be as good as we think we are. It is OK to admit we don't have all the answers and, more importantly, to ask for help when we don't. Good self-awareness reveals to us when we need to do just that. The other point to remember is that, in some people, their low self-awareness may mean that they underestimate their skills and therefore compromise their confidence.

Another benefit of increased self-awareness is that it puts you in a better position to adapt your behaviour to different situations, and engage with different people in different ways. Should you want to, that is. Some people prefer to interact with all people in exactly the same way, possibly in the laudable belief that they are presenting their true and consistent self all the time, to everyone. A consistent self, offered on a sort of 'take it or leave it' basis. Actually, higher self-awareness helps you achieve just that, but it also offers you the flexibility to adapt your behaviour when you choose.

This relates to another very practical benefit of increased self-awareness: better communication. So, when you want to influence or motivate different types of athletes or coaches, you are able to draw on a repertoire of communication skills that are better suited to getting your message across to their style rather than yours. The ability to adapt your behaviour in this way is part of *self-regulation*,[8] which is the second element of the EI model.

Finally, just a quick mention of a supporting point about self-awareness and communication: body language.[9] Body language, or non-verbal communication reveals far more about our message and intentions than words could ever do. Self-awareness of our body language results in our increased ability to keep our body language consistent with our message. It also helps us read other people's body language better and respond to the message or emotion that is communicating. In this way, self-awareness is at the heart of our ability to build understanding and trust in our working relationships.[10] We'll return to body language in Chapter 5 (see pages 89–91).

HOW SELF-AWARE ARE YOU?

Here's a short questionnaire to get you thinking about your level of self-awareness (based on Scheier & Carver, 1985).[11] Rate each statement using a scale of 1 to 5, where 1 = strongly disagree and 5 = strongly agree.

1. I am quick to notice changes in my mood _____

2. I usually worry about making a good impression _____

3. I often think about my reasons for doing things _____

4. Before leaving the house, I usually check how I look _____

5. I sometimes step back (in my mind) in order to examine myself from a distance _____

6. I am concerned about what other people think of me _____

7. I generally pay attention to my inner feelings _____

8. I am concerned about my style of doing things _____

9. I know the way my mind works when I work through a problem _____

10. I care a lot about how I present my self to others _____

Add up your total. Higher scores tend to correlate with greater self-awareness.

HOW TO BECOME MORE SELF-AWARE

Self-awareness has many benefits, of which those listed above are just some of the key ones. If it is so beneficial, how can you improve it?

There are several techniques to help you become more self-aware. Unfortunately it is not an overnight job and you won't become supremely self-aware by going on a course, or even reading a book like this one. It takes time, and successful people continue to develop their self-awareness for the rest of their lives.

Reflective practice

A good place to start is reflective practice, which has been defined as 'thoughtfully considering your own experiences in applying knowledge to practice'.[12] In other words, reflective practice is about making sense of your experiences in terms of the actions, thoughts and emotions that you had at the time and after you've had the time to mull them over. By looking inwards to identify both the motives behind your behaviour and, just as importantly, how you can make improvements were that situation to reoccur, you are deepening your self-awareness.

It may not be the easiest or most comfortable of exercises, but reflective practice is something that all good coaches and practitioners engage in. Those that claim they don't, have probably become so good at it that they do it non-consciously. If you are interested in a no-nonsense method of reflective practice, see 'A simple model for reflective practice' below.

A SIMPLE MODEL FOR REFLECTIVE PRACTICE

The following model by Marchel[13] provides three simple levels for your reflection:

- Level 1: Descriptive – simple description of the event or situation
- Level 2: Analytical – analysis of context and consideration of the reactions of people involved
- Level 3: Integrated – discussion of your own reactions and feelings and their consequences on your assumptions, attitudes, behaviours and future practice.

For an example of reflective practice in action, read Danny Kerry's interview (see pages 198–206). It will give you an idea of an elite coach whose self-awareness really benefited from reflective practice when push came to shove.

Reflective practice is your own critical appraisal of your actions and emotions, which helps you turn experience into learning – a point illustrated very powerfully by Jared Deacon:

> I do a lot of reflection and questioning of myself … If I've investigated the issue from every single point possible and I still come back to 'this is the thing to do', then that gives me more confidence to take it on.

Seeking feedback

However, it is true that we are sometimes not the most accurate or objective observers of our own behaviour, which makes reflective practice challenging. In his interview, Nik Diaper illustrated this point when he talked about the feedback he received after being rejected for a job for which he had applied in one of the major sports (see page 149). The feedback was tough to take. But being a reflective person, Nik was determined and changed the behaviour that was causing the unfavourable perception of him by some others. For a different story about someone dealing with tough feedback, check out the interview with Danny Kerry when he talks about the feedback after his team returned from the Beijing Olympic Games (see page 201).

One way to increase the accuracy of your own observations of your behaviour is to use the next tool in developing self-awareness: seek feedback before it is given to you. Asking a trusted colleague to give you effective feedback provides a way of sense-checking your own assessment of your behaviour and performance. The more specific the feedback can be to a recent event or situation, the more powerful it will be in enhancing your self-awareness.

However uncomfortable it may be, providing and receiving feedback is a feature of high performance. It is the conversations that are left unsaid that are the most corrosive to effective working relationships.

A SIMPLE MODEL FOR PROVIDING FEEDBACK

Providing and receiving feedback can be an uncomfortable process for some, but it need not be and is also an essential activity in high-performance working relationships. One simple model that helps to frame good feedback is the AID approach:

A – Action. Describe the action or behaviour that you have observed.

I – Impact. Describe how that action or behaviour impacts on what you are both trying to achieve.

D – Do. Describe an alternative action or behaviour that the other person can do to improve the situation.

Get a mentor

The way to take your feedback to the next level in raising self-awareness is to get a mentor. You may already have a mentor, or someone who provides effectively the same support. Either way, it is someone who can act as a sounding board, trusted adviser, wise counsel and/or expert. That is someone who can not only give you specific and timely feedback, but also help you to relate that to the changes and improvements you would like to make.

Performance profiling

You'll be well on the path to improved self-awareness if you follow some of the above suggestions, but you may want to keep track of how you are doing and put some numbers into the mix. The final technique for improving self-awareness will help you do just that: performance profiling.

Performance profiling[14] is widely used in elite sport to help athletes, coaches, support staff and senior management focus on and develop their skills. The technique identifies a series of critical-performance criteria, against which current and desired performance ratings are assigned. The critical performance criteria usually describe a range of knowledge, behaviour and skills that are central to achieving excellence in that role or field. The owner of the profile rates their own performance against the selected criteria and can validate these by asking those who work close to them to also provide a rating of the owner's performance. By comparing their ratings with those of their colleagues, the owner can raise their self-awareness about their strengths compared to how others see them.

Related to profiling, some of the most helpful tools for self-awareness are psychometric profiling questionnaires, including the Bolton and Bolton model, to which we refer in Chapter 6 (see pages 107–108).

There are also some more humanistic approaches that have a role in developing self-awareness, such as *Mindfulness*.[15] The practice of mindfulness helps individuals act more in accordance with their values and aspirations.

That's probably enough techniques for the moment! As mentioned, many of our interviewees talk about the contribution of their self-awareness to their performance. We asked Deirdre Angella (see page 130) if it was possible to accelerate the development of self-awareness?:

> The easy answer is 'yes'. I guess it comes back to people's willingness: how important is it to you to be more self-aware, do you understand what self-awareness is and how important a skill do you think it is? It is that whole thing of 'we don't know what we don't know' and unless you are prepared to take the risk and do some work with self-awareness, then you will never know. Much of it is to do with self-questioning, having some key questions to ask yourself is really important. Skills-based awareness can be very important, such as mindfulness.

FIG. 1.4 Self-awareness builds self-confidence

TAKING SELF-AWARENESS TOO FAR

Like any good thing, too much focus on self-awareness can be counterproductive. For a start, over-analysing things can lead to a state of relative paralysis and even end up knocking back self-confidence and self-esteem. This is particularly true if you have a strong self-critical streak anyway. It is important to remember that effective self-awareness is as much about reflecting on what you have done well, in addition to what you could do better. So your work on self-awareness should start with a positive mindset about the performance benefits it will bring. It is best to engage someone else to give you some constructive feedback and possibly guidance in the early stages of exploring your self-awareness.

Developing self-awareness is an endeavour that should be undertaken in measure, checking yourself regularly so that you don't become too self-absorbed or too self-conscious.

SUMMARY

Self-awareness is about realising who you are and what drives you to do the things that you do. But it is true that most people spend little time thinking about themselves in this way. However, all the successful coaches and practitioners that we have worked with have a high degree of self-awareness.

From a more practical perspective, self-awareness is about understanding your personality and how much it controls your life. It is about being more in tune with your current mood and how that drives the emotion and behaviour that is seen by others. It is about accepting ourselves so that we can concentrate on building an understanding of others (i.e. empathy) and foster effective relationships with them. That means we can communicate, influence, motivate and lead to a level which reaches our true potential. In other words, self-awareness helps you to be the person that you want to be to succeed in the high-pressure environment that is elite sport.

Everyone can develop their self-awareness further, and there are some proven approaches to help do that. Reflective practice and seeking feedback are a good foundation to a strategy in this area. Having a competent mentor adds some real value, as well as gaining some quantitative input through performance profiling. Beware of becoming too bogged down in all this internal focus, though. As important as it is, time and effort spent on it needs to be balanced with developing other skills and an external focus on those whom you are trying to help: the athlete.

Ultimately, it is our responsibility to know ourselves truthfully. In doing so, we can take conscious and positive action to define ourselves according to our values and core motivation, rather than being driven by underlying semi-conscious motives, reactive emotions and possibly unhelpful compulsions. Self-awareness is like any talent: it's worth practising.

CASE STUDY: VALUES INTO PRACTICE

DAVE CLARK

Head of Fitness, Irish Rugby Football Union

FIG. 2.1 Dave Clark

Returning to his biokinetics clinic after a lunchtime run on Cape Town's Table Mountain in late October 1992, Dave Clark received the call that he had dreamed about for most of his adult life. The request was for Dave to come and run the warm-up training session that afternoon for the Springboks (the South African Rugby Union national team). The Springboks had gathered in town to prepare for their tour of Europe, following their readmittance to international rugby earlier that year. In preparation for this, the team's coach had asked Professor Tim Noakes, Discovery Health Professor of Exercise and Sports Science at the University of Cape Town and South Africa's premier sports scientist, to recommend someone to take the team through their paces before the practice session. Dave Clark instantly came to mind.

At first, Dave hesitated to believe the message, but he quickly decided to head down to the Springboks' training ground to check out what was happening. Fifteen minutes later he was met by an expectant squad of 30 players, many of whom he admits were his sporting heroes. Dave maintained his cool and saw this as an opportunity to apply all of his sports science enthusiasm to elite-level athletes. Turning to the coach, Dave asked keenly: 'So what's the plan this week, what do you want me to do in the warm-up?' The coach replied with pragmatic precision: 'You've got 40 minutes, so just fuck 'em up!'

Whatever the coach's intention, Dave's warm-up prepared the squad well, impressing the coach enough that he was invited back to lead the warm-ups until they left for Europe. This proved a pivotal moment. From that unexpected summons onwards, Dave developed a highly successful career to become the world-class sports scientist and applied conditioning coach that he is acknowledged to be today.

His rise is founded on his commonly appreciated humility combined with a conviction in his methods that focus on one goal only: improving the athlete's performance. Many athletes attribute, in part, their medals on the world stage to Dave's precise and impactful interventions.

As a South African, Dave grew up in a culture that lived for and loved its sport. But making a career out of sport in a country isolated by the apartheid sanctions of the 1980s was a challenge. Initially, teaching offered Dave a channel to combine an enthusiasm for sport with a means of earning a living. But while he strove to be the best teacher he could, what Dave really enjoyed was the coaching process. So in a move characteristic of his spirit of adventure and determination, Dave took himself to the United States for a couple of years to play and coach rugby union.

With his international yearning only partially sated, Dave returned to South Africa. Within a short while, Dave heard about a new course at the University of Cape Town called Sports Science. For Dave, the proposition that you could exercise-test someone and then influence their training based on the results was an exciting step forward from basic physical education. So, Dave resigned from his job, sold his house, got engaged to Ingrid, married Ingrid and moved to Cape Town – not necessarily in that exact order, but all within the space of three months.

The course itself not only played right into Dave's inquisitiveness, but also took him way out of his comfort zone. Rising to the challenge, Dave completed his BSc honours in sports science and then his master's degree while at the same time opening his biokinetics clinic in Cape Town. Under Dave's leadership, this soon became one of the largest cardiac and orthopaedic rehabilitation centres in Cape Town. As his reputation grew, Dave made a bid with a couple of colleagues to provide fitness coaching services to the Western Province Rugby Union. Known as 'Province', the senior team had the biggest supporter base in South Africa's Currie Cup and is based at the home of South African rugby, Newlands stadium, where Dave was a season ticket holder.

It is at this point that we return to Dave's descent from Table Mountain and the call from the Springboks. Dave's modesty downplays this event as one of those fateful days when the right person happens to be in the right place at the right time. In any case, Province, having heard about Dave's work with the Springboks, soon called him and gave him a contract for the next year as their fitness coach, a role Dave would keep until he left South Africa in 1995.

Before we jump too far ahead, it is worth pointing out that Dave was appointed as fitness coach to the Springboks for the period of time that covered their 1994 tour of New Zealand. The Springboks versus New Zealand is always considered to be a battle of the giants in South Africa. The Springboks had yet to return to the form they had achieved before the years of isolation and they lost the first two tests and drew the last. Results like that in a nation with a passion for rugby meant that the coach lost his job.

Kitch Christie was appointed as the new coach and was to take the Springboks to their 1995 Rugby World Cup victory. However, he didn't appoint a fitness coach. And, on the day that the Springboks beat the All Blacks team in the 1995 World Cup final, Dave was in Arizona to take his CSCS (Certified Strength and Conditioning Specialist) exam with the NSCA (National Strength and Conditioning Association, United States), having self-funded the trip in his desire to develop his skills. That qualification was to prove decisive in Dave's next career move; this time as national fitness coach for the Welsh Rugby Union.

With typical drive, Dave applied for the job, was appointed, moved the whole family to a new continent and started in post in Wales inside of two months, in late 1995. Dave allows himself to moderate his modesty slightly when recounting these events:

> As much as I'd like to say that I've kicked down doors to be where I want to be, I guess there's been a bit of 'being in the right place at the right time' … But I am quite clear about this: I was qualified appropriately and did the right thing with the opportunity.

Reflecting on this, Dave acknowledges that he has a strong drive combined with core principles, describing himself as 'a man of conviction with a hard edge': 'Success in high-performance is balancing where you sit between conviction and compromise.'

Anyone who has worked with Dave will know that he is prepared to stand his ground in a forthright manner, when he has the evidence and the conviction that the situation warrants. But these days, rather than force his point through, he strives to make the case logically and scientifically and to take people with him, rather than antagonise them. This tactical influencing is something that Dave recognises as an important skill:

> The people who are really great high-performance deliverers, have that as a touch. It's not strategic, it's more of a tactical touch, situation by situation.

Dave explains that there is often a pressure for young coaches and practitioners to respond immediately when challenged, but that is not always a useful approach:

> The guy I respect is the guy who makes it look like he 'has got time on the ball'; the one who takes a bit of time before he responds, even if he already knows the answer. Because if I come back too quickly, I may lose you. I guess as a younger Dave Clark, this is where my error possibly lay. Because straight away, my answer would come out: Why not? But now, I've learned to take people along

the road with me, so I don't come back so hard and fast with my responses. In a high-performance environment, a more directive style can sometimes be required. But even then, the ability to listen and take people along with you is still key to that.

It is these influencing skills that have refined Dave's approach and enabled him to work successfully with some of Team GB's leading athletes. Although they are non-technical skills as such, they are central to Dave's practice philosophy now.

If I am in a situation and I see the block, I don't go straight through that door anymore. I might go around the side or I might give it some time to see if I can develop another key to that. But it is a fine line: at some stage you may want to find a subtle way to use the science to explain the potential gain for instance. If I think that the person can grasp the science, then I'll use that to help persuade them of my proposed course of action.

FIRST-HAND VIEW

Dave and I worked together for the Welsh Rugby Union when I was WRU national coach. Integrating sports science is always a challenge but Dave always gains respect and credibility from the people he works with. He is able to support and challenge coaches in a way that puts the development of the players and the team at the forefront of all decisions. He adopts a holistic approach to development of the athlete and the person. He can build excellent rapport with players of all ages and communicates effectively. He is self-aware and aware of the differing learning styles that players may have and therefore how he has to differentiate his coaching to build on the positive working relationship that he develops.

Kevin Bowring
Head of Elite Coach Development, RFU

Dave points out that while it is important to develop influencing skills to get people on board, sometimes you have to make a judgement call that further effort isn't worth it at that time. In fact, in some situations when you are on solid technical ground, you have to be willing to stand firm and not shy away from a possibly forthright conversation. 'At some point in time, you have to be able to say, "No, I don't go there" and that is where it bumps up against the conviction end of the scale.' In other words, unless you have the conviction in what you are proposing as well as the explicit buy-in from the coach and/or athlete, it is practically impossible to be effective.

Dave recalls that working for the Welsh Rugby Union (WRU) with Kevin Bowring, then the national coach, helped him to develop these skills. The period was clearly an enjoyable time for Dave, but after a change in national coach at the WRU, he found himself between jobs. Not for long, however, as an opportunity arose in 1998 at what

FIG. 2.2 Dave coaching

is now the **sport**scotland institute of sport to build the strength and conditioning service at the nascent institute. It was absolutely what Dave wanted: 'It was a multi-sport situation, I couldn't have written that job description better.'

This was very early days at the Institute, and Dave was one of only five employees. It also coincided with a time when strength and conditioning practitioners across the UK were starting to organise themselves into the UK Strength and Conditioning Association (UKSCA), something Dave gave an enormous amount of energy and commitment to getting off the ground. This wasn't without its challenges, and Dave's influencing skills were needed at the highest level, as well as his drive.

Recounting this era, Dave is asked about why he really cares about what he does, but maybe his modesty causes him to hesitate a little with his response:

I don't know. I'm quite clear that my passion is one of my strengths. It is something that I don't work on, it is something that just is … If you've convinced me and taken me along with you, then I would deploy my passion. I am passionate about my work and that is probably why I do what I do.

As you can read in the quotations from the likes of Chris Hoy and Campbell Walsh (see pages 26 and 24), this passion is recognised by all who work with him and is combined with conviction, yet Dave remains open to alternative views and approaches. So how does Dave cope with alternative approaches from others, even some athletes, where the passion either isn't evident or just plain isn't there? 'You come with the technical expertise and bring a certain amount of passion, but the energy to be the athlete has to come from the athlete.'

Dave recognises that the level of passion and commitment of an elite athlete correlates to the culture and leadership of each sport. He cites the example of the sport he currently works with, canoe slalom, and the positive culture of athlete engagement and responsibility that pervades there:

I've learned a lot in the five years particularly in the canoe slalom programme and particularly from Jurg [Gotz, head performance coach, canoe slalom, see pages 163–171]. If an individual athlete comes to me and says, 'I really want to work hard', I'll say, 'Fine, I'll give you the keys to do that.' This programme has athletes that work like that and bring the ownership and their own leadership. It is a huge privilege to work with them in that way.

But even within the programme, or within a squad and over the course of a cycle, there can be a wide variability in an athlete's motivation; you need to be able to work with that. So that when competition time comes, the effects of stress mean that the athlete may rely on you more, or during the hard training of the off-season or winter months they may want you to be more directive. You need the sensitivity and feel to be able to read that and adjust your approach accordingly.

So what advice in this area can Dave offer to coaches and practitioners starting out in their careers?

It is about learning the skills to see what is confronting you and respond to that. When you start out, you need to have a few bankers, both technical and positive behaviours, [which] you know you can fall back on [and which] will either buy you time or deliver results for you.

Dave considers his approach to developing the athlete and coaches' trust in him has been central to being an effective practitioner:

The athletes need to have trust in me. If they don't totally believe in what you're doing, you won't get the results. Chris [Hoy] had trust in me in that way. Although Chris would have a discussion with me at the start of each cycle to scope out the plan, thereafter he would apply himself to that plan. Remember, it was a little bit more simple with Chris because it was just him and I, as he was running his own track programme, and we focused on getting him as strong as we possibly could in the squat, in order to convert that into pedal power.

Quite a revealing statement, that: you have to encourage Dave to talk about his work with Sir Chris Hoy. He doesn't look for recognition in that way and doesn't want his comments to be misconstrued.

The telephone call to work with Craig MacLean and Chris Hoy came just before they departed for the Sydney Olympic Games in 2000. Dave had spent a busy year setting up a network of strength and conditioning coaches across Scotland, and part of his remit was to provide strength and conditioning support to elite Scottish athletes abroad if necessary. Into that sphere came Craig and Chris, based in Manchester and interested in learning more about what Dave could do for them. Dave watched the guys lift weights and afterwards discussed some ideas on what could be improved, but with the Sydney Olympic Games imminent, the conversation focused on the post-Games situation. Once recovered from winning silver in the team sprint with Jason

FIRST-HAND VIEW

Firstly, he's a 'good guy', and this makes any kind of relationship with him easy. He talks straight without any bullshit. I believe he always has the performance or well-being of the athlete as the first consideration. He is very open to being questioned about his recommendations ... why are we doing that exercise?, why are we doing this many reps at this time in the year? Equally important is the fact that he will then give a considered response ... a clear explanation, with concrete examples, of why he believes it is the right thing to do ... or he is open to looking into it and see if an alternative may be better. He is not too proud to change the plan and admit that something else may be better.

Campbell Walsh
Olympic silver medallist canoe slalom

Queally, Chris and Craig spent January and February in Scotland training with Dave. Soon after, Dave got the call to clear his diary and attend a GB Cycling pre-World Championships training camp in Germany. The relationship grew and by the end of 2001, Dave was seconded to work with the GB track sprint group up to the Athens Olympic Games.

However, it wasn't all plain sailing from that point. Any high-performance environment will be populated by those who are passionate about what they believe, and they will make a stand for it. Track sprint cycling in the early 2000s was no exception, and this proved a decisive learning point for Dave. A debate developed over the length of Chris's taper for a major event – the traditional long cycling taper of a couple of months or the shorter nine-day taper proposed by Dave. In the end, Dave's view persuaded Chris: nine days is what Chris wanted. But not everyone agreed: 'It was one of those classic situations where I knew that it didn't matter whether I'd won the day or not, I'd lost the overall battle.'

This, plus the way the system worked at the time (which put the EIS under pressure to deliver all the services to sports in England), meant that after the 2004 Olympics in Athens, Dave's role with GB Cycling team was not renewed. Although Chris Hoy still consults him from time to time, Dave has moved on to work with other teams. Dave reflects ruefully: 'It could have been dealt with far, far better.'

Dave describes a useful example of how to use influencing skills to introduce an innovation into an athlete's training. To detail that innovation here would compromise competitive edge, but we can indicate that it related to the nature of the squat lift that Chris and the other sprint cyclists were doing. Dave looked at the way they lifted and thought that they could achieve just as effective power development and at the same time reduce the risk of the frequent lower back injuries they were suffering. He made the case for changing the foot stance while preserving muscle activation. For many cyclists and coaches, this was counter-intuitive to their existing technique. However, Dave persuaded them to adopt the new technique, and soon the cyclists were squatting heavier loads that transferred into greater power through the pedal. Dave didn't persuade them with facts alone; his view was built on intuition and understanding the sport, and was also informed by years of experience: 'I didn't *know* that at the time [i.e. that muscle activation was preserved in the alternative stance], but I knew that – if you know what I mean.'

Subsequent studies have proved Dave to be right, but this is a great example of influence in high-performance arenas. In such arenas, the full facts are not always available if you want to make cutting-edge interventions that get the athlete on the podium. But with the deductive logic and, just as importantly, the trust of the athletes and coaches, a case can be made. However, that alone doesn't win the day. Dave persuaded people on this one because he combined the logic and conviction with the ability to explain the proposal in a way that enabled others to relate to it.

I've got a very strong philosophy about strength training and its place in developing performance. I am confident in my technical ability, through strength, power and postural interventions.

FIRST-HAND VIEW

What I liked about working with Dave is that he is very calm and considered, he does not try and force his beliefs and training ideas on you, rather he presents you with the evidence relevant to cycling and lets you decide – there is no ramming it down your throat. To his advantage Dave is not a flamboyant character, he calmly gets on with his job, he is good fun to work with and is very passionate about what he does for athletes. He lets the results the athletes he works with speak for themselves.

Sir Chris Hoy
Multiple Olympic gold medallist

That quality of legitimate confidence is much in demand in elite performance sport, so it is no surprise that before long Dave started working with GB Canoe Slalom. On this occasion, the Scottish connection was Campbell Walsh, who sought Dave's support in the year before the Olympics in Athens. Here again it started with a discussion about the functional nature of strength. After observing training on the bench-pull machine, Dave noted that the machine didn't replicate the full roster of the paddler's propulsive moves. A conversation followed:

Dave: So, Campbell, when your feet are under the deck, are they flapping
            about in the wind, or are they pushing against a foot plate?
Campbell: No, against a footplate, which I sometimes actually kick out because
            of the force of my stroke.
Dave: So you can't be pulling with your feet flapping in the wind in the
            gym. You've got to have them planted, otherwise you're not working
            the whole chain: you're missing an opportunity.
Campbell: Kerching! That makes sense to me!

That seemingly simple, yet incisive proposition started Dave's work with GB Canoe Slalom. That responsibility remained part of Dave's day job while he ran the team of strength and conditioning coaches in Scotland. Dave clearly thrives with these diverse responsibilities and is happy to work out of the limelight in a humble way, yet be full of conviction with that hard edge. This attitude is apparent in his response when asked about his advice for young practitioners: 'You need to be very clear early on in your career why you do this.'

With characteristic humour, he expands:

You don't do it for a chapter in a book. And also not for a thank-you, don't expect that. If you can't look at yourself in the morning and say, 'I feel good because that programme I wrote for that athlete has made a real performance difference', then don't do it.

CHAPTER 2
VALUES INTO PRACTICE

In his own words, Dave Clark is a man of 'conviction with a hard edge'. It is a statement that provides an insight into what makes Dave tick, what he is driven and guided by: his values. We didn't need to ask Dave directly, 'What are your values?' These came out as he recounted various stories in the interview. In fact, asking someone what their values are probably gives you a rose-tinted view of the reality. Sure, people most often reply with a list of values that they *believe* they believe in. But it is only when you see the values come out in practice, in how they actually behave in the 'moments of truth', that you get a sense of what their critical values actually are.

So reading through Dave's interview, what do you think Dave's values are? You may want to start your list with that tagline Dave was so clear about: 'conviction with a hard edge'. What does that suggest to you? The obvious element is conviction, in that Dave has to really believe in what he is doing: he has to understand and buy into the evidence base, the science; he has to believe that what he is proposing will make a performance difference for the athlete; he has to believe that the athlete buys into the work and effort that Dave is proposing, and he has to believe that his colleagues, coaches and the sport also buy into his proposal. And, in turn, that they believe in Dave's ability to deliver.

FIG. 2.3 Dave and Sir Chris Hoy

That is just the start, as there is also the 'hard edge' element to the statement. What does that suggest to you? In the examples that Dave talks about, there is clearly a determination for Dave to stand firm when he believes that he is on solid technical ground. But this doesn't mean that determination is driven by the desire or need to enforce his ego. Far from it, as one of Dave's other values that comes across very strongly, without him saying so, is humility:[1] although happy to receive recognition when it is legitimate, Dave does not seek it. In our interview with him, Dave was at pains to recognise the talent and hard work of the athletes, coaches and his practitioner colleagues long before he would acknowledge his own contributions. Reading Dave's interview further indicates values such as self-motivation, commitment, consistency, fairness and humour. However, Dave's humility would probably appreciate the spotlight being taken off him for a while, so we'll draw on a couple of the other interviews in this book.

If you are reading this book from beginning to end, you will have already encountered Jared Deacon's very self-aware statement of consistent values (see pages 2 and 6). If you've dipped in and out of various chapters, you may well have read how Danny Kerry's values have come to the fore at various times in his career (see pages 198–206). Danny's interview also raises the importance of values in a team setting, in that shared values can deliver agreed behaviour standards and drive performance upwards. He talks about the time when that shared value system wasn't in place at the time of the post-Beijing review, and the power of shared values when they were developed and bought into by all of the team via the 'golden thread'. For the rest of this chapter we'll explore what values are and why they are important. We'll also ask some questions that will help you clarify what your own values are and how you can make them work for you.

WHAT ARE VALUES AND WHERE DO THEY COME FROM?

A person's values are their basic beliefs that particular ways of behaving or a state of existence are preferable to another way of behaving or state of existence. Each value contains a judgemental connotation that embodies the person's notion of what is right and what is wrong. Because of that, values are often linked to a belief system and act as an ethical guide to behaviour, especially in times of uncertainty or stress. They are implicit within decision-making, in that a person tends to makes choices consistent with their values.

We form our values in the early phases[2] of our lives, influenced by family and culture. They tend to be quite resistant to change, unless challenged by the aftermath of significant emotional life events.[3] As an example of the early imprinting of values, the biomechanist Paul Brice refers to the origin of his values of consideration and always doing the best that you can for an athlete, coach or colleague in Chapter 4:

> My parents have always engrained me to be respectful of people, have good manners, say please and thank you, all of these are fundamental things. They all ferment themselves in everything you do. If you've got that, then you have a certain level of wanting to do the job to the best of your ability, to bring your A-game to the table.

WHY ARE VALUES IMPORTANT?

Our values are important because they constitute the foundations of our evaluation of particular situations, our behaviour within them and, often, our emotional reactions to them. While personality profiling and other psychometric tests are very useful in providing some insight into the reasons for our behaviour, the profiling of values has proven to be a far more accurate predictor of the quality of our decisions.[4]

The decisions we make and the behaviour we display when times are tough are even more informed by our values. Dave Clark has faced many tough times and 'moments of truth' in his career, where he has had to make decisions based on his core values. That 'conviction with a hard edge' clearly came into play when he held firm in his appraisal of the best tapering session for Chris Hoy before a championship. Dave's values of conviction and integrity may well have cost him further work with GB Cycling as the EIS took over (although Dave did continue to work with Chris Hoy and is credited as his strength and conditioning coach). At the same time, Dave didn't compromise his integrity, and that integrity is why many athletes and coaches trust and value Dave to this day.

So, on an individual basis, our values define us and provide an ethical compass to our actions. But on a day-to-day basis, our values may not be explicit, such that other people would know that we hold them to be important. Or we may have yet to develop a level of self-awareness where our own values are indeed known to us. In any case, it is helpful to be more explicit about our values when we get the opportunity to share them with others, as this leads to people understanding us better and, more importantly, interpreting our actions correctly. Being open about our values leads to fewer misunderstandings, less conflict, more trust and better collaboration.

Many coaches are open about their values and sometimes encapsulate them as a *coaching philosophy*.[5] More often a coach will express their values as a set of guiding principles and consequent behaviours that inform their coaching practice, rather than as a formal list of values. Coaching philosophies can be quite focused on just the coach and athletes' roles in the training and performance environment. However, they can also extend to expectations around athlete attitudes and general behaviour, including sportsmanship. Having such a philosophy is not unique to coaches, as many applied practitioners also develop their own as Sarah Hardman outlines in her interview (see pages 93–101).

Indeed, there is a strong train of thought that all good coaches and applied practitioners should consciously develop and refine with time what their coaching/service delivery philosophy is, as this guides who they are and how they work. Sometimes these philosophies also encompass the ethics covered in relevant professional or organisational codes of conduct.

As well as at an individual level, values are also very important at the team and organisational level. Teams – and here we mean support teams just as much as those 'on the pitch' – operate far more effectively when they have a joint purpose and a way of working that is defined in shared behaviours drawn from common values. Under such conditions, trust can prevail and in performance terms, this enables more and calculated risk-taking to occur, which is essential for elite-level performance, whatever the context.[6] In the same manner, organisational values are critical to enhancing the sense of belonging of its employees and network, as well as building confidence with clients, customers and funding agencies. The English Institute of Sport (EIS)[7] and **sport**scotland institute of sport[8] both provide explicit organisational values on their websites.

When talking about team and organisational values, it is worth noting that an individual's publicly stated values can sometimes be at odds with their privately held ones: they may have different or, indeed, contrasting individual values than those required for their role. For example, Jared Deacon experienced this when there were changes to the EIS structure in the North East after the Beijing Olympic and Paralympic Games. You can read the details in his interview (see pages 7–8), but suffice to say that Jared's personal values won out in the clash between individual and role values. It should be remembered that although individual and role values can sometimes be inconsistent, this situation doesn't need to end up in discord. Sometimes we find ourselves in a role where we have to take actions we wouldn't choose, but we don't always have the luxury of running things all our own way. One key point to remember is that values change across sports and sports institutes, and as a practitioner you need to be able to reconcile your own values with those of your employer. In practice this may mean, where you have more than one employer, that there are different expectations of you from those different employers, both of which are as valid. You may therefore need to reconcile how you work within that environment.

HOW DO I KNOW WHAT MY VALUES ARE?

As covered in the last chapter, there are many benefits to knowing who we are and why we do the things we do. In all of this, a good place to start is by clarifying what our values are. For some of us, these are already apparent to us and, possibly, to those around us. For the rest of us, we may not be that clear about what our values actually are. Although we may have a sense of what is right and wrong and where that comes from, we may be yet to articulate this as a list of values. If you would like to make some progress on this, try the exercise 'How to clarify your values' below.

HOW TO CLARIFY YOUR VALUES

Think about some 'moments of truth' for you:

1. Have you ever pushed yourself beyond what you thought you were capable of doing? For example, you might have had to ski a difficult off-piste section when you took a wrong turn at the top of the mountain. Or you may have free-climbed an overhanging section that you never thought you could. Or you may have given

a presentation that went down really well although you dreaded it. Hopefully, you get the idea: think about when you achieved something beyond your perceived capability.

2. Now think about a situation where you were a lone voice, where you stood up for something or someone when nobody else was prepared to do so.

3. Finally, think about a time when you have walked away from a job, a client engagement or important situation because you just didn't agree with what was happening or with what was expected of you.

In these three 'moment of truth' scenarios, you will find your values if you reflect on why and how you took the actions involved. Was it any of the following: courage, determination, fairness, integrity, adventure, creativity, learning or optimism that was at the heart of your behaviour? Or something else, perhaps? In any case, these pressure situations do more to reveal our true core values than everyday situations can. When push comes to shove, we tend to revert to type – and 'type' means the core of us, with all the niceties and subtleties stripped away.

If you find that this all seems like hard work, stick with it or discuss it with a trusted colleague, mentor or friend who'll give you an objective answer.

If you still find that too onerous, you may want to look at *commitment* as a value! Failing that, check out the box 'What really matters to you?' (overleaf).

HOW DO I MAKE MY VALUES WORK FOR ME?

Whatever your values are, it is very useful to be ready to spell them out if a key situation arises, such as an interview or when joining a new team. This skill becomes even more important the higher up you go in an organisation, but the people who can do this early on in their careers tend to stand out. This is not to say that the values you have today should be carved in stone. Indeed, the power of *significant emotional events* in challenging and sometimes shifting our values throughout our lives is well understood. But with a developing self-awareness and regular reflective practice, most elite coaches and practitioners, such as the ones interviewed in this book, are able to describe what really matters to them. That essential yet understated ability can nurture trust and collaboration as well as inspiring athletes to follow the lead, confident that the coach or practitioner knows what really matters.

Another way to make your values work for you is to develop the behaviours that positively align with your values. Behaviours developed in this way will often become strengths because there is so much conviction behind them. There is more to be gained from developing strengths (unless there are some 'mission-critical' weaknesses), as these can become signature strengths and make you stand out from the crowd.[9]

WHAT REALLY MATTERS TO YOU?

This is an exercise to identify which values you are prepared to fight for and which ones are merely 'nice to have'.

Firstly, it is easy to generate a long list of values that appeal to you. In fact, here is ready-made list to save you the effort:

accomplishment, accountability, accuracy, ambition, challenge, collaboration, commitment, compassion, competency, courage, creativity, credibility, dedication, dependability, dignity, discipline, diversity, efficiency, empathy, empowerment, enjoyment, equality, excellence, flexibility, friendliness, fun, generosity, honesty, independence, individuality, innovation, integrity, learning, loyalty, optimism, persistency, quality, respect, responsibility, security, service, teamwork and wisdom

This is not a comprehensive list, so you may wish to add some more. Once you have a final list, select the five values that are most important to you. Then ask a trusted colleague or friend to challenge you to justify why these are important to you; offer examples from your own experience.

Once you have completed the explanation for all five, ask your colleague or friend which were the four most convincing explanations; you will have to drop the fifth value from your list. You can no longer have that as a core value. Maybe you like it and agree with it, but it is peripheral and not what really matters to you. You can see that you may have to engage your influencing skills; check out Chapter 6 if you are a little rusty on these.

Next, take this one stage further and ask your colleague or friend to identify which was your least convincing explanation from the remaining four values. You may find this uncomfortable, but it is worth seeing how strongly you can make the case and how convincing that is. You will discover the values that are non-negotiable, the ones that really matter to you. As a reward for your effort in this exercise, you will be able to articulate your values at any future time with examples you feel strongly about.

One tool to consider helping you is the *core qualities*[10] model. This model invites you to identify a core quality or value and then map the associated behaviours, as demonstrated in Figure 2.4 opposite.

The core qualities model helps to explain how values can influence our behaviour in practice. Like any good thing, too much can lead to problems, identified as a *pitfall* in this model. To stop you going into the pitfall, the model encourages you to practise the *challenge* behaviour. Taking the challenge behaviour too far is itself not helpful and referred to as the *allergy*.

FIG. 2.4 Core qualities model

Source: Ofman, D., *Core Qualities: A Gateway to Human Resources* (Scriptum, 2002)

We can illustrate this model with one of the values that you often hear cited in high-performance sport: commitment. So how does the core qualities model help to understand the implications of that value in practice? Figure 2.5 takes commitment as a core quality and moves it around the quadrant.

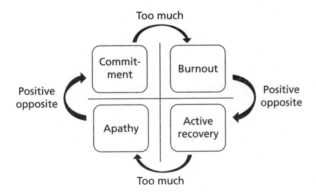

FIG. 2.5 Commitment in the core qualities model

As you can see, too much commitment can lead to the pitfall of burnout. Burnout is a dangerous condition for an individual to find him or herself in. We'll cover pressure and stress in Chapter 9, but for now it is worth noting that the path to burnout is fraught with declining performance, more impetuous risk-taking as well as poor judgement and decision-making – that is, if a person experiencing burnout has the focus or energy to make a decision at all. Bad enough for the individual, but you can probably imagine the performance implications for the sport or organisation.

This is not an argument for less commitment by any means. Elite sport, as with any high-performance environment, can thrive only if inhabited by people who are willing to give their utmost commitment for a sustained period of time. The principle that this model highlights is that 100 per cent commitment requires the challenge of including active recovery time, and nowhere is this more important than during times of extreme stress and pressure, such as a major Games or championships. (This is something we will cover further in Chapter 9) You wouldn't expect your athletes to train and compete without active recovery, so why would you put yourself at risk in this way? While many sports and supporting organisations pursue a duty of care to protect individuals from burnout, it is also true that some sports and supporting organisations inadvertently foster a culture where people who do not look after themselves will eventually suffer. Ultimately, the individual is in the best position to know how far to take their value of commitment, so that they make that value work for them, rather than against them.

SUMMARY

We discuss values early in this book because values are the foundation for the high-performance behaviours that are covered in the remaining chapters. Values are our basic beliefs and principles that guide our choices and behaviours.

Our values are particularly influential when it comes to those 'moments of truth', the occasions when we are called to take action when there is greatest uncertainty. Some of our interviewees referred to how such times and events as a real test of who they really are as a person. Under tough circumstances, their values were the one reliable source of guidance, when they couldn't rely on anyone else.

Knowing where our values come from is an important stage of self-awareness and helps us to develop consistent and reliable behaviours, especially when we are under pressure. Our values are developed early in our lives as a result of our experiences, our families and the culture that we grew up in. For most of us, those values remain fairly consistent throughout our lives and for others they can change as a result of major life events. Through it all, our values remain the foundation of our behaviour and guide the quality of our relationships and the purpose of our work. Identifying what those values are can take some self-searching, so the tools and core qualities model described above can help.

Having clear and well-grounded values is only the entry ticket to high-performance sport; making those values come alive for you in a consistent and reliable manner, is the way to win.

CASE STUDY: MOTIVATION AND DIGGING DEEP

PETER CUNNINGHAM

Head of Sports Science and Sports Medicine, Artemis Racing

FIG. 3.1 Pete Cunningham

Driving over the causeway from Weymouth to the Royal Manor of Portland, there is a sense of chaotic calm, Chesil Beach providing the tranquillity on the right (or, more aptly, starboard) and the unusually unruly waters of Portland harbour raising the tension on our port side. These waters are noted for yielding fine sailing conditions; yet the occasional high winds can callously capsize even the world's best sailors. In August 2011, strong winds challenged the sailors at the London 2012 test event. Triple Olympic champion Ben Ainslie capsized in his second race but ended the day as joint leader of the Finn class. So, not only do you have to have your sailing wits about you, you need to be fit and strong to fare well. And there is one man who is most often credited with helping GB's elite sailors become fit and strong. He is Pete Cunningham, latterly head of sports science at the Skandia Team GB Sailing, and we are here to meet him.

The Royal Yachting Association (RYA) Performance Centre is located at Osprey Quay. Amongst the mêlée of boats, masts, sails, workshops in containers and

Portakabins, warehouses and offices, it is a light industrial building, the nearest thing to what Team GB's sailors call home. An unexceptional external appearance is deceiving; once inside, the sense of purpose and focus on exceptional standards and winning are very evident. You see it first in the eyes of the sailors that move in and around the building with that paradoxical combination of relaxed determination. Maybe it is the look of confidence; it is certainly not one of complacency. Even if you wanted, you could not be complacent for long in a building that is adorned with pictures of some of GB's sailing victories, as well as the text on large banners adorning the wall: 'The definition of insanity is doing the same thing over and over again and expecting different results.'[1]

Pete Cunningham doesn't dwell on the banners for too long as he shows us around. He doesn't need to be reminded of the sort of performance values that have made him central to elite sailing in the UK for nearly 20 years. This small warehouse packs in a double-height workshop, strength and conditioning gym, physiotherapy and consulting rooms, kitchen, offices and meeting rooms – all making efficient use of every square centimetre. (It is a sailing facility, after all.)

Facilities have progressed a long way since he started working with the RYA in 1993. At that time, Pete was appointed to one of the few applied sports science roles in the country. It is easy to forget that while the science of sport has been around since the ancient Greeks, it is only in the last couple of decades that demand for the discipline has spread beyond the services of academic sports scientists.

Pete first started working for the RYA on a part-time basis while completing his PhD on the physiological demands of elite sailing. This work was part of the then Sports Council-funded Sports Science Support Programme (SSSP). Although it was a part-time role, Pete found himself in full-time demand.

> I spent a lot of time taking bloods after races, looking at heart-rate data. Virtually every weekend for the first year or so, I was at a training camp somewhere or at a racing event, so I got to know the sailors really well. It was a good way to get involved.

So what motivated Pete to make such a commitment to this role?

> Well, partly because it was something I enjoyed, I wanted to feel I was helping. Partly I wanted to solve a puzzle – I wanted to know what the physiological demands of sailing were.

In communicating his subsequent insights about these demands to the wider sporting and scientific community, Pete found himself on a collision course with some of the more established academic authorities. Old school maybe, but they were still capable of seriously rocking the boat for Pete. But elite sailing was changing at the time, and Pete could see what impact this was having on the sports' physiological demands:

> Speed off the start-line was critical, it became much more dynamic. It was becoming much more physical and that has a massive physiological impact.

FIRST-HAND VIEW

Pete has been one of the members of staff in our governing body that does actually really make a huge difference. Pete is technically very capable, working hard to study the latest academic developments and network with other sports science professionals to make sure he is at the top of his field. But it is his other skills that make him stand out from the crowd. Pete, quite unusually amongst specialists, sees his primary job as getting his athletes to win gold and his secondary job as being the team's lead physiologist. It is a subtle but significant distinction and not always easy to get right. For example, when is it better for Pete to allow a sailor to concentrate on the technical over the physical for a while, or when is better to muck in and unload a container full of boats and masts? Difficult decisions to make, but Pete seems to have a knack of getting that balance spot-on.

Iain Percy
Double Olympic champion

How did Pete manage to challenge the established views of the old school?

We [with Tudor Hale] published a few papers and presented at British Association of Sport and Exercise Sciences conferences early on, using a load of field data. There was a bit of scientific rigour behind it and the RYA was fully behind what we were doing.

In any case, there is nothing like some medals to quieten your critics:

My PhD was on the demands of single-handed sailing and we got a gold medal in each of the three single-handed classes at the Sydney 2000 Olympic Games. So we must have been doing something right.

Lottery funding for performance sport had been introduced only two years prior in 1998, so the foundations for those Sydney medals appear to have been partly laid down in the long hours and dedication before then. Pete was a key part in that, but he wouldn't put it that way himself. Far from it:

To be honest, for success in sailing the first priority is that they are a talented bunch of sailors. They're pretty good athletes as well.

There is also no sense whatsoever that Pete derives any pleasure from proving himself right or others wrong. There is, however, little doubt that Pete's priority is to help the sailors win gold; being a leading physiologist is very much secondary to that.

Sydney 2000 was an achievement. At the time, Ben [Ainslie] got the gold in the Laser and Iain [Percy] got his first gold in the Finn class. It was as if we'd done a pretty good project together that had culminated in them getting the gold medals and a knowledge for me that whatever we had done physically, was in the right ballpark.

Those results helped to bring round the other sailors within the elite squad. Until then, many were known as excellent sailors, but not that many were known for their fitness. The Sydney results provided the pointer as to the marginal, but sometimes significant, gains that could be achieved with the correct sports science strategy.

Really, the physiology went forward from there. We developed what we call our *gold standards* physically. For each sailing class, we have standards in aerobic fitness, anaerobic fitness, upper body strength, leg strength, leg endurance and so on. We have criteria that we expect athletes to reach.

Is this about just getting the sailors stronger?

No, the key is making them train in the right area that is going to make a performance impact. Over the past 18 years, I've gained quite a good knowledge around that. Obviously they change the Olympic classes now and then, and that gives you a new challenge. For example, the new class this time [for the London 2012 Olympics] is women's match racing. So I've been doing quite a bit with them on the water to see how hard it is. It is a new boat as well; we're now working with the Elliot. They're much shorter races as they are at a much higher intensity when they sail.

Even though there are the standards and the criteria, it is clear from listening to Pete and from those who talk of him that he is a very pragmatic man. By his own admission, he has numbers and targets swirling around in his head, but he is not hidebound by them. From his earliest days in sailing, it seems that Pete has always been willing to get stuck in, to help out where the work is needed. Maybe this has something to do with Pete's life before sailing.

Or rather, that there almost was no life for Pete before sailing. He was shot while being mugged by a gang in broad daylight in some far-off Caribbean port. Pete ended up in hospital for two weeks before he was flown back to the United Kingdom for a long recovery. During that time he reflected on his previous six years in the Merchant Navy as a navigator with Shell. Pete had joined after his A-levels, having been selected for one of 12 apprenticeships from over 10,000 applicants. Although Pete loved the work (after all, it was all about numbers), he wasn't sure that he wanted a life with such risk: 'I was relatively lucky, but it was the catalyst for me to say, "This isn't the life for me."'

The Merchant Navy's loss was sport sciences' gain – and, more particularly, GB Sailing's gain. Pete's love of the sea goes back to when he was a child with a father keen to teach his three sons dinghy sailing. Later on, as a teenager, the craze was windsurfing

FIRST-HAND VIEW

Peter Cunningham worked for the RYA as an applied scientist for nearly 20 years, being one of the first to have this kind of role in the country, during which time he always displayed the key characteristics needed to succeed in high-performance sport.

- A massive passion for performance, a commitment to excellence and a willingness to work the time and hours to achieve that.
- Good social and communication skills and an ability to get to know the athletes and gain their trust. At the same time being able to maintain the correct balance between friendship and professionalism – 'you are not their friend, but are friendly with them'.
- The ability, while being selfish about one's own development, to be selfless in the desire to assist athletes to succeed.
- The ability to move beyond using the measurable standards of academia; in this environment there is only one thing that matters and that is the athlete's performance.
- Trust and integrity, so that both sailors and management know that any decisions or judgements made are always for the good of performance.

Stephen M. Park OBE
RYA Olympic Manager

and his dad made him his very first windsurfer. So started Pete's passion for a sport, which remains with him to this day. It wasn't an obvious forgone conclusion that Pete would forge his second career in performance sailing. After completing his undergraduate degree, Pete contemplated a return to the Merchant Navy. Shell wanted him back. However, at the last minute, Pete got the call inviting him to join the SSSP working with the RYA. Pete acknowledges that while opportunities like this present now and then, it is the prepared mind that grasps them.

When he returned from the Sydney 2000 Games, Pete took advantage of the opportunity that the sailing medal table presented:[2]

All the sailors were full-time, much more professional than four years earlier. They really wanted fitness testing, they all wanted updated training programmes, how to lift weights properly, to be able to do big compound lifts. With that the physiology really changed behind sailing, I would say.

Pete could now refer to role models such as Ben Ainslie, Iain Percy (double Olympic champion) and Shirley Robertson (gold medallist, Europe class, Sydney 2000; Yngling class, Athens 2004):

It became the norm that people had training programmes. We had pretty good role models that really helped. They're still good role models now: you'll still see Ben in the gym every day. It's interesting because some of the younger people coming in look at the likes of Ben and 'Percy' and think: 'Crikey, they're really talented, they do really well.' Well, in reality, they work bloody hard, they're real grafters. As a younger sailor, you need to see that. These guys really pound themselves and in their mid-thirties, they're still in great shape. That's rubbed off really well on some of our younger sailors: people who wouldn't look amiss in most sports when bench-pressing 1.3/1.4 times their bodyweight.

Significantly, as well as the athletes, coaches also became more receptive to the potential advantages of the sports science programme throughout the Athens and Beijing Olympic cycles:

A lot of our coaches are ex-world class athletes, so they have come through the system. They were on the World Class Programme in the early days, so they know about the physiology, they know about the strength and conditioning, they know about the nutrition. That helps, as they have a pretty good understanding about where we're coming from.

FIG. 3.2 Pete mixing recovery drinks

Even so, there appear to be some effective checks and balances in the system:

> For some of the older school coaches, the boat set-up comes first. Getting the boat right, getting the rig right, getting the sails right and then it's, 'OK, you can go to the gym now!' So I still think that there is a little bit of conflict sometimes. But perhaps that sort of conflict is quite healthy because you can overrate your area as the be-all and end-all. To win is a combination of skills in several areas.

As well as developing relationships with the coaching staff, Pete also built up his support team over the Athens and Beijing cycles. He had to: the competition was not far behind. Other nations were taking notes, and that required even greater vigilance to achieve those marginal gains as well as capability across all the support disciplines. Plus there was the development of expertise required to support the Paralympic sailing team:

> You have to be pretty meticulous these days. I wouldn't say that we're a million miles ahead of everybody on the sport science side in sailing now. I'd say that we probably were eight years ago. Everybody looks at our system and everyone knows that we have a gym here and knows what we do. The Americans are trying to copy it: they have a warehouse just up the road here trying to replicate what we do.

There is not much that goes on in the Performance Centre without someone being able to explain to Pete why he or she is doing it:

> We need to be pretty precise in everything we do: we work towards a goal in each area as opposed to training for the sake of training with no real performance improvement. Otherwise, you just end up standing still.

While maintaining a keen overview of everyday activities, Pete's strategy has been to build an integrated sports science team, now 10-strong:

> Half my job now is managing the team, making sure that they work well together. It's quite easy to overstep your area. I'm very conscious that it's not my role these days to give the strength and conditioning [S&C] advice. In the same way, I think that it's very hard for Steve [S&C] not to give physiology advice. Each area overlaps a little bit and we have to be very careful that the sailors get the same message from all of us.

So how does the team achieve this?

> We have a few systems in place, including monthly meetings for the whole sports science and medicine team. At those, we review each sailor on the performance programme. We look at their training, where they're progressing and where they are not. We have a comprehensive online data collection and management system to track each athlete's programme.

FIRST-HAND VIEW

Over the last 18 years, Pete's role has changed. However, there are a few things that have remained constant. An understanding of where he and his colleagues can make the biggest difference, selling those to the sailors, and then focusing on those areas. A pragmatic approach to changing the behaviours of the sailors, most of whom had a history of good sailing, as opposed to a history of good conditioning.

Chris Gowers
Head Coach, Skandia Team GBR

Expanding from technical matters, what sort of people fit well into the team?

Well, the very first thing I look for is enthusiasm, passion: someone who is not just here because they want a job in sport. It's long days and if you think that you're going to come into sport and work only the hours it says in your contract, then elite sport is not for you. Above all, no matter how good you think you are as a sports scientist or doctor or physiotherapist, you have to get on with people and be really enthusiastic and passionate about what you do.

What is Pete's advice when it comes to getting on with people in an environment that necessarily invites its fair share of egos?

One standpoint, which I have with the sailors as well, is: 'Let's be brutally honest with each other.' If you're honest, don't hide behind corners and don't say what you think people want to hear. As long as you're honest and you've got good grounding behind it, then you can't be judged wrongly.

Does this lead to conflict and, if so, how does the team handle that?

We have some pretty frank discussions amongst the team and we don't always see eye to eye. But we air our differences and see which way to go. Honesty is the best policy. If you've got any issues, let's get them out straight away and chat about it, as opposed to harbouring them and feeling bitter about it. I'd say we've got a pretty good team in that respect, everyone's opinion is valid. Whatever you say is a worthy comment.

In building the team, what is Pete's approach to managing people?

Well, they're a relatively hard bunch to manage, as they're quite set in their ways! It's quite hard because you spend a lot of time with them, often sharing a room for a month on camps and competitions and then you have to manage them. It is an interesting balance to achieve, being the boss of people you get to know really well. But I try to create an environment where you don't feel as though it is not your right to say something. We try to be open.

When talking of 'being open', Pete reflects on how he encourages his team to communicate openly with the sailors, coaches and the wider management team:

It's too easy to send an email. You learn so much by just having a chat with someone, just chewing the cud with them. You can often then get them to open up a little bit, which they'd never do in an email or on the phone. That can often give you some information that can help you build the relationship with the sailor or coach. If you're hiding behind your laptop, those really useful and quick conversations just don't happen. We're pretty clear now about what the culture is. A few people are really good at it now, at just mingling and chatting and being in the face of people a little bit, you know. Rather than hiding away and not really knowing who's in the gym.

There is a balance to be struck here, as Pete is conscious that support staff can become too friendly with the athletes:

That overfriendliness is not something I promote. It can end up with cliques developing if you're not careful. It can happen anywhere, but strength and conditioning is a good example: you get a few people who are really receptive to the S&C people and want as much support as they can get. Where there's other people who need the support but don't ask for it and because they are not really pally with the S&C team, they may feel shunned a bit.

This professionalism extends in the social arena. When success is delivered, surely it is good for people to celebrate?

Going out with the sailors at the end of an event for a drink: we don't condone that. If the sailors want to go out for a few beers, then let them go and do their own thing. There are enough support staff and coaches for the practitioners to go out for a beer with. That professional line between support staff and the athletes is very important.

Pete is clearly very considerate of his team and talks generously about each one. It is easy to see why they are so respectful and supportive of each other, always ready to rise to the pressure of competition.

Beijing [Olympic Games 2008] was phenomenal. As a team we came back with six medals.[3] But there were real big hurdles like: no wind. So there was a massive weight loss programme for everybody; we had a super-skinny team. Nathan (Lewis, nutritionist) did a bloody good job for us on the weight loss side. Adrian was involved and Steve Gent, our S&C guy. Some of our sailors had to lose 10 kilos and we had to keep them healthy. And we always knew that there could be the odd typhoon coming through (it blew 30 knots in Ben's last race), so we needed them to be strong, fit and light. We did a load of work behind the scenes that nobody was aware of in a range of areas, and it was pretty successful.

Pete believes that the time is now right, both for himself and the sport, to move on and let someone else take Team GB to the next stage. Besides, he has other great sailing challenges ahead as he joins Artemis Racing in their quest for the 34th America's Cup. It seems as though Pete will once again be hands-on: not only is he head of sport science and medicine for Artemis Racing, he is the only sports scientist there at the beginning. Although it is initially a part-time role, it looks as though Pete's schedule will take him away with the team most weekends at the start, working all hours. No doubt he will be taking bloods, heart-rates and mucking-in wherever he can. He can't wait.

CHAPTER 3

MOTIVATION AND DIGGING DEEP

Chapter 2 ended with a look at commitment as a value. Motivation is the driving force that delivers commitment, so it is appropriate now to look at motivation. You may well have studied athlete motivation in your coaching and applied practitioner courses, but this chapter is about your motivation.

The fact that you've picked up this book probably means that you are already motivated to work in elite sport, or at least to learn more about what it is like to work in it. Alternatively, you may already be working in elite sport or another high-performance setting and looking to develop your skills further. Either way, you are likely to be a fairly motivated individual. This chapter aims to help you work out where that motivation comes from and, just as importantly, how to nurture it so that it can sustain you during the good times and the challenges.

Motivation is the process that is responsible for instigating, cultivating and sustaining the behaviour that helps us to achieve a number of outcomes, such as performance goals and personal development. It also encompasses humanistic elements such as achieving our potential and defining a sense of purpose.

FIG. 3.3 Elite athletes are motivated, but where does your motivation come from?

Motivation is very complex and characterised by many overlapping and competing theories. So this chapter will cover a couple of the key ones that we have seen work well for successful elite coaches and practitioners. This is not a comprehensive review of motivation, and there are plenty of suggestions for further reading if you are interested.[4]

MANY SOURCES OF MOTIVATION

Our interviewees illustrate some of the many motivational drives that exist. In the previous interview, Pete Cunningham refers to being motivated by his love of the water, a strong sense of curiosity and by the inherent enjoyment he gets from the work. Jared Deacon illustrates self-motivation through goal-oriented behaviour in striving to compete at the Olympics (see pages 2–3).

While Nigel Mitchell is also clearly self-motivated (see page 111), he also refers to being motivated by the desire to prove people wrong when they thought he wasn't capable of the task, which is an external driver. From another perspective, Ali Rose refers to her motivation coming from a desire to help athletes get better, often involving complicated problem-solving (see page 78). In Chapter 4, Paul Brice describes an interesting motivational journey: he still has his initial drive of a strong curiosity and a desire to improve the quality of his practice (see page 55), but more recently he has also been motivated by the challenge and personal satisfaction of helping others to develop: he recruited and took responsibility for the development of two PhD students in 2010 as trainees within the biomechanics group at UK Athletics.

While their motivational sources and processes are as unique as their fingerprints, all of our interviewees know that their motivation does not cascade from a perpetual fountain. They have all experienced times when their motivation was stretched and diminished. However, they all built it back up again through reflection on what their core motivation is and what their dedication to elite sport means to them. If you would like a quick 'pulse check' on your motivation, try the exercise 'How self-motivated are you?' opposite.

SOME KEY MOTIVATIONAL CONCEPTS AND THEORIES

So how does an understanding of your motivation help when times are tough and you have to dig deep in order to make sense as to why you chose to work in a highly-demanding world? First you have to understand the source of your motivation.

As discussed above, our interviewees have a great deal of self-motivation, which leads us to one of the key concepts of motivation: intrinsic and extrinsic. Intrinsic motivation occurs when an individual evaluates that the task itself has merit, either as a laudable purpose in itself or as a means to an end to another worthy outcome, or just because the task is inherently enjoyable. Pete Cunningham provides an example of his intrinsic motivation when he refers to his early work with sailing and taking

HOW SELF-MOTIVATED ARE YOU?

Rate the following statements according to your level of agreement or disagreement with them:

1=strongly disagree, 2=disagree, 3=neither disagree nor agree, 4=agree, 5=strongly agree.

	1	2	3	4	5
Because I am resourceful, I know I can get through when faced with difficulties and unexpected events					
I get a strong sense of satisfaction when I've done a good job					
I like to set myself challenges					
When things aren't going so well for me, I remain positive					
If I work hard and apply my skills, I will achieve my goals					
If I make a mistake, I always learn from it					
When I perform well it is usually down to me, rather than down to luck					
When faced with a challenge, I can usually find several solutions					
I usually look for the upside possibilities when there are changes at work					
I meet my deadlines					
I celebrate when I achieve something challenging					
I regularly set objectives and goals to achieve or complete the things I want to					

Add up your scores. If you scored:

42–60: Congratulations, you are highly self-motivated. In order to keep yourself in that state of mind as often as possible, reflect on what is going well and what it contributes to your motivation (see later sections).

24–41: You are self-motivated to some extent, but there is definite room for improvement. To be able to rely more on your own motivation, try some of the techniques suggested in the next two sections.

12–24: You may have a level of self-doubt that is holding you back. There are some techniques throughout this book that can help you realise your potential and build your confidence.

physiological measures at races every weekend for a year. Self-motivated people like our interviewees and successful elite athletes[5] generally have a high level of intrinsic motivation.

Extrinsic motivation also plays an important role and occurs when the individual sees value in the task, because completion of that task will bring some reward or recognition. Extrinsic motivation therefore involves some form of external regulation, such as obtaining rewards (e.g. winning the gold medal) or avoiding punishment.[6] After all, while we may not seek it, we all appreciate some recognition sometimes and that is extrinsic motivation.

Turning to theories of motivation, one of the most influential in the world of sport is *self-determination theory* (SDT).[7] SDT 'maintains that an understanding of human motivation requires a consideration of innate psychological needs for competence, autonomy, and relatedness'.[8] This theory smartly fuses elements from several different theories, including *cognitive evaluative (goal-setting)* theory and *basic needs* theory, two of the 'grandfather' theories of motivation.

Goal-setting motivation theory is based on the practical reality that some of us like to achieve end-points or states as a result of our actions, such as a certain grade in an exam or a job as a senior Applied Practitioner in high-performance sport. This theory is classically put to work every day in the guise of *performance objectives*[9] (and sometimes incentive plans), which many sports and organisations set for their athletes and employees. While performance objectives can indeed focus and increase an individual's effort, such motivational techniques can often be found wanting. For example, have you ever looked down your list of performance objectives and found that some are more appealing than others? This is because the objectives contain different experiences: some would be about demonstrating our skills and others may be about developing new skills. Furthermore, some of those goals might hold a desirable outcome for us (e.g. you work more in a particular sport as a result of a successful exploratory project) and others might yield an outcome that we're less happy about (e.g. you finish working with an athlete because your work was successful and you are no longer needed).[10] Different goals have different behavioural and emotional consequences for us.

This is where SDT provides a more sophisticated approach to understanding our motivation because SDT differentiates the content of goals according to our perceived needs. In particular, SDT proposes that we are motivated to satisfy particular psychological needs: *competence, autonomy* and *relatedness*. In that way, SDT recognises that the motivational quality of our goals is determined by the extent to which they will satisfy our needs for growth and development. Ali Rose illustrates this point when she explains that her motivation comes from helping people through solving complex problems and injuries (see page 78). More dated needs theories (such as Maslow's *hierarchy of needs* and Herzberg's *two-factor model*) assume that needs alone are enough to drive our motivation, but SDT recognises an additional factor: the motivational climate. This refers to the level of support that the individual perceives they receive from their manager, coach or peers. This includes the extent to which the culture and management practices encourage an individual to develop their skills, strive for autonomy and make him or her feel part of the team or organisation.

SDT can present a useful framework to assess your own motivation and how to raise your motivation if you find it flagging. For example, are your goals realistic and challenging enough? Just as importantly, do those goals sit well with your needs to develop your skills or to develop a sense of independence in your work, or do they help you feel part of the team or sport or organisation? This model can also help you ask some serious questions of yourself as to why you are working, or keen to work, in a high-performance and often highly pressured environment. In order to flourish in that environment, you will need some well-grounded motivation, which is easier to nurture if you understand where it comes from. This reflection will also help you strengthen your self-awareness, as discussed in Chapter 1 (pages 13–14).

The SDT model can also help you understand how other people are motivated – although, as mentioned above, motivation is highly complex and interwoven with other factors such as personality, so caution is required to prevent errors in interpretation. However, the more we understand about another person's motivation, the better we are able to relate to them and build a more effective working relationship. More of that in Chapters 5 and 6.

RECOGNISING WHEN YOUR MOTIVATION IS WANING

Our motivation is not a fixed constant; it ebbs and flows along with our mood, our sense of purpose, fulfilment and engagement with our work. However enthusiastic we may feel about an initial goal, there is often a point when we lose momentum and can feel like the goal is out of grasp. Some projects seem to go on and on and progress seems elusive, so our energy and determination can take a knock. Recognising when we are in a motivational slump and taking control of it can help to us to keep focused and continue to enjoy the challenge. Try the exercise below, 'Picking yourself up', to help you identify when you need to pick yourself up.

PICKING YOURSELF UP

There are two parts to this exercise. Firstly, it is about understanding what drains our enthusiasm and, secondly, about recognising what action we can take to pick ourselves up again.

Make a list of your responses to the following questions:

1. What motivates you?
- _____
- _____
- _____
- _____
- _____
- _____

2. How do you feel when you are motivated?
- _____
- _____
- _____
- _____
- _____
- _____
- _____

3. What demotivates you?
- _____
- _____
- _____
- _____
- _____
- _____
- _____

4. How do you feel when you are demotivated?
- _____
- _____
- _____
- _____
- _____
- _____
- _____

Your responses will help you develop strategies for how to read the early warning signs of demotivation and how to push yourself forward again.

In order to help, here are some of the typical responses that people have to the above questions:

1. I am motivated by:

Having a challenging goal
Receiving recognition and positive feedback for a job well done
Receiving a reward for good work completed
Working with others
Learning as a result of the challenge or from working with others
Helping others as a result of achieving the goal

2. When I am motivated, I feel:

A sense of achievement
Energised
Capable
Refreshed
Positive
Fulfilled

3. I am demotivated by:

> Unclear goals
> Boring or pointless work
> Lack of recognition for good work
> Difficult people to work with
> Unfair or low financial reward
> Lack of support or help

4. When I am demotivated, I feel:

> Down
> Moody
> Flat
> Tired
> In a rut
> Restless

This exercise helps us be 'in tune' with the current state of our motivation. By focusing on what motivates us and dealing with the factors that demotivate us (as much as possible), we can raise our overall motivation. That requires us to know how motivated we are, so being more 'in tune' with our motivational state is part of our motivational strategy.

TECHNIQUES TO HELP YOU DIG A LITTLE DEEPER

How do we restore our motivation when times are tough, when we start to question why we make so much personal commitment at such great personal cost? Figure 3.4 identifies some helpful techniques that are described in more detail below.

Focus on what really matters

Often we get overwhelmed before we get demotivated. When we have just too much to do, our energy and focus can diminish along with our drive for the key results. The way forward is to focus on what really matters. Pick one goal that is important, focus your energy on it and complete it. You will gain a sense of satisfaction, and momentum will start to build again.

Reflect on what is going well

When you are in a motivational rut, taking some time to reflect on what has gone well and what you have achieved already will provide a motivational boost. Make the effort to create a list of what you have already achieved in the project or towards your

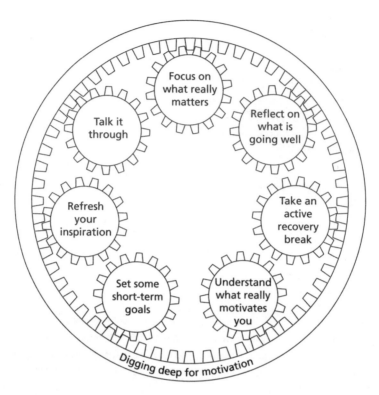

FIG. 3.4 Techniques to nurture your motivation

goal, including what you may consider as small achievements. Recognising in this way that simply getting started is an achievement in itself, will remind you of your capability and rebuild a sense of purpose and momentum.

Take an active recovery break

A change is as good as a rest, and our motivation needs a rest every now and then. You may well be able to keep relentlessly pushing yourself through a slump in energy and motivation, but a quick break will recharge you. Try to take an active break before you become exhausted, and you will manage your energy and therefore motivation in a much smarter way.

Understand what really motivates you

If you have followed some of the approaches suggested in Chapters 1 and 2, you will already be well on the way to understanding the source of your motivation. If you understand where motivation comes from, it is much easier to take control of it.

Set some short-term goals

When you need to dig deep, it is useful to set some tactical goals for yourself, just to get you through the immediate challenge. They don't have to be massive or particularly meaningful; rather, they should be short-term stretch goals just to keep your momentum going.

Refresh your inspiration

When you are in the thick of the challenge and losing motivation, it is easy to forget why you are pushing yourself so hard in the first place. Your original goal, persistence and energy came from someone or something that inspired you. That inspiration can become a little hazy when you are labouring hard and seemingly making little progress. As with motivation, inspiration benefits from the occasional topping up. We discuss this further in Chapter 10, but in the meantime it is worth reminding yourself of the original inspiration upon which you made the commitment and sacrifices to help you achieve your goals.

Talk it through

If you are in a motivational dip, it is useful to talk through the reasons and possible remedies with a trusted colleague of friend. Even better would be to talk them through with a mentor, someone who understands your situation well and who won't judge you. Your mentor can also help you maintain (or maybe develop) a positive mindset, which is important in order to counteract the negative thinking that can preoccupy some of us when things aren't going our way.[11] Reflecting on what is going well and how your abilities are contributing, rather than undermining yourself, can also help to develop a positive mindset. If you are not used to it, or find it uncomfortable, then practise positive thinking.

SUMMARY

A high level of motivation can help you achieve extraordinary heights in your chosen field. However, motivation is not a fixed entity and many of us experience peaks and troughs in our levels of motivation as we move through the highs and lows of our careers. One way to smooth that out is to be very clear about where our motivation comes from, so that we know how to restore it when needed.

The many theories of motivation provide some insight into the core drivers of motivation.[12] SDT helps us to anchor our goals into the deeper needs that motivate us, which enables us to manage our motivation rather than taking it for granted.

There are times when our motivation is challenged, when we lose our drive and we have to dig deep to get ourselves engaged once more in striving towards our goals. Recognising in our mood and behaviour the early warning signs that tell us we are feeling demotivated can help us to take early action.

Our ability to dig deep is key to achieving excellence in high-performance sport. Successful athletes have to do it all the time, especially after the setbacks of a disappointing performance or an injury. Coaches and applied practitioners often experience periods of diminished motivation also, but there are strategies to help us all dig a little deeper when needed.

CASE STUDY: GETTING YOUR MESSAGE ACROSS

PAUL BRICE

Senior Biomechanist UK Athletics, English Institute of Sport

FIG. 4.1 Paul Brice

'Are you bringing your *A-game* to the table?' That is a question that many athletes, coaches and applied practitioners were asked as they put in the hard yards of training that lead to the London 2012 Olympic and Paralympic Games. The appearance of the phrase within the UK Athletics (UKA) vernacular is attributed to Dan Pfaff, director of the UKA Lea Valley Performance Centre, just a few miles from the site of the London Games. Pfaff is the highly regarded US athletics coach who has guided 33 Olympians to seven medals, including Donovan Bailey, the 1996 100m Olympic champion.

The significance of the challenge implied in those few words resonates all too well with Dr Paul Brice, UKA biomechanist. For Paul, it doesn't make sense to bring anything less to the table and he has been pursuing that excellence since he was a teenager:

> I am driven by doing the best I can, almost verging on being a total perfectionist! I think that's probably a good strength and sometimes a big weakness.

There is certainly a sense of 'Let's get on with it' in conversation with Paul: his every sentence has a brisk pace to it, an energy that opens up the possible, and the promise of what his chosen subject can offer. It really is quite infectious – maybe because his enthusiasm comes across as so well-grounded, so rooted in common sense and is delivered with downright plain-speaking. It may seem a paradox, but what you find in Paul is a tranquil eagerness.

Tranquil is probably not a word that Paul's physiotherapist would have used to describe him. She was treating his cruciate ligament injury, picked up as a result of playing as a 16-year-old professional footballer for Crewe. In Paul's view, the problem wasn't the knee; rather it was that the injury wasn't getting better, despite weeks of treatment. Paul was far from tranquil about it and was driven to find a faster resolution. Furthermore, he wanted to understand some of the fundamental mechanics behind the problem:

> I decided to take a much more hands-on, active role in my recovery from injury. I wasn't confident in the information being delivered to me and when people told me rehab would take 11 months, I thought 'I can do it quicker than that'. I needed to, as this was make-or-break for my football career. But there was no real plan or any clear direction or logical progression. I was inquisitive as to why, not in an arrogant sense; I was really interested to learn, to understand what was possible based on the facts and not opinion. So I read research papers, travelled all over the country to visit experts. The desire to play football as a full-time job was something I had to give 100 per cent attention, a once-in-a-lifetime opportunity. Through some difficult times and conversations, I managed to return to play within six months.

FIRST-HAND VIEW

Paul is one of the most valued members of the support staff. The minute he walks into the office, folks are gathered around his desk with questions. His people skills are excellent and he has a great knack for making the complex seem simple when interacting with athletes or centre coaches. Paul is always seeking input from the coaches and athletes in terms of what they are working on, what they think are key components to mechanical efficiencies, and then overlays this with the current trends utilised internationally by leading mechanists. It is rare to find a pragmatic practitioner in this realm who has such intuitive insights combined with a huge dose of common sense. I have worked with biomechanists for over 35 years and there are few in his rank.

Dan A. Pfaff
Performance Centre Director, UKA

Paul admits that there was a big risk in his strategy, as the injury could easily have recurred. But at 16 going on 17, he realised that he it was an even bigger risk to place his career in the hands of a practitioner who didn't seem to have the same focus and attention to detail that he had. Not surprisingly, this plays out in Paul's work ethic to this day:

> I feel I've got to do the best I can. I know it may sound a bit cheesy, but it is more than a job: it's about their [the athletes'] career. If they've been given unique genetic qualities and they have access to the best service available, then we should be aspiring to give them the best service. People I work with every day and the resources that we've got inspire me, so I've got no excuse not to aspire to be really, really good. If you're doing a job, then do it to the best of your own ability. You're there to make a difference to the athletes.

The knee incident not only reveals something about Paul's driven and inquisitive nature, but it also marks the inception of his biomechanics career. It shaped his interest in the discipline, and he went on to study sports technology at Portsmouth University and then Chichester University for his PhD. While at Portsmouth, Paul did anything he could to work with sport, it was his passion after all; it also 'cemented his passion for biomechanics':

> I've always been a good sportsman and played football and athletics at county level. But I've always been fascinated as to how can I push myself? I want to know what I can do and that goes with everything I do. For example, I didn't just want to buy a flat, I wanted to buy a house that was totally run-down and then rebuild the house while I had a full-time job. I don't tend to do things by half!

So Paul didn't just do the course, he also went along to local athletics, football and cricket clubs in a bid to develop his biomechanics skills.

> I did anything I could to work with people. I used to get involved as much as I could, including physiological and psychological testing. I was interested in the results, but also how they applied their areas of science.

At the same time, his thirst for knowledge and understanding led him to complete a number of coaching qualifications.

> It gave me an appreciation of what it was like to coach and a basic understanding in observing what is both good and bad, with the ultimate challenge of trying to fix it.

Paul clearly has a great deal of respect for good coaching, although he recognises that the actual skills can be hard to define:

> When you've experienced a good coach, you know what a good coach is. It is really difficult to define, but that whole attention to detail is key. A good coach

first identifies what the problem is and then they are almost relentless in their pursuit of fixing that problem. Because if that problem is going to cause you an injury or limit performance, then you've got to do something about it. For me, what a good coach does is to focus on that problem in order to effect permanent change. They are not worried that it is going to take weeks or months; they know they have to fix it and stick to the plan. I also like the way they're very creative and innovative about how they do it, but they never deviate from the problem they need to change.

Aston Moore [UKA technical lead for jumps and coach to the triple jumper Phillips Idowu] is probably one of the best coaches I have ever worked with. Ted King [UKA Jumps coach] as well. To have these as your first two coaches, I was truly blessed. They had an understanding of what biomechanics was, they could engage me, and that gave me a massive acceleration in my ability to communicate with people.

As well as having the good fortune to work with some of the best coaches, Paul recognises some other key influences. One was Neil Smith, his PhD supervisor:

He was very, very bright but he was also good people-wise. He has this ability to take massive amounts of information and just pick two or three things and say to the coach: 'That is what you need to focus on.' I would always give too much information, but he had the ability to see what was really important and critical to performance.

Paul compares that approach with that of another well-known biomechanist he knew in his early days:

Another academic, probably the cleverest person in biomechanics I have ever met to this day, unbelievably clever, but what stood out for me was that they had no ability to communicate with people. That showed me that it is not just about being clever. You have to be able to put it in a language that coaches and others can understand.

After completing his PhD at the University of Chichester, Paul accepted a role working partly for Birmingham University and partly for the English Institute of Sport (EIS). His goal, however, was to work full-time for the EIS and he took all the opportunities he could to learn from other more experienced practitioners. After eight months his opportunity arose and he started working full-time for the EIS with UKA.

Phil Graham-Smith at the University of Salford is someone else who has helped him through his career:

Phil was a real inspiration. What stood out from the onset was his enthusiasm for the sport and also the discipline. A unique ability to openly share his knowledge, talk through experiences and without actually telling me directly, he showed me where I actually was. I thought that I was this massively clever academic lad who could change the world, but through creating certain situations, Phil helped me see that I actually had a long way to go. I see it now, but I was definitely limited in my ability to use my knowledge. It was a bit too much about the science for me. Someone once said to me: 'If you have only got a hammer in your toolbox, then everything is a nail.' That sums it up for me. I now understand about the variety of skills you need to get through to people.

Although Paul's natural domain is the models and measurement of biomechanics, he is equally at home with communicating effectively with people and building relationships. While this view may have raised an eyebrow of two in the younger Paul, he recognises that these are the key skills that have delivered the success in the role that he loves. As well as being an excellent biomechanist, he says,

> You have to be creative about the way you communicate. I used to think: 'Well, there's the information, that's got to make sense because it shows you something you can gain from and it's going to make you better.' So surely they'll do it? But more often than not they didn't. I learnt a massive lesson; the art of the role is not to just produce complex scientific data. The real art is the ability to engage with coaches and athletes, and allow them to utilise the data/information to inform daily training to improve performance. Communicating well with each person is a unique puzzle, and solving that really drives me.

As well as being able to get his message across on a one-on-one basis, Paul reflects on how his presentation skills have improved and where he has drawn influences to help him in this area:

> I look at the people who for me are really good at what they do. I try to analyse the skills that they have that I could learn. For example, Neil Black [UKA head of sports science and medicine] is brilliant at getting engagement from the audience when presenting. He has a real passion for whatever he's talking about and that inspires the audience. Now maybe it's hard to be inspiring about biomechanics, but I'd like that passion to come out. I know that I'm not there yet, but I'm working hard at it because you should be passionate about what you're doing. I don't want to be a Neil Black or a clone of anyone, but try to learn skills from them in order to get my message across. You may only get a group of athletes for an hour and you've got to make the biggest impact you can in that hour. So you've got to work on these types of skills.

Paul also recognises that if you want to work with and influence some of the most talented coaches in the world, you have to invest what you think you haven't go much of – time.

> I didn't go in and bombard them with everything I could do. I went to Aston and said, 'This is where I've come from, what are you guys after?' I just went in and tried to do the things that he wanted me to do. And I tried to do them really

well. Start with the basics and slowly build the support from there, don't be obsessed with trying to show everything you know. I spent hours and hours watching training; I was fascinated by what Aston was saying in training and trying to get my technical eye in. I would write down all the little things that I saw and then ask Aston about them. I don't think that we do that enough. You've got to spend a little bit of time in their world for them to spend hopefully some time in yours. That at the beginning makes a real difference.

Getting to know the sport, the event in particular and building relationships with the coaches and athletes are central to Paul's approach now. This hasn't always been easy; some people were wary of what biomechanics could really offer them and others were cautious about letting a newcomer cause ripples in an established setting. It is natural that some people can feel threatened by the perceived invasion of sport science, especially if they don't really understand it. So how does Paul approach this? One point he makes is about the importance of always being honest and dealing with issues, as in this example:

Well, I have struggled to connect with some coaches. I can engage and relate with a lot of people, but one coach and I clearly didn't get on. Part of the problem was that this coach had had some very bad experiences previously with some practitioners who let him down. I asked him to join me for a beer, and we had a very frank discussion. We talked about the many issues between us, particularly how he perceived me to be too confident and arrogant. We found a common ground, cleared the air and the working relationship improved. Since then, I've seen a different guy. I learned that I have to keep him informed about everything I'm doing and every conversation I have with anybody about his athletes. Fair enough. I know that now and I wish I'd sorted it out earlier.

FIRST-HAND VIEW

The area of biomechanics is absolutely vital to gaining that extra one or two per cent. This is especially true in the horizontal jumps where good technique can literally make or break the performance. It is in this area of biomechanics that Paul Brice excels.

Paul is not only an exceptional biomechanist, his knowledge of the technique required for success rivals those of some of our best coaches. He is a great communicator and is able to take complex biomechanical issue and break them into easily understood concepts, which enables some of our less scientific-minded coaches to understand. He is diligent, thorough and inventive and will often work with a coach to arrive at unique solutions to old problems.

Aston Moore
National Event Coach, UKA

Not only is Paul much more willing to have the difficult conversation now, he has also improved his ability to read how others are reacting to him and what he is saying:

> I'm now quite good at picking up when people are upset with me, from their behaviour, what they're saying and their body language. I'm not scared of having those conversations now, whereas before I'd avoid them at all costs. For the relationship going forward, it's actually the best thing to happen. As soon as you deal with it, it doesn't manifest into something massive.

What about when things are going well; what sort of person does Paul work well with?

> I can get on with most people. All athletes, coaches and colleagues range from being really easy to get on with to what some people perceive as being bloody difficult to work with. I seem to get on with most of them. As a person I am much more comfortable receiving constructive feedback than any type of praise. I believe this is primarily what drives me, my obsession to constantly improve as a practitioner to be as effective as possible.

FIG. 4.2 Paul Brice working with Jessica Ennis, heptathlete

So Paul is now in a key position of trust within UKA. It's one that he has clearly built up from the hard graft of getting to know the sport, the coaches and the athletes as well as by his openness, honesty and willingness to assert his view when he has the facts and data behind him. Being an excellent biomechanist is probably just the entry ticket to this, yet an essential element. Paul is trusted to work with the coaches in a role that informs, helps, challenges and develops consistent biomechanical analysis and standards of athlete performance. With each coach for every event, Paul has developed a *Critical Determinants of Performance* (CDP) model, which identifies the key biomechanical parameters and helps to focus training and rehabilitation initiatives. The CDP model has helped Paul develop relationships with coaches by providing objective analysis of the principles and the related training and performance data. Introducing change is always an interesting test of your ability to persuade people and get them working for the change instead of against it:

> The CDP model came out of the blue for some people, so there was some resistance. But CDP is not just biomechanics, it is being very specific about how we use it. I knew that introducing it was a going to be a challenge. So I sought the opinion of people I respect before I started. They all said it made logical sense. So I was even more convinced that this was the way forward. I needed to get some wins quickly, so I thought, Who was the person who was likely to engage with this the most? I sat down with Aston Moore and we worked out how we could use it in triple jump and long jump. Then Aston started using it in his technical feedback. So I thought, where is the next win? I decided to go to the coach who I thought was likely to give me the most challenge: Steve Rippon [Scottish Athletics head of facility and lead field events coach]. I knew he would challenge the thought process more than anyone else, not because he was difficult or opposed to change, far from it, but he would not just accept what I was saying – and rightly so. It took a great deal of time and a lot of discussion. But after eight months we had something we could both agree to; it was well worth the effort.

In the summer of 2008, events meant that CDP had an even more important role to play: helping Jessica Ennis change her long jump take-off foot from right to left. In June 2008, Ennis was diagnosed with stress fractures of the navicular and metatarsal bones, which meant that she missed the Beijing 2008 Olympic Games. Over the next year Ennis, changed her take-off leg in the long jump.

> Ennis's long jump was a massive risk. The CDP model helped in that we could monitor progression of critical elements such as stride length patterns into the take-off board and resultant efficiency of the actual take-off. We had to be objective to see what was and wasn't working compared to jumping off the right leg. It started off as an injury-prevention type exercise, but ended up as an actual performance gain. She is definitely off-loading on the right foot now and jumping further now off the left foot: there aren't many people in the world that can change legs in long jump, never mind trying this within the constraints of a heptathlon and then jumping further as a consequence. It was a massive risk, but

the support team behind the athlete [Toni Minichiello, UKA national coach for combined events and Ennis's coach since she was 11; and Alison Rose (see pages 74–83) her physiotherapist] deserve to take credit for thinking about this beforehand: high jump and long jump are both high in impact load and force and could potentially contribute to increased incidence of injury. You have to off-load the right foot, so we either change the high jump or the long jump take-off. My view is that changing the take-off foot in high jump is really, really difficult, virtually impossible, so we all agreed that the long jump had to change.

With that amount of risk and the high-profile nature of the situation, how did the team behind Ennis manage this?

Like with many big decisions, a lot of people had opinions, a lot of people potentially putting doubts in the coach's and athlete's head. Toni managed the situation really well: he set clear expectations that this is a long-term project, but we still need to be able to compete at a certain point. If we're not at a certain level 10 weeks before competition, then we'll revert to her other foot.

How did Paul manage the risk of using his CDP?

Well, we concentrated on the two elements that the CDP told us made the big difference: getting her leg coming back towards the centre of mass and then not landing so far in front of the body. We knew that would reduce the amount of load and we also knew that she had an enormous amount of horizontal speed, so she only had to get the leg in the right position and she would jump 6.30m, 6.40m. She jumped 6.43m at her first competition out, so that was a massive relief.

At the time, there were plenty who were ready to decry what was being attempted. How did Paul manage his critics?

A lot of people said that the things we were focusing on weren't right. I didn't take it personally. I just stuck to the facts: these are the things that are important to jumping; these are the things that are potentially influencing injury; these are the things she does badly and these are the things that we are doing to improve that. Everyone can find fault with things and has a view, but this model focuses on facts not on opinions.

That sounds like there could be some intense pressure?

The realisation for me is that this job is about pressure. You just have to embrace it. If you don't embrace pressure, you're in the wrong job. Because winning medals sounds glamorous, but the athlete has to deliver and you have to prepare them as best you can to deliver on the day. Anyway, I love it. If there wasn't any pressure, it would be boring!

Paul doesn't suggest that all is deafening harmony, but he is very clear that he is where he wants to be and loving every minute of it:

> I need to be inspired by the people I work with. I just want to learn as much as I can and as fast as I can. I'm obsessed about information and developing myself. I want to be the best that I can. I'm not really sure how far that can go, but I know that I am in the best environment to do it.

CHAPTER 4

GETTING YOUR MESSAGE ACROSS

In his interview, Paul Brice quotes some advice that a mentor gave him early in his career: 'If you have only got a hammer in your toolbox, then everything is a nail.' Paul said this in the context of the need to relate to different people in different ways, using a variety of skills. Over the next three chapters, we'll be covering some of the skills that can enhance the effectiveness of our ability to communicate and the quality of our working relationships: the skills that enable us to successfully work with different types of people (athletes, coaches, performance directors) and in different situations (training, competition, when things are going well – and not so well).

This chapter starts with an overview of the communication process, which is more intricate than the basics of one person giving a message and another person receiving it. In practice, there are more complex steps and subtleties involved, which we map out. Once this is done, we'll look at a practical tool that can help us get our message across to different audiences and through different channels, such as face-to-face, by email and when presenting to groups. Finally, as well as a method to help structure that message, we'll identify some of the powerful emotional techniques that convert agreement into action.

THE COMMUNICATION PROCESS

When we communicate with one or more people, there is usually a reason behind it: to provide information, to check understanding, to persuade, to encourage action or possibly to inspire them to change their behaviour in some way. The subtext to all this is about the building of understanding and trust between us. This can happen during a casual chat with a friend as much as during a purposeful conversation with a coach. Either way, there is a very similar process at the heart of the endeavour, which involves a sophisticated choreography of message, words, body language, hearing, listening, interpretation, visible responses and feedback. As Paul Brice says, there is much more to communication than just the words (see page 59).

Understanding the key elements of the communication process enables us to identify and develop the composite skill sets. For the purposes of simplification, Figure 4.3 describes the key elements of the communication process.

As you can see from Figure 4.3, the simple act of getting our message across involves far more than just the words we say. Although the words we choose, as well as the structure that we give to our message are vital for clarity, we communicate far more about the intention of what we say by our body language and our voice (tone, pitch and pace). If our body language and voice are out of sync with the words we are saying (i.e. the message encoding), then the message we actually send can be different from the one we mean to express with our words.

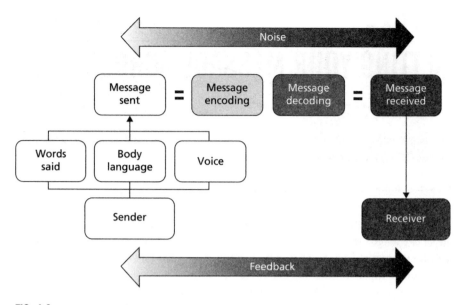

FIG. 4.3 Simplified communication process

There is another juncture that is also ripe for misinterpretation and that is the message decoding by the receiver. The receiver of the message will have his or her own filters, biases and priorities, or 'noise' as represented in Figure 4.3. The result is that they may hear certain words over others, or interpret certain phrases according to their expectations and not ours. They may only hear part of, or a selected part of, our message and this may be happening at an unconscious level for them. Which means that the message received is rarely exactly the same as the one that is sent.

However, body language cues from the receiver can help us to interpret whether our message is being received as intended. We consciously and subconsciously scan for these signs (such as a nod of the head or eye contact) in order to check the reaction that the receiver has to our message. As you may imagine, this is not a very reliable system. For one thing, the receiver may mask their reaction with misleading body language (unwittingly or otherwise) and we may indeed misinterpret the body language we see.

So what are the skills that can help in different stages of the communication process?

DEVELOPING AN EFFECTIVE MESSAGE

Paul Brice gave an example in the previous chapter of the dangers of falling short in communications skills (see page 58). An effective message is concise, organised, gets to the point and gains the receiver's attention by using the right language for them. This holds true for a number of communication channels: speaking one-to-one; writing emails and some types of report; and presenting to an individual or group of people – all skills that applied practitioners in high-performance sport are required to do.

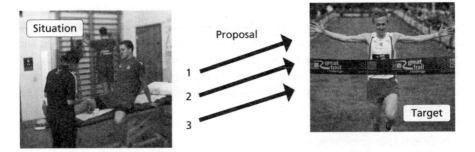

FIG. 4.4 STP: from A to B and how it can be done

A useful tool for developing a message that others can understand is: 'Situation, Target, Proposal' (STP). Although STP is a problem-solving tool, it also serves to organise the key points of our message into a logical order and enables us to focus on the intended impact of that message or desired outcome.

Situation

This element of STP describes how things are now. Some questions to ask when developing or writing the situation are:

- What is the key issue and what is the current state?
- What are the contributing factors, perspectives and opinions that are operating?
- Who is involved and in what role or capacity?
- What is helping or hindering the movement towards the target?

Target

If the situation describes the starting point, the target describes the desired endpoint or how things could be or maybe how you would like them to be. Some questions to ask for this element are:

- What are you trying to achieve, accomplish or even avoid?
- What is the purpose of achieving the target, how will it make an impact?
- Who has bought into this goal or desired outcome?
- How would you know when you have achieved the target, how would you measure it?

Proposal

This is a description of what is needed to take the issue or situation from the current state to the target, or endpoint. Some further detail to this element would typically involve the description of one or more of the following: strategies, plans, actions, processes, pathways, roles and responsibilities.

Most regular face-to-face communications and emails do not need a comprehensive account of the proposal. However, including some form of proposal or solution in your message can engage the receiver more. As long as you are within your remit and sphere of knowledge and experience, demonstrating that you have thought through the issue and have some ideas about solving it will generally gain better reception than merely describing a problem with little or no suggestions for how to resolve it.

Using STP not only increases the impact of your communication, but it also saves time and effort. It helps to organise thoughts before speaking or writing an email, which can help prevent possible misunderstandings by ensuring we know what we want to say and why we want to say it.

STP also works very well when you get those quick opportunities to catch someone's attention and leave them with a message and a possible solution. For example, if you have only five minutes to talk to a coach or an athlete after a practice session as they walk back to the office or changing room. Without being overbearing, a logical STP structure can help you to get your message across very effectively in those valuable few minutes.

In our interview, Paul Brice refers to Neil Smith, a sports scientist who inspired him because of his ability to identify and communicate the salient points of complex situations or issues (see page 58). STP can be very useful in highlighting these salient points and lifting them out of the background noise, because it helps you focus on what really matters: the target and the impact.

In order to get started on using STP, try the exercises below in the box 'STP – developing structure to a message'.

STP – DEVELOPING STRUCTURE TO A MESSAGE

1. Firstly, read the following email from strength and conditioning coach Nick to athletics coach Steve:

Hi Steve,

I've been working with Jack on his Olympic lifts over the last month and the problem is that he has poor range of motion, so he is not very good at getting into the catch position at the end of the power clean. He is keen to do the lift properly, but he's not going to make much progress until he can sort out his flexibility. I don't want to push him too hard until he has this, as it won't help him. I've spoken to the physio last Friday about this and he has spoken to Jack. The physio says that they can help Jack, but Jack hasn't been available to put in the extra time for the sessions with the physio. Jack says that he doesn't have the time right now what with all his current training schedule. As we've talked about before, Jack getting his technique correct is important for him so that he can lift enough weight to

have an impact on his power and strength when running, without
increasing the risk of injury. He can do all the other gym work pretty well.
So could you free up some of Jack's time so that he can put the effort in?

Thanks
Nick

2. Now, take the information in the email and make some bullet points about the
Situation, Target and Proposal in order to generate a STP structure.

Situation: • _____

• _____

• _____

• _____

Target: • _____

• _____

• _____

• _____

Proposal: • _____

• _____

• _____

• _____

Imagine if you were Steve receiving the original email. The email wanders around
following Nick's agenda and comes across as though he is passing on a problem that
Steve has to address. In fact, Nick is just trying to get Steve's buy-in to the service
that he is providing.

Using the STP structure you have developed from the original email should
highlight what the real issue, target and proposal are. Using that within an email is
more likely to lead to Steve's support, without Steve having to use more of his time
than necessary.

STP QUESTIONS TO ASK

Read the statements below and write some STP questions that would help you understand more about the issue.

1. Swimmer James is on podium potential funding. One area of performance that lets him down is his starts and turns. For example, if he were able to match the turns of the world's best swimmers, he would reach the Olympic final in the 400m Individual Medley. Both James and his coach believe he is getting faster, based on his improving overall times. The coach is considering putting some dedicated resource towards improving James's (and possibly his other swimmers') starts and turns. As an applied sports scientist, what would you want to know to help pull together an STP to use as a response to the coach?

   Situation: • Here's how I see it... _____

                • _____

                • _____

                • _____

   Target: • _____

                • _____

                • _____

                • _____

   Proposal: • _____

                • _____

                • _____

                • _____

2. As an athletics coach, you have been working with some track athletes for a couple of years, under the guidance of a head coach. Now the head coach wants you to take charge of several of the athletes on your own, without his direct supervision. The athletes may not be too happy about this, considering they joined the training group because of the head coach's reputation. You are a highly competent coach, identified as a future head coach, but how will you gain the confidence of the athletes who will be transferred to your group?

This example calls for some creative licence from you, as not all of the information is available, but the point is to come up with the right questions and place those is a logical structure. Your questions will have more impact as a result of doing so.

Situation: • _____

• _____

• _____

• _____

Target: • _____

• _____

• _____

• _____

Proposal: • _____

• _____

• _____

• _____

IT'S NOT WHAT YOU SAY, IT'S THE WAY YOU SAY IT

Having a logical structure to your message really does help to get that message across. Sometimes it will be appropriate to include some facts and data in that message in order to add some evidence to your proposal. However, while logic and structure may gain you agreement to your message, it is the emotion behind that message that is more likely persuade your listener to take action as a result of that message:

Logic + data + structure = agreement
Logic + data + structure + emotion = agreement and action

By emotion, we mean conviction: it is hard to convince someone of your message if you yourself don't fully believe it. And that doubt can manifest in our words, our tone of voice and our body language. Others pick up on that doubt, either subconsciously or consciously, and that leads to our message being undermined.

All of our interviewees have inspired athletes, persuaded their peers, fought against the status quo and won battles against a sometimes-entrenched system, because they had conviction. Not that they walk around like obsessive evangelists, but they do know how to pack a punch to their message with legitimate conviction. This is something that Jurg Gotz excels at (see pages 163–171), as explained by the canoeing performance director John Anderson: 'His high level of emotional intelligence and people skills mean that he is outstanding at understanding people and knowing how best to communicate with each on an individual basis to get buy-in.'

It is also interesting to check some of Dave Clark's comments as another example of conviction (see pages 18–26). In fact, Dave describes himself as a man of 'conviction with a hard edge'. In another example, Dave talks about the importance of legitimate conviction: 'The key thing in many success stories is that there is a good person at the middle of that: someone who has clarity of conviction and the courage to stand and drive that conviction.'

Dave goes on to illustrate this with a situation where a strength and conditioning coach was not using a back squat test with an athlete because the team physiotherapist was against doing so. Dave makes the point that if the strength and conditioning coach believes that the squat test is the right approach, he should make a case for it, rather than just simply acquiescing. Dave paraphrases what he said to the strength and conditioning coach: 'At least convince me whether you understand that squatting is the right thing.'

The passion of the protégé is awakened as he makes a cogent case explaining why he believes he is right, so Dave says:

> Now go and win that argument with that physio. If you've made a physio upset, then live with it. You are responsible for that and if you truly believe that you are right, you should make the case.

One final example of communicating with conviction is from the interview with Danny Kerry (see pages 198–206). Danny talks about the long road to centralising the Women's Hockey programme, which started before the Beijing Olympics in 2008 and took several years to achieve. Crucial to winning people over to Danny's conviction in the benefits of centralisation was the emotion he put into his message, his appeal to ultimate reward. He said to his team:

> What use is it aspiring just to be an Olympian? We're funded to win medals. You aspire to medals! Look at the sports that win medals, look at cycling, look at rowing, look at sailing – they all have centralised programmes. And we're a team sport, think of what we could achieve if we were together!

A powerful message indeed, with echoes of STP. But just as importantly, packed full of belief and potential.

Apart from conviction, other methods of adding emotional appeal and interest to your message are the use of metaphors, analogies, examples and anecdotes. A metaphor is a figure of speech that uses one concept to describe another. One example often used in swimming is to imagine that you are a dolphin, flowing naturally through the water – a useful image when swimming using the underwater kick. Metaphors, used thoughtfully, can be great ways to leave a memorable image in someone's mind. This connects with the point you are making, which by association also becomes more memorable. Coaches often use metaphors when explaining techniques as a way of helping the athlete understanding the feeling of the particular move.

An analogy can be very useful when you want to provide a contrast or comparison of concepts in people's minds. For example: As an athlete, you need to eat quality food. After all, you would not expect an Formula 1 racing car to perform at its best using petrol from the local garage.

Brief examples and anecdotes add colour to your message and sometimes provide evidence strong enough to convince your listener that you have a point. These two techniques particularly appeal to the wide appeal of storytelling: most people like a good story. Storytelling techniques – such as having a beginning, middle and end as well as a turning point associated with your key message – can help you to get your message across even more effectively. When using stories, be careful about how you use jokes: what is funny to you may not be funny to everyone else in the circumstances.

SUMMARY

The complexities of communication can be broken down into component skills, which in turn can be practised independently and then reunited into overall communication excellence. Breaking down communication in this way is rather like deconstructing a swim stroke into component drills practice and then combining those specific drilled-in skills into one flowing stroke.

This chapter has addressed just two of those skills: structuring the message and the importance of emotion in turning a message from background noise into a purposeful action, even if that action is just making sure someone is informed.

In the next couple of chapters we will look at further critical communication skills, such as questioning, listening, body language and adapting your message to different styles of personality. Finally, at the end of Chapter 6, we will look at how all these skills come together to deliver effective communication and how they can foster productive working relationships.

CASE STUDY: CONNECTING WITH OTHERS

ALISON ROSE

Physiotherapist, the Coach House Sports Physiotherapy Clinic

FIG. 5.1 Alison Rose

When an elite coach is prepared to arrange and fund your flights so that you can be at a competition to support their athlete, you probably know that you are making a significant impact on that athlete's performance. Ali Rose received exactly that vote of confidence from Toni Minichiello when he insisted that she be on call to treat Jessica Ennis during the IAAF World Championships in August 2009. As described in the previous chapter, Jessica Ennis had to switch from right to left take-off leg for the long jump (see pages 62-63). It was a risky endeavour by Jess and the team around her, but it eventually paid off. However, Minichiello knew that there was one person who was more likely to be able to fix any potential problems Jess may encounter between the gruelling seven events: Alison (Ali) Rose. In the event, there were no serious injuries and Jess went on to claim the world title.

It probably helped that Ali had worked at the previous four athletics World Championships; the 2002 and 2006 European Athletics Championships; the previous three Olympic Games; and every World and European Cross Country Championships since 2003. But perhaps more importantly, Ali had been a crucial member of 'Team Ennis' over the previous year, helping her to recover from the stress fracture of her foot. Ali appreciated being a member of a close team:

> Working with that entire team at that time was great. Jess is an amazing athlete anyway, very conscientious and always looking forwards which is a skill in itself. So you obviously had very good materials to work with.

This wasn't Ali's first experience in working with world-leading athletes. Indeed, from her early days as a physiotherapist Ali had designed and implemented prehabilitation and rehabilitation programmes for many of Team GB's Olympians, including some of the key medallists at the Sydney, Athens and Beijing Olympic Games. If you speak to any of these athletes, you will discover what Jessica Ennis found: Ali is not only a very talented physiotherapist but also an acute reader of an athlete's state of mind. This is one of the reasons why athletes warm to and trust Ali: she understands what they are going through and is able to build their confidence in her treatments and their consequent performance.

Perhaps Ali's own athletic career as a talented marathon runner provides her with some understanding of the athlete's challenge, but not all ex-athletes can dedicate themselves selflessly to the service of others. Dame Kelly Holmes, double Olympic champion in the 800m and 1500m events at the Athens Olympic Games, is one of many well-known Olympians to recognise the quality of Ali's work. As the reality of winning two Olympic gold medals started to sink in, one of the first people Kelly publicly thanked was her physiotherapist Ali Rose. Ali had been working with Kelly for two years before the Athens Games (2002–2004). Prior to that, Kelly's potential had been thwarted by a continuous string of injuries and she was losing the belief that she would ever be injury-free. Her coach (Margo Jennings), doctor (Bryan English) and other support staff, including Zara Hyde Peters, worked together to execute a training and race plan that limited overtraining and kept Kelly injury-free. It was unusual for Kelly to remain free of injury for so long before a major competition, and although this may have been somewhat unsettling at first, Kelly's confidence grew – and that had performance dividends. According to Ali, the growth in Kelly's confidence was a significant factor:

> Behind the scenes, seeing the confidence come back to her as she realised that she was remaining injury-free was key. Free from injury, she was able to remain more consistent in training and therefore become fitter and therefore more able to achieve the results she did. It was the change in confidence levels as she became more resistant to injury that was rewarding to be a part of.

Anyone who has worked with Ali will realise that teamwork is very important to her:

> Team-wise, that was a really special team with really good supportive people that all worked together in a challenging situation with a delicate athlete, which then obviously got the best result you would ever want.

FIRST-HAND VIEW

Alison needs no introduction as far as her abilities as a physiotherapist, but as any member of a support team it is the 'over and above' qualities that help make the real difference in our programme. The key attributes that aid Alison in her world-class delivery are her obvious understanding and experience of the elite competition and training environments in sport, and her willingness to understand the specific differences that are connected with diving. Alison oozes confidence in her work, her communication is always honest and accurate, and she also makes me feel like she is totally committed to helping us. To back all of this up, she is a lovely person to have around with a real easy-going personality. A real trust has developed and I feel we are lucky to have Alison as a part of our team.

Adrian Hinchliffe
GB Olympic diving coach 2004 and 2008

Ali joined the team as a result of Kelly's initial trust in her because Ali had spent 2002 working with Gerard Hartmann, a physical therapist based in Ireland. Hartmann was one of the most sought-after physical therapists in the track and field world, but for Ali to spend a year under his tutelage raised a few eyebrows amongst conventional physiotherapists. However, Ali has always had, and still has, the curiosity to seek such fresh and effective treatments to sharpen her practice. Kelly was looking for a different approach, and Ali had that to offer.

Part of what Ali offered was also an empathy with the predicament that elite athletes often find themselves in, for Ali had herself been an ambitious runner and no stranger to the physical cost of dedicated training. When studying physiotherapy at the University of Edinburgh in the early 1990s, Malcolm Brown coached Ali to a level where she eventually represented Great Britain. But subsequent injuries took their toll and Ali retired from competitive running in 2000.

Ali's early years had seen her bought up in a sporting environment, one where she was good at both swimming and running. Running, however, won when Ali realised that, at the age of 15, a choice was required if she was to progress, and the good club structure, coaching support and mentoring from an elder athlete meant the track's benefit was the pool's loss.

Ali's interest in the human body had been ignited while reading physiology and anatomy at Dundee. Intrigued by how the body worked, she changed track from medicine to physiotherapy. After her graduation, Ali worked at Edinburgh University's Fitness Assessment and Sports Injury Clinic. As a young physiotherapist, this provided invaluable experience to work alongside skilled and experienced practitioners and other disciplines such as nutrition and podiatry.

Ali's own performance goals were still alight at this time, and in 1999 she moved to work in Australia to have a final push at making the GB Olympic Games team, taking a job at a clinic that had a contract with the Australian army. That role suited Ali well at that time:

It was a great job for me. I learnt a lot working with a steady flow of amazing and compliant patients. The comparison with what I do now is that these normal people had to have an elite-level body in order for them to do what the army wanted them to do. A lot of them had chronic problems that they didn't want to talk about because there was a risk that they could be medically downgraded. So many of them didn't come to clinic until they were desperate, by which point you really had to be smart about how you treated them. I did a fair amount of deep work, and most often it worked for them.

Here things took an unexpected twist. Injured and not on the team, Ali was phoned 10 days prior to Team GB arriving at the pre-Olympic Games holding camp in 2000 by Neil Black, then UKA head physiotherapist. He had fallen off his horse and broken his leg and said, 'Do you fancy working at the Olympics ... and we'll pay you.'

Regrettably for Neil Black, but arguably good news for Ali Rose, UKA needed an urgent replacement for him. It wasn't just a case of being in the right place at the right time: clearly some influential people believed that Ali was also the right person to stand in for one of Team GB's most highly regarded physiotherapists. Some of the endurance coaches (including Malcolm Brown) knew that Ali had what it takes to treat some of GB's best medal prospects, under pressure. That experience proved formative when it came to treating high-profile athletes in a highly pressurised environment:

It was one of the most amazing things I've ever done. Work-wise, it was ridiculously hard with long hours and loads of athletes. The physiotherapy team was fantastic and the support and management team were as well. The athletes were on great form and everyone was on such a high that you just got on with it and did the work. I got good feedback from the athletes I worked with, so that helped my confidence.

How did Ali cope with the pressure of working 18-hour days treating very high-profile athletes who were amongst some of Team GB's main medal contenders?

Difficult question ... I think that the athletes helped, because they came across as normal people. They treated me as a normal person. The athletes being as friendly as they were made me feel part of the team that they wanted to work with. Treating some was terrifying, as they preferred and needed to be treated 'just so'. But the army job was great experience for that, in that it gave me a lot of confidence in treating the same people on a daily basis. In the lead-up to the Games, I did treat many athletes daily. The physio and medical team was also very supportive, in particular Mark Buckingham, who really looked out for me. Four years later, in Beijing, we did far less work, because the athletes were so healthy. But in Sydney a lot of the athletes had injuries and we were working around the clock to make sure they were ready for race day.

As well as willing to do the hard work, Ali clearly has the technical and manual skills to excel in her field. But Ali also credits and rates the importance of her intuitive skills in being able to spot and resolve minor movements or postures that potentially hinder an athlete:

> Some of my best results come particularly with the complicated people: For example, I watch them walking and I just know that despite the fact they've come in with a sore foot, I may well start by treating their left shoulder, which may be the one thing that is stopping them getting better. For me, it's intuitive as much as anything.

For Ali, it's hugely important to keep her mind open and it is when Ali is running that some of her best insights and solutions arise.

> I've always had an intuition about my work, but not really realised the importance of it. I try to keep my mind open to what I'm detecting, but at the same time I try not to think too hard about it in order to let my hands sense what is happening.

Ali maintains an openness to new ideas and encourages her team to do the same at her own clinic, the Coach House Sports Physiotherapy Clinic (CSPC). Ali set up the clinic in early 2003, having spent the previous year at the Hartmann clinic.

Openness to and having new ideas gets you so far, but actually persuading others of your new ideas and implementing them can be a far greater challenge. Ali understands this all too well when it comes to working with new coaches and sports. An example of this is Ali's work with diving following the Athens Olympic Games in 2004. At the time Ali was working part-time with the English Institute of Sport and was treating the diver Tandi Gerrard. (Tandi and her partner Jane Smith just missed out on a medal at the Athens Olympic Games, finishing fourth in the synchronized three-metre springboard event.)

FIRST-HAND VIEW

It is difficult to put everything Alison does into a single snappy quote. I suppose that's a quote in itself! Alison provides a superb level of rehab and pre-hab; her ability to work closely with myself as the coach and support the development, improvement and problem-solving within the athletes' training programme is invaluable to me and other members of the team of practitioners. The ability to explain simply and take into consideration the other training demands helps build a robust and successful training environment.

Toni Minichiello
Coach, combined events, heptathlon and decathlon, UKA
Coach to Jessica Ennis

Tandi had long-term problems with an incredibly stiff middle and upper back. In treating Tandi, I realised that Tandi's core stability needed to improve. Diving tended to use some fairly old-school ideas and expected their divers to do 80–100 hanging pike-ups from wall bars everyday. Yet Tandi had a very weak core and abdominals, which was why she was experiencing some of these problems. Following some consistent work on her core strength, Tandi's back improved. Tandi was pleased and she persuaded Ady, the coach, to see what I was doing to support Tandi. [Adrian Hinchliffe was head coach at City of Leeds Diving Club, and GB Olympic diving coach 2004 and 2008.] At first, I don't think Ady was too impressed, as I was advocating some key changes to the conventional diving exercises. But after our long discussion, Ady decided to support the changes, which we eventually introduced across the programme.

Ali stresses the importance of getting to know both the sport and the athlete:

I learned a huge amount from Tandi, because I don't dive. You do need to learn from your athlete. We started building up a series of diving-specific exercises and implemented them through the club.

This was a risky strategy because Ali's proposals were substantially different to the approach taken by diving for many years in this area. However, Ady's leap of faith paid off:

As a result, injury rates plummeted and Ady was thrilled. So it snowballed from there. Ady prides himself on his approach to injury prevention and we have relatively few injuries now. Injury prevention is a key part of the training implemented in Leeds by the coaches.

How did Ali initially learn about the impact of the critical performance movements of divers?

It took a great deal of observation and a good knowledge of the body anyway, so that you can see if there are any physical limitations that might prevent them doing certain movements. Then learning from the coach about what they are specifically looking for, so that you can marry that up with the physical examination. It helps when the coach compares and contrasts the divers in terms of what movements or skills they have, so that you can connect the different movements to performance ability. Seeing this on film helps a great deal: the difference between bad movement patterns and good movement patterns. Also it is helpful to talk to the athletes themselves, as many of them are good at describing the movement and the feeling that they want during the dive. It is important for me to be able to visualise the required movement so that I design a stretch or intervention that will lead to improvement of help to prevent an injury.

In order to bring these changes about, Ali had to draw on more than her powers of observation, creativity and manual skills. Influencing skills might be of help here. After all, people buy into what you're proposing only if they buy into you:

> Being a runner helps, as runners believe in you anyway. But having Kelly be so generous in her public thanks to me has brought a lot of people to me on the basis that I treated Kelly. It becomes self-fulfilling to some extent: the more an athlete believes in a physio, the more they'll do their exercises and the more likely the athlete is to get better.

Ali's ability to build quality relationships with athletes, coaches and colleagues has been central to her impact on athletes, the practice of physiotherapy in British elite sport and the wider system. These abilities are built from difficult experiences, as well as the good times.

> When Jessica got injured, although we were all gutted and absolutely distraught, we still had each other to rely on and no one was blaming each other. The team is really supportive and because everyone behaved so positively, we all carried each other forward. Whereas there are teams where you don't have that honesty and openness between all the people in the team. These are the situations when it goes through your mind, 'Is it really worth me being in this situation?' If the team doesn't gel, it can be very stressful and you only need one difficult personality type to make things difficult. It is where you get the arrogance and individuals thinking that they are the most important. But we all rely on each other and there is no one in our team that is more important than Jessica. It's the same with diving. The handpicked team that Ady has put together and the way he leads them and got them working together; it takes a lot of skill to do that.

FIRST-HAND VIEW

Ali operates beyond the normal boundaries of conventional practitioners. She, like the world-class athletes she treats, is always looking for the edge which will improve performance; she seeks out the best and goes to learn from them, a key attribute being her openness to learning despite being a world class practitioner. She understands the psychology of elite athletes. A problem that is small at the start of the training year, when reproduced prior to a major event takes on a different meaning to the athletes. Ali recognises those meanings and the implications. Finally she values the role of the coach. Rather than excluding the coach from the relationship between her and the athlete, she embraces it. So the coach finds themselves being educated along with the athlete. She is a person of integrity.

Malcolm Brown
High-performance athletics and triathlon coach
Coach to Alistair and Jonathan Brownlee

FIG. 5.2 Alison Rose

So how does Ali focus on getting the job done when there are difficult people to work with?

> I've been lucky that I haven't been in that situation very often. But when it happens, I think it is about being consistent: finding the way to explain clearly why you think something is happening and how you can improve it and checking that you've got that message across. The danger is when you get people within a team who don't want to share the care of the athlete with anyone else. It becomes a difficult situation and the person to lose out is the athlete.

On the more positive side, what are the qualities of people that Ali appreciates working with?

> Well, I look for people to be honest and have similar goals. It has to be fun, challenging and everyone has to learn from the work. I try to create an atmosphere where you can implement new ideas and I value working in teams that are all-inclusive, where we're open with each other and discuss issues if they arise. When a team works together, that is how you get the best out of all those people. I don't think that any of us will ever know everything, so you need to be able to pool and share your ideas. If your idea doesn't get used or doesn't work, then not being precious or coming up with another one [helps]. Being open-minded enough to acknowledge that another idea or approach could work better than yours.

FIRST-HAND VIEW

Alison understands elite performance in a way which allows her to relate to the athletes, understand their motivations and know how to get the best out of them. Most importantly she brings a rigour to her work which ensures that goals are achieved.

Jack Maitland
Director of Triathlon, Leeds Metropolitan University
Coach to Alistair and Jonathan Brownlee

Taking that a stage further, Ali comments on the type of people that influence and inspire her:

There are some ridiculously good physiotherapists out there with hands-on skills that I can only aspire to have. I admire those people who are open enough to share these skills. I have been taught by and am mentored by some physiotherapists with expertise in chronic complex injuries. I love the challenge of dealing with those types of patients and I've been on courses for these injuries, where the physiotherapists that have taught … have been amazing. I really appreciate it when someone has an openness to sharing what they do, and that doesn't always happen.

In recent years Ali has extended her skills from physiotherapy to managing the CSPC. Based on her experiences of recruiting and managing a team of physiotherapists, what advice does Ali have for new practitioners?

Just immerse yourself in as many courses as you can and then practice the skills you've learned. Be prepared to learn from other physiotherapists. It helps if you're willing to get immersed in sports and observe the athletes, even if you do that for free, as it is important to build up the experience. Try to get experience where you're working under pressure; rugby is a good example of that, where you've got to treat and fix people quickly. Observing, asking questions and being open to admit you don't know something.

Looking back on her achievements, where does Ali still get her motivation?

I get an incredible buzz and really learn a lot from treating patients with chronic complex injuries, which can have multiple causes. Because they are such complicated injuries to treat, I have to use all the skills that I've learned from all the courses I have done. I can then apply these skills back into the sporting field on much more healthy individuals. To treat someone who has had chronic pain for years and they finally are able to sleep through the night is hugely satisfying.

Seeing those changes in people is very motivating: you can see how much it means to them, how much it affects their daily life, their relationships and their working life. My biggest driver, my biggest buzz is being able to make a difference to someone's life.

CHAPTER 5

CONNECTING WITH OTHERS

In her interview, Ali Rose refers to the importance of being able to connect with both her clients and her peers. Athletes such as Dame Kelly Holmes, Jessica Ennis and the Brownlee brothers have benefited not only from Ali's technical skills but also from her skill in being able to understand their needs and concerns. Ali's ability to connect in this way is bound in her intuitive recognition of what is going on with an athlete's body while training and sometimes even from just the way the athlete walks into the treatment room. Ali can deduce a great deal from the body movements and postures that she observes, powers complemented by some incisive questioning and listening skills. These are skills that are just as pertinent to Ali's work within the sports science and medicine teams supporting some of Team GB's best athletes as they are to her 'technical' physiotherapy ones. Ali also gains an intrinsic enjoyment from connecting with her colleagues in the all-inclusive way she describes (see page 81).

Connecting with those we work with means being able to build a bond that stimulates trust, interest, engagement, challenge, high standards and loyalty to name just a few benefits.[1] Very few people have the luxury, or possibly the misfortune, of truly working alone, which means that connecting with others whom we work with is an essential skillset: one that can be developed to achieve excellent and productive working relationships.

This chapter starts our exploration of how to achieve this with some straightforward techniques and approaches. In the first three chapters, we looked at the individual attributes of achieving excellence in high-performance sport. We began with self-awareness, then looked at values and finally at motivation. All of these can be described as 'closed' skills in that they are relatively stable whatever the situation, just as is true of closed skill sports or techniques. As with sport skills, so with 'people' skills: there are 'open' skills, such as connecting with others and influencing, which need to be adapted to get the best result depending on the circumstances.

In Chapter 4, we started to move across the frontier between closed and open skills, in that getting your message across requires flexibility of approach when communicating with different people. However, in getting our message across, we run the risk that we are in 'transmit' or 'push' mode only and not taking into account the needs of others when sending that message.

This chapter starts to help us take the needs of others into account, thereby migrating our message from 'push' mode to 'pull' mode. A message in 'pull' mode is based upon an understanding of the receiver's interest or need. Therefore it is far more likely to be effective, as it is built on our understanding of the needs of the other person or people and hence more likely to have an impact by achieving support and action from that other person. Our understanding of that other person's interest or need is created by questioning and listening, two of the techniques we will cover in this chapter.

QUESTIONING SKILLS

You have probably got to where you are today by being able to ask some useful questions. After all, asking good questions is a great way to learn. So why is this a skill singled out for specific attention? Well, although you may be used to asking questions in your everyday life, the ability to ask quality questions in a conscious manner is central to building effective relationships of any kind, essential to influencing others and critical in diffusing difficult situations and conflicts. The challenge is that many of us are not as good as we think we are at asking quality questions. Maybe that is because we take this skill for granted, or perhaps we have yet to experience the power of great questioning. In any case, the ability to ask good questions is a core skill when it comes to connecting with others.

If we want to do this successfully, that means understanding more about the other person: what they know and what their views and attitudes are for example. Asking timely and pertinent questions is the best way to achieve that connection. We gain more information from asking open questions, as opposed to closed questions. Closed questions can be useful, but run the risk of eliciting one-word or short answers. For example, 'Do you think that the rehabilitation strategy will work?' may receive only the one-word responses of 'Yes' or 'No'. So closed questions may not reveal much new information or understanding. Open questions, on the other hand, generally encourage more plentiful answers. For example, it is very difficult to provide a one-word response to the question 'What is it about working with athletes that you like or dislike?' Further examples of open questions include:

- Please can you tell me more about why you use that particular drill at that time in the training session?
- On what do you base the athlete's periodisation plan?
- How do you think that athlete will respond to the challenges of the rehabilitation strategy?
- What are the factors that contribute to the athlete's take-off speed from the board?
- How is the team getting used to the new tactical configuration?

Starting open questions with 'how' and 'what' are the mainstays of encouraging someone to share information, techniques, views and attitudes. You could also start with 'why', but beware that this can sometimes be interpreted as interrogatory and may elicit a defensive response rather than an engaging one. For example, the simple question to a coach, 'Why does your athlete keep getting injured?', could be interpreted as an implied criticism of the coaching routine, even though it was an innocent enquiry about the contributing factors.

Used well, open questions can elicit more information, encourage people to open up and help to reveal views and opinions of those asked. Try the challenge in the box 'Asking open questions' to improve your open questions skills.

FIG. 5.3 Elite coaches and practitioners know the art of a good question

ASKING OPEN QUESTIONS: NOT AS EASY AS YOU MIGHT THINK

Ask a colleague or friend to work with you on this open question skills practice. Firstly, think of a situation for which you would like to find a solution or way forward. For example, maybe you want to take up scuba diving, or paint the bathroom. In any case, you need a situation where your colleague or friend can coach you to help you work out what you could do to move that situation forward. The other person also needs to think of a situation for themselves.

Then coach the other person to help them find a way forward or a solution to their situation. But do this by asking questions that begin with only 'what' or 'how'. Many people find it challenging to confine their questioning in this way, but it is a great way to practice asking open questions.

Closed questions are not all bad, however, and they have their part to play in connecting with others. They are particularly useful for seeking engagement ('Do you agree that we need to talk about this now?'); checking understanding ('Have I got this right: does the athlete need to place in the top eight to qualify?'); and clarifying agreement ('Now we've talked this through, do you agree that the athlete would benefit from a performance nutrition strategy?').

In most situations, a combination of open and closed questions is appropriate. A strategy of starting a conversation with closed questions and then moving to open questions can help to gain initial interest and then confidence that you are interested in them and what they have to say. Although it is best to avoid creating an atmosphere of interrogation, probing and leading questions also have their place in helping to draw out further information and agreement.

Questioning skills are a fundamental component of any coach's or sports practitioner's toolbox. Asking good questions of the athletes and coaches that you work with (for example, about their technique, their awareness of movement, their attitude and how they are physically feeling) encourages them to think and can even precipitate those 'Aha' moments that reveal a new truth or perspective to them in a way that enables them to positively change their technique, approach or point of view. Good questions enable athletes to develop insight and take action for themselves.

LISTENING SKILLS

Great questions need great listening, so that you really hear, understand and process the responses. (Remember Chapter 4 and the communication process model, pages 65–66). In fact, listening skills are just as important as questioning skills when it comes to connecting with people we work with. Taking just one of our interviewees as an example, Nik Diaper (see pages 146–153) has listening skills that are much appreciated and a hallmark of his relationships with coaches and athletes. Tom Dyson (Lead Coach – Adaptive Boats, GB Rowing Team) says:

> Nik's communication skills in this role have been key. He has always listened carefully to my requirements, identified the main parameters and applied logic to discern if an athlete might be who we are looking for.

And Jayne Ellis (Paralympic Coach, Great Britain Cycling Team) says: 'Nik has a very strong quality in that he is able to listen carefully and fully understand the needs of the athletes and coaches.'

Unlike Nik, many of us are actually not that good at listening, for a whole host of reasons. For a start, we can be easily distracted and find our mind wandering off while the other person is speaking to us. Or we may find that what they are talking about just doesn't interest us very much. Other blocks to our effective listening are when we are overly judgmental about what the other person is saying, or we might be filtering out what we want to hear – in other words, hearing what we want to hear, rather than what is actually being said. For those and other reasons, most of us can considerably improve our listening skills. It is worthwhile doing so because ratcheting up this skill set can lead to more understanding, less misunderstanding, less conflict, more clarity and better influencing skills to name just a few benefits.

Actually, you already are a very good listener. When you want to be. Think back to the times when you have been genuinely interested in what someone else has to say. Maybe it was when an athlete described what it was like to win their first senior medal, or when a coach described how her team outwitted the competition under the pressure of a final. In any case, at that time you were very interested and had no problem listening. And this is the key to listening skills: actively choosing to listen. When we make the choice to listen, we are more attentive, more responsive and more effective at building relationships with others. But only active listening creates the right environment for trust and understanding to develop between two people.

Active listening requires a conscious commitment and effort to listen attentively, which means recognising and managing our own personal blocks to listening. Self-awareness helps to reveal what those blocks might be. Some of those blocks have been mentioned earlier and others are described in the box 'Blocks to listening'.

How, do we get better at listening? Like all skills, listening can be improved with practice. The box 'Choosing to Listen' gives you some techniques to help you develop your active listening skills.

Think about your reaction when someone is really listening attentively to what you have to say. Rather pleasing, isn't it? When people take an interest in us in this way, it helps to build trust and understanding; it helps us connect so much more effectively with them. That is why listening skills are among the most important we can develop and keep on developing.

BLOCKS TO LISTENING

Rehearsing: when we are too busy thinking about what we are going to say next.
Comparing: when we are filtering or interpreting what someone is saying through our own experience or judgements. For example, you know you are doing this when you catch yourself thinking in response to what someone is saying, 'That's not how I would have reacted'.
Mind-reading: a classic block to active listening when we try to second-guess what the speaker really means by what they said. When we think that we know what the other person is really thinking, we have effectively stopped listening.

CHOOSING TO LISTEN

Ask a friend or colleague to recount a recent experience in some detail. Recognise your own personal blocks to listening so that you can be aware of them if they occur during this exercise. While your friend or colleague is talking, periodically ask them to pause and then paraphrase what they have told you so far. Do this a few times during their talk, and then summarise the key points back to them when they have finished. Make a note of how accurate your paraphrasing and summarizing were. Did you add anything in or miss anything out? Did you emphasise points that interested you more, or did you recount the points with the original importance given to them by the speaker? By practising this a few times, you will be able to develop more attentive listening and more accurate recall.

NON-VERBAL COMMUNICATION

Questioning and listening skills are the foundation of our effectiveness in being able to connect with others. But we should also pay attention to our non-verbal communication if we are interested in building successful working relationships.[2] Non-verbal communication encompasses the messages transmitted by our body language in our eye movements, facial expressions, posture and gestures, as well as the variability of the tone, pitch and pace of our voice.

Sometimes our non-verbal communications are synchronised well with the words that leave our mouths and at other times they are at odds with the message we think we are giving. The trouble is that people generally (subconsciously or otherwise) rely on our non-verbal communications when they are decoding the intention of our message, especially if these are inconsistent with the words that we are using. So it is important to be aware of our body language and to ensure that it is consistent with our message.

The key components of non-verbal communication to consider when questioning and listening are illustrated in Figure 5.4 and described below.

FIG. 5.4 Key components of non-verbal communication

Eye contact

Making eye contact with someone when we are questioning or listening to him or her is vital in building trust and rapport. It is unwise to make too much continuous eye contact, as this can cause anxiety in the other person. So averting your gaze every now and then for short periods of time can help to keep the amount of eye contact more natural.

Facial expression

Keeping an interested, relaxed and authentic expression will help you gain the other person's belief that you are engaged in what they have to say. Like most things, it is worth considering getting feedback on your expressions, either from others or using a mirror. Does your face say or give the impression that you want it to?

Posture

Maintaining a relaxed and open body posture will help the other person to relax and be more open as well. Folded arms, however comfortable, do not communicate a particularly relaxed and open disposition, and can be interpreted as defensive. So it is generally better to keep your arms unfolded. When possible, facing the other person communicates more interest, rather than occupying a side-on posture. Leaning forward slightly now and then is also helpful to communicate your interest when you are questioning or listening.

Gestures

A thoughtful use of hand gestures (for example, counting points raised on our fingers) can reinforce the key points of questions we may be asking. Beware, however, of this being interpreted as finger pointing. Head gestures, such as an occasional nod, can reinforce the message that we are attentively listening.

Voice

Keeping a relaxed voice will convey a confidence and help to build trust. Varying the pitch, tone and pace of your voice can help to reinforce key questions or points you are making, as well as maintaining the energy of the conversation. Particularly important in supporting your questioning and listening skills is the use of silence. Just staying quiet after you've asked a question and occasionally having the courage to allow a pause in the conversation can encourage the other person to share more information or express additional views.

SUMMARY

Connecting well with those whom we work is essential if we are to be successful. Building those connections means understanding more about the other person and relating our information, opinions and insights to their perspective. In that way, we turn our way of engaging with others from one of pushing our agenda to one of relating our information and views to their needs. So that means that what we have to offer is easier for others to accept, as we have helped them to build the connections to their own agenda.

Those connections partly arise from our questioning and listening skills, as well as our awareness and use of consistent non-verbal communication to support those skills. Other elements, particularly the presence of trust, are also important to building successful working relationships. We will explore these in the next few chapters.

However, questioning and listening skills are a very good place to start, as they are the foundation of all the higher-level skills such as influencing, inspiring and leading as well as managing conflict. All of our interviewees agreed that it is essential to keep developing questioning and listening skills throughout their careers. Indeed, many stated that excellence in high-performance sport is less about having the right answers and more about having the right questions.

CASE STUDY: INFLUENCING OTHERS

SARAH HARDMAN

South Lead Physiologist, English Institute of Sport

FIG. 6.1 Sarah Hardman

Sarah Hardman is testament to the fact that it takes a great deal more than academic qualifications to succeed as an elite applied sport scientist. As lead physiologist for the English Institute of Sport southern region and a central member of the physiology team behind the success of Team GB's rowing squad, Sarah is held in high regard by many in the system as a very effective and influential physiologist.

And yet Sarah Hardman does not have the *standard* requirement of a PhD, which may come as a surprise to some, given her current position and responsibilities. She certainly has the academic rigour and capability to complete one and she may well yet do so one day, but for now, this certainly does not hold her back. In fact, Sarah's non-technical skills are just as highly valued as her technical expertise, if not more so. The abilities to plan and organise, to build relationships, to influence at the highest level in the system and to garner the trust and confidence of all who work with her, whether athlete, coach or colleague, have marked Sarah out as one of the UK's leading applied physiologists.

Perhaps it is not surprising that Sarah has risen so high, as she has nurtured an ambition of achieving her potential in sport since her teenage years. Like many, Sarah combined a love of sport (playing tennis at county level in her early years) with a keen interest in human biology and physiology. Her interest led her to do a sports science degree, a course described by her parents as 'so you'. And so it proved as she completed first her undergraduate degree at Sunderland University and then a master's in physiology at Manchester Metropolitan University. Here she had her first chance to work in an applied capacity, providing support to England Netball as part of the then Sports Council-funded Sports Science Support Programme.

With applied careers in short supply, Sarah was all set to take a position as a research assistant working with the late Professor Tom Reilly, when she was offered the role of physiologist at the Welsh Institute of Sport (WIS) in 1999. Along with the Lilleshall Human Performance Centre and the British Olympic Medical Centre, the WIS was one of the precursors of the current institutes of sports. WIS offered a glimpse of the future for integrated sports science, sports medicine and coaching support for elite athletes. Although it may not have felt like it at the time, for Sarah joined WIS when staff changes meant that she had no boss or real work programme. While this might seem disconcerting, in truth it is not an uncommon situation to find on-going changes at your new place of work, which means that your role is not quite as you were initially led to believe. Under these circumstances, rising to the challenge as Sarah did is key.

Sarah had also helped set herself up well for being accepted at WIS by gaining a substantial amount of experience with elite athletes during her master's studies. It took considerable commitment and a fair amount of persuasive skills and time, but Sarah managed to get voluntary work with disability athletics, women's football, badminton, netball and wheelchair basketball. This valuable experience not only helped to convince WIS that Sarah was the best candidate, but it helped Sarah start to understand how to build key relationships with athletes and coaches.

Once at WIS, Sarah began working in a multi-sport capacity, though with a particular focus on netball. At the time, Wales Netball had both a New Zealand performance director and head coach, and as New Zealand was one of the leading nations in the sport, this provided some much-needed performance focus for the

FIRST-HAND VIEW

Sarah is diligent, conscientious and thoughtful. Coaches are a hard and sometimes unpredictable phenomena to work with and she engages with us with flexibility and patience. However she is professional enough to ensure that principles in sports science are maintained and is a leading example of the maxim 'In opening up new areas, be bold in what you try but cautious in what you claim!'

Darren Whiter
GB Rowing team coach

team. It was also a good opportunity for Sarah to work with professionals committed to a performance mindset:

> The performance director had a vision that they wanted to change the culture and get the athletes into a performance mindset, rather than just playing for their club. In Wales at the time, it was all about the Commonwealth Games, which was a great kick-start to my career because of the focus it provided.

Sarah went with the team to Singapore in 2001 to gain some early experience of the challenges of working and living with coaches and athletes away from home, on tour:

> The fact that they took me on tour meant that they trusted me and wanted my input, but on my first tour it took some sorting out as to how I could work best with them. I had a good relationship with the coach, but she didn't always buy into the advice I was giving. At the time, I thought that it was a good idea to take all sorts of measures, but looking back, I probably could have dropped a couple. The coach probably thought that the logistics of what I was doing ate into some of the training time, and that was probably true.
>
> At one time the coach was having a tough time with a lot of stress at home. She took it out on me and I was privately quite upset about that for a while. The next time I saw her, she said: 'I really do value you and think that you're doing a good job.' I think that she realised that she had been stressed and had taken it out on me. Of course, now I wouldn't take it personally because I know that it is part of high-performance. At high-performance level you will get frustration, conflict and stress, and as a support practitioner you will often bear the brunt of that. But that doesn't mean it is about you or what you are delivering. Training camps are high-pressure situations; I now have a much better self-awareness and know what my hot spots are. It is important to know how you are likely to react to certain situations – what is your comfort zone and what is your nightmare?
>
> It can also be a challenge when you're a practitioner and you are staying with some of the players. Fortunately, I was sharing an apartment with some of the senior players and they understood some of the pressures.

In 2002, the Manchester Commonwealth Games provided Sarah with the opportunity to work at her first multi-sport event. While this was a very positive experience, it also highlighted to Sarah the challenges of not being fully accredited and outside of the Games village.

> For me, it was really hard because I was staying in a house and the team were in the village. So I was separate to my peers; everyone I worked with was in the village and I had to travel in every day. I felt that it was all going on [in the village] and I was missing out. I had to have a bit of a chat to myself and focus on what I was there to do. It was really hard for me at that age, my first multi-games experience and being separate. That was a really good lesson for me. I

loved it once we got going, particularly sitting down and having the key conversations with the athletes and coaches.

Here Sarah reiterates a key point, that successful applied practice is not about being in the laboratory, it is about the trust and hence conversations that you have with the coaches.

After the Manchester Games, high-performance sports science delivery evolved further in the UK, with the foundation of UK Sport and the English Institute of Sport (EIS). As funding expanded, more opportunities became available with the Athens Olympic Games less than two years away. Momentum also increased at WIS as new people joined and a real sense of team purpose and support developed.

> We all had the ultimate drive to help the athletes to get on an Olympic podium. We had a mutual respect; very like-minded and we all brought something to the table. We worked hard and played hard as professionals. A high level of trust built and it was a good time.

FIRST-HAND VIEW

It is communication that is at the heart of both the successes and the dysfunctions in multidisciplinary teams. Sarah has an openness and approachability which keeps others in the team on board with her, and makes the athlete feel that she is completely present with them. This is not easy to achieve, but Sarah's demeanor and level of self-awareness in her dealings with others, combined with her extraordinary capacity for organisation and planning, creates a sense of calm which is priceless in an elite setting.

Joanne Elphinston
Physiotherapist

Sarah's main focus leading up to Athens was working with the badminton squad and latterly GB Badminton, helping them with their acclimatisation strategy. How receptive was the sport to Sarah's work, even though there were a couple of Welsh players in the squad?

> A couple of the coaches were fine and the buy-in from the players was good. The performance director was behind the strategy, so that helped. It took some time to get everyone on board, so we spent a lot of time on courtside at Milton Keynes to build the relationships.

GB Badminton performed reasonably well in Athens, with Nathan Robertson and Gail Emms winning silver, but changes at WIS meant that Sarah's focus moved on to athletics and the build-up to the Melbourne Commonwealth Games in 2006. Given Sarah's experience was mainly in racquet sports and netball, this was quite a departure, so how did Sarah manage that?

I was mainly working with a group of middle-distance runners [including a young Dai Greene, the 400m hurdles world champion in 2011] and with Paralympic track and field athletes as well. At the time, it was quite daunting. So I just went to the track and spent time with a couple of the key coaches. But I felt that I had big shoes to fill, as the physiologist before me had done such a good job. However, people had faith in me and I discussed my plans with the coaches and physiologists who were good sounding boards, such as Andy Jones [Professor of Applied Physiology at the University of Exeter and UKA physiologist] and Charlie Pedlar [Centre for Health, Applied Sport and Exercise Science, St Mary's University College].

So four years after Sarah's experience at the Manchester Commonwealth Games, the set-up was somewhat different at the Melbourne Games: this time she was fully accredited and staying in the Games village. However, as with any multi-games event or championships, there was a high level of pressure on everyone in the team.

I had learned to accept that it was going to be very long days, and planning my schedule so that I had the occasional downtime helped. I managed the pressure by taking myself off for a run most days and making sure I didn't get too hungry! You need to have your own downtime and Matt [Cosgrove, sports science manager at WIS, Sports Council Wales and subsequently with Welsh Cycling] was a good manager who understood the importance of being able to get away every now and then. I ran my own programme, which meant early starts, but my work was often complete by evening sessions. There are swings and roundabouts to everyone's role, so you take the breaks when you can. I roomed with one of the media people and not with other sport scientists, so I was fortunate that I could get a real break from the work.

Returning from Melbourne, Sarah continued her role with athletics but was now ready for her next challenge. A management role had more appeal than an academic one at this stage, as Sarah sought to strengthen her skills in planning and organisation. The right opportunity came up when an EIS position working full-time with GB Rowing came up towards the end of 2006. Sarah decided that it was worth applying to see how she would be considered for a role at that level. Success came her way and she moved to Bisham Abbey in early 2007, leading the delivery of physiology services to Rowing and managing the laboratory and staff at Bisham.

Within three weeks of starting, Sarah was asked to go on a rowing camp. The pressure was on, as Sarah was the only person there to provide physiological support to GB's top rowers and the head men's team coach, Jürgen Gröbler. While Sarah received great support from the national governing body physiologist, Al Smith, she was very much on her own at the camp. It was also a complicated role, labour-intensive with the monitoring of a range of different types of sessions. Not only was Sarah learning about rowing, but also she had to do it fast because it was Olympic qualification year.

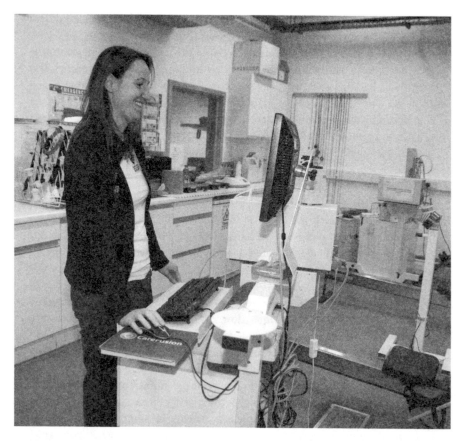

FIG. 6.2 Sarah checking athletes' data

The learning curve was very steep. It felt like they chucked me in the deep end with bricks on my feet and no life jacket. Not in a bad way, but just to provide me with the challenge to learn quickly. Jürgen was great, it was his idea to take me, as he told me that was the only way to learn.

So how did Sarah teach herself to swim fast in this environment?

Well, getting to know people was the key element. Spending the time learning about rowing was important, but there's nothing better than spending the time getting to know the athletes and coaches.

At the same time, Sarah was very aware that the service quality and culture of the physiology laboratory back at Bisham Abbey needed an upgrade to make it world-class. Not because of any shortcomings by the staff, but more because expectations were advancing quickly and Sarah wanted to make sure that the laboratory standards were second to none. To manage the change required some assertive leadership, as the existing culture could have held progress back.

I was advised by senior managers that there had been no direct management of the department previously and, as such, an overly relaxed culture had developed. So I thought that they needed some leadership and direction. It took some time to consolidate what needed to happen. But once we had that, I was very vocal about where we were heading and made sure that we got there, mainly through some very detailed planning and assigning responsibilities. Pulling everyone together as a team to deliver was important. As was accepting that we weren't going to achieve everything in the short time leading up to Beijing, so prioritising was critical.

Sarah gained an important insight as to how to get people to take ownership and responsibility for their actions:

Trust was a big issue, really. On the one hand, I didn't want to micro-manage, but on the other, could I trust that what I expected to happen when I wasn't here (on camp, for example) would actually happen? Helping people to develop was sometimes a challenge: a couple of members of the staff didn't realise what I meant by *world-class* and frustration can build up in those circumstances: 'Well, why don't they understand?' Then someone asked me, 'Have you asked them what *world-class* means to them?' That was a light-bulb moment, as I then worked on how to coach them to define their own interpretation and standards.

It took some time to consolidate the new team, and even though Sarah knew that the team would be short-lived, she knew it was worth the effort. So it proved, with the inevitable changes after Beijing, as happens when the system reflects after each Olympic Games. The post-Beijing review brought about some far-reaching changes for sports science and medicine delivery within the EIS. The new strategy meant that national governing bodies were given direct funding and responsibility for sourcing sports science and medicine services. They became the direct customers of service providers like the EIS. Inevitably, there was some turmoil, as the system gradually adapted to the new structure. Many people saw changes in their roles and their managers, and some lost their jobs in high-performance sport altogether.

There was a period of redundancies and physiology was hit quite hard, but it is much better now for lots of reasons. It is interesting about that balance between the technical skills and those that could work well with the coaches and athletes: the people that stayed had good relationships with the sport they worked for.

Good interpersonal skills can be critical, then, and your job can sometimes literally depend on them. But can you train people to have these skills as well as the self-awareness that they are built on?

Yes, you can, using coaching techniques such as asking good questions to help people work out the answer for themselves and to help them understand more about themselves, such as how they react in certain situations.

FIRST-HAND VIEW

Sarah Hardman stands out as a world-class practitioner. She is a very welcome calm presence in a frequently highly charged atmosphere of intense training. She will bend over backwards to find a way for every athlete to complete a training session, even if that involves setting up a completely different piece of equipment in a different location at a different time. Sarah gives the same priority to our training needs as we do ourselves and she will persevere until things are done to our own exacting standards. It is fantastic to have someone working in the team who demands from themselves the same level of performance as we do and who takes the same level of pride in her work as we do. And above all, one of the special things that Sarah exhibits is genuine care and concern for the athletes.

Katherine Grainger
Mulitiple Olympic medallist, GB Rowing

This clearly has implications for future recruitment, so Sarah was invited to expand on the characteristics that she would look for in a new member of her team:

Attention to detail, a genuine passion to do the job, self-awareness and an ability to know when to be a sponge: when to observe and listen and learn, and just realise the opportunity they have and use that opportunity and not bulldoze their way in. Often when we interview, or when we have people with experience, they'll come in and they'll be so passionate and so enthusiastic, but to their detriment: Because they'll come in with that 'I think you should do this' attitude, and you can't do that with a coach.

A genuine passion for the job? What does that look like?

An example would be the situation where a practitioner knows that there is some squad training happening, but they don't need to be there. But actually they'll give up another day to go and see the athletes do what they do, just to give them support.

For Sarah, rowing provides a good example of where that support is given by coaches, athletes and applied practitioners to each other across the elite squad.

The team ethic in rowing is phenomenal. They all train in the same place. They all support each other: when the Olympic guys have finished their races, they'll wait to watch the Paralympic guys racing. The team dynamic within rowing is very, very strong. The culture in rowing is 'we just get on with it'. They're not flashy. They're just hard-working and passionate about what they do and very, very good at planning.

GB Rowing is a particularly tight-knit team, so how did Sarah manage to build the working relationships and influence some of the programmes?

> One example is on the adaptive [Paralympic] side: working with the coaches to characterise the training and identifying what to monitor and when to monitor it. We now have a generic bank of data to work with. Coaches now come to me with case study questions for individual athletes, we're now at the stage where we can do some real bespoke and specific physiological support with the athletes. This is based on their trust in what I'm doing on the back of my suggestions for a physiology support programme for the squad. We've now added in other disciplines to the testing, so the approach is working well.

As Sarah's role continues to evolve, her role has been adjusted to include the role of physiology lead for the southern region of the EIS, something that means she spends much of her time coaching physiologists on how to build relationships with the sports, athletes and coaches. Sarah's ability not only to build those relationships herself, but also to coach others on how to master those skills is why the system rewards people with interpersonal skills on top of their technical excellence. For Sarah, these are two sides of the same coin:

> You can't have one without the other and be successful. It's the only way to get the job done.

CHAPTER 6

INFLUENCING OTHERS

Like Sarah Hardman, those who achieve excellence in high-performance sport, have to be very good at influencing others. The ability to affect someone's opinion or behaviour is a highly regarded and rewarded talent in any walk of life, especially very competitive ones. What exactly do we mean by *influencing*? In a nutshell, it is getting others to buy into your vision and having the skill to convince others to accept and sometimes take action based on your perspective or agenda. As with any talent, the ability to influence can be deconstructed into specific skills and drills, then practised and developed. In fact, you have been developing your influencing skills all of your life. In all of our relationships, be they with family, friends or work colleagues, we exert some level of influence to put our point across or indeed to persuade others to agree with us and, hopefully, go along with our ideas and actions.

How effective we are at persuading others depends on our ability to communicate and build relationships. Not, of course, forgetting that the essential component of whether others respond to our influencing effort is the trust they place in us. In that regard, influencing is very different to manipulation, where the intention is to impose views or actions towards an outcome that is selfish or possibly detrimental to others. As well as not being about manipulation, this chapter is also not about influencing as a result of power and authority. While those may be legitimate conditions for some forms of influencing (for example, during the extreme pressure of a major games), those in charge often, rightly, have to dictate what happens. It is generally more effective to persuade others when you do not have clear control over their actions, and that is the focus of this chapter.

What is very clear about the 12 people interviewed in this book is that they have an influence in the UK high-performance sport system that extends above and beyond their job title. Through their exceptional influencing skills, they continue to achieve an impact that defies the confines of their job description. Whether they have been inspiring athletes to make extraordinary efforts, persuading colleagues to take calculated risks or making system-wide changes, their ability to influence has been central to their success. Read the interview with Sarah Hardman for an example of influence in action when Sarah started working with GB Rowing (see pages 97–101). Sarah talks about how she started to influence rowing coaches by developing and introducing a physiological monitoring model. Some of our other interviewees have influenced and introduced changes against the tide of opinion, such as Jurg Gotz and his call to move to a class-based coaching system (see page 166) and Nigel Mitchell, who was able to change the delivery of sports performance nutrition in the UK (see pages 113–114).

With those examples in mind, this chapter explores how to increase your impact, to metaphorically punch above your weight in the workplace by using influencing skills. Firstly, we'll look at the component skills of influencing and how they are related to the skills we have previously covered in this book. Then it is worth understanding the different styles of influencing, so that you can practice and develop a range of techniques to influence different people in different situations.

THE NATURE OF INFLUENCE

On one level, there is nothing magical about being able to influence. It is a combination of persuading (when you want to convince someone to do something) and negotiation (when you are seeking a mutually acceptable outcome). Everyone influences: think of the time you have persuaded friends to go where you want to for an evening out or when you have impressed someone enough to offer you a job as a result of an interview. That positive influencing happened because people trusted you and believed in what you were saying or suggesting. You were able to put across what you wanted in a way that convinced them that was the best option. On top of that, the principal skills involved are really just an extension of those we have already covered in previous chapters: self-awareness; values; motivation or intention; communication and connecting with others or rapport. Figure 6.3 maps the skills covered in previous chapters to influencing skills.

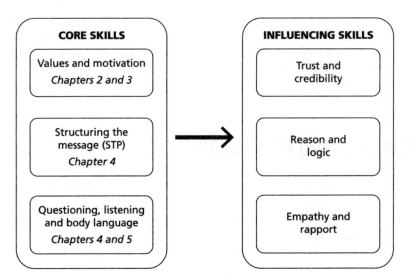

FIG. 6.3 Influencing: built on skills covered in previous chapters

The next sections describe how the core skills covered in previous chapters can be developed into principle influencing skills.

WITHOUT TRUST ...

In the absence of coercion or power, it is impossible to influence unless there is trust. Trust, as the saying goes, is hard won and easily lost. But what exactly is trust? Trust between two people is like the baton change in a sprint relay: we don't always see the detail, but we certainly know when it doesn't work. So we need to slow it down, to understand the individual steps involved. Trust comprises two components: the perception of competence and of intention. For someone to trust another person, they have to believe that the other person knows what they are doing (i.e. they are at least competent) and that they are working towards a common goal or an intrinsically worthwhile outcome (i.e. they have an honest and worthwhile intention). Jared Deacon makes this point in his interview: 'I find it easier to influence ... the ones who believe in you and what you're doing.'

Remarkable competence, or expertise, is often very influential on its own. Being an expert places a person in an influential position, as people can defer to and sometimes take actions based upon this perceived superior knowledge and understanding. Many of our interviewees are considered to be experts in a particular sport or practice: a position that contributes to, while not explaining the totality of, their influencing skills.

However, at the beginning of a high-performance sport career, it may take a while to prove to coaches and performance directors that you are competent, let alone an expert. But it won't take too long for people to work out your intentions and whether they believe in them. You probably won't be surprised that our self-awareness, values and motivation play a substantial role in the authenticity that people judge us to hold and therefore their willingness to trust us. That is why we cover these concepts and skills in the preceding chapters.

Trust is necessary, but not sufficient on its own for influencing to be successful. Some further techniques are required, including making a case for people to buy into.

PUSH, PULL AND PERSUASION

The championing of a case, or the advocating of an action, is a common approach when people consciously seek to influence. Sometimes our training (particularly within science and medicine) encourages us to believe that the irrefutable facts and beautiful logic of our argument alone are enough for people take the action we are seeking. Yet while it is very important to make a case with facts, reason and clarity of message (as pointed out by Dave Clark, see pages 20–21), this approach provides only the entry ticket to the game of influencing. Paul Brice neatly illustrates this principle:

> I used to think: 'Well there's the information, that's got to make sense because it shows you something you can gain from and it's going to make you better.' So surely they'll do it? But more often than not they didn't.

Paul is now very influential across UK Athletics for a number of reasons, not least of which is his ability to relate his message to the needs of different people. His influencing approach is now more about relating his case to the needs of the person he is trying to influence through questioning and listening skills (i.e. pulling), rather than just providing information (i.e. pushing). A pulling approach to influencing is generally more effective than a pushing one. You do need your argument and logic ready, which is why the STP model can be useful (see pages 67–71). But you also need questioning and listening skills to help you identify the needs of the other person so that you can then relate your proposition to those (see pages 85–89).

Positivity is very important when you are trying to influence most people. The STP model draws our focus to the positive upsides: the target along with the proposal for how to get there. Within that structure, your influencing efforts will benefit substantially from choosing positive language. Some work on your self-awareness should reveal the attention you pay to your choice of words and how these affect thought and emotions in others. For example, the use of hesitant phrases, such as 'I mean', 'Isn't it?' and 'You know' undermines how well a speaker comes across.[1] This effect is even more pronounced when the listener does not have much time, a common occurrence in high-performance sport.[2] Bearing that in mind, which of the following statements is more persuasive?

- I'm afraid that athlete might not make the qualifying time with the deadline so close.
- With some specific and targeted sessions, the athlete has a good chance of qualifying.

Both are factual and accurate, yet one presents a more positive perspective. Some may call that *spin*, and they would be right if the intention were to mislead or deceive. But if there is an objective reality and a genuine belief that the athlete could qualify, the power of positive language could make all the difference to an athlete's career.

The right words at the right time can support your influencing efforts. The field of neurolinguistics provides some further insights into the relationship between words and the higher mental processes (or meta-programmes) guiding other mental processes related to our thoughts, emotional reactions and behaviours.[3] Subscribers to the practical application of neurolinguistics (i.e. neurolinguistic programming, or NLP[4]) often contend that particular words appeal more to holders of one meta-programming trait than to another.

One example is the NLP concept of how meta-programmes result in traits that filter information received according to different preferences. In the case of being motivated either to move towards a desired outcome or to move away from an undesired outcome, words can make all the difference. Someone motivated to move towards a particular goal is more likely to be persuaded by words and phrases such as: *achieve; possibility; what we could accomplish; obtain;* and *likelihood.* Whereas those motivated or concerned to move away from an undesired outcome or bad situation are influenced more by words and phrases such as: *reduce the risk of; avoid; minimise; get away from;* and *put some distance between.*

While the choice of language is important when seeking to influence, it is a subsidiary contributor to the principal skills. However, once you have made progress with the core skills, it is worth experimenting with some of the language techniques. Well-chosen words can make a difference, but they will miss their mark if they are used insincerely and in the absence of an understanding of the other person's situation, views and feelings.

FROM ANOTHER'S PERSPECTIVE

If you want to be successful at genuinely influencing someone, then seeking to understand their perspective is a necessity.[5] If we are able to appreciate how the other person sees a situation or an issue as well as have some insight into their opinions and feelings about the matter, and what they want to achieve from a situation, then we are better placed to relate our case to their wants and needs.[6] By using their perspective to explain our position, we are making it much easier for the other person to accept our case. For example, a classic comment you often hear from coaches is the equivalent to 'So what? How will it make the boat go faster?' In other words, how will what you suggest help the coach achieve his or her goal of a better athletic performance? This was the way that Chris Price was able to influence Amy Williams to stand in freezing cold water after training sessions.

> Chris was giving me words of encouragement and keeping me focused on what I was doing and why I was doing it, whilst I stood there shivering! He said something like 'when you are standing on that podium in Whistler, you will think back to times like this and be grateful that the discomfort and effort were all worthwhile.'

Another example is the manner in which Dave Clark persuaded Chris Hoy and Craig MacLean to change their squat lift technique. Dave not only had the facts at hand to make his case, he related his solution with a clear understanding of the critical performance requirements of cycling (see page 25).

You have probably heard expressions such as 'see it from their perspective', 'walking in another's shoes' and 'listening with your heart as well as your ears'. All of these convey the concept of empathy, whereby you sincerely seek to recognise and understand the other person's views and feelings. In that way, empathy is the cornerstone of influencing. Questioning and listening skills open the door to understanding and appreciating someone else's views and feelings. When we display an understanding of another person in this way, we are demonstrating rapport, or the ability to be 'on the same wavelength'. Rapport will be thin, if not absent, without empathy and effective working relationships are very hard to foster without rapport.

Some people aim to supplement empathetic rapport with the use of body language that mirrors that of the other person.[7] While body language and vocal mirroring happen quite naturally when two people are genuinely in rapport, consciously applying this to relationship-building has its risks. For a start it can distract from the core empathetic work of actually listening and understanding. In addition, the person you are trying to build rapport with can notice and interpret simulated rapport attempts as a lack of authenticity or even mockery.

While empathy provides us with insight into another's perspective, understanding something about their personality also provides us with some paths to influencing.

IT TAKES ALL SORTS

Developing an insight into a person's values, motivations, perceptions and behaviours provides us with some understanding of their personality. Reacting to and dealing with people's personalities is something that you have been doing all of your life. We can take that to the next level with some understanding of how different personality types can be influenced by different approaches. While we are all individuals, there are personality traits and types that share behaviour patterns. By observing and recognising these patterns, we can flex our own language and behaviour to better match their preferred way of receiving communication – remembering, of course, to maintain our authenticity and honest intentions when doing so. Otherwise, we can come across as fake and be interpreted as manipulative.

However, with the honest intention of trying to reach out to different personality styles, this is legitimate influencing territory. There are many theories of personality that describe traits, types and styles, so for the purposes of illustration and focus we'll cover just one here. A cautionary note: the concept of influencing different personality types is not based on hard science and other personality models are available![8]

The model referred to here[9] describes two key dimensions of personality: assertiveness and responsiveness. Figure 6.4 shows the top-level styles associated with the relevant extents of task and people orientation.

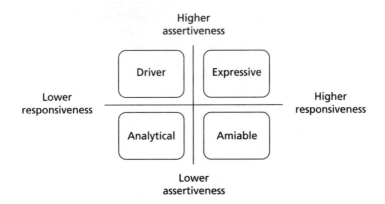

FIG. 6.4 Different personality styles defined by extent of assertiveness and responsiveness

The four styles are associated with different preferences for communicating and receiving communication. If you can match your style of communication to the other person's personality style preference, you are likely to be more persuasive. The table 'Influencing different personality styles' summarises the different personality styles and some techniques for how to influence them.

INFLUENCING DIFFERENT PERSONALITY STYLES

Personality style	Influencing techniques to try
Driver: tend to be assertive, task-oriented, formal, determined, self-reliant, decisive, efficient, competitive and focused.	• Keep your arguments brief and to the point. The STP model will be useful. • Where possible, connect your proposition to what they have said, making it consistent with their perspective. The self-confidence of a driver means that if you want them to run with your idea, you are better off using some skilful questioning and listening to enable them to come up with the idea themselves. • Drivers are drawn to competition and winning, so point out how your idea can either help them win or avoid losing. • Expertise and authority can be persuasive for drivers, so it can be useful to refer to the support of an expert or leader if you have it.
Expressive: tend to be assertive, people-oriented, animated, friendly, enthusiastic, outgoing, spontaneous and fast-paced.	• Expressives are generally optimistic people, so referring to a positive potential outcome will help to gain their interest. • Expressives respond well to friendly relationships, so investing some time in getting to know them and showing that you do will increase their receptivity to your ideas. • Expressives understand the concept of 'win-win', a situation in which there is mutual benefit for both people. So if you can help them, they are more inclined to help you.
Analytical: tend to be task-oriented, systematic, formal, organised, methodical, accurate, logical and happy to work alone.	• As with drivers, analyticals respond well to expertise, so explaining how your idea has expert backing or relates to the work of an expert will help them get on board. • Analyticals are not very comfortable with risk, so explain how your idea will help reduce risk and reassure them about any perceived risks to you idea. • Analyticals are drawn to facts and data, so including those in a STP structure to your message will help.
Amiable: tend to be supportive, people-oriented, informal, relaxed, friendly, agreeable, helpful and dependable.	• Amiables are comfortable when there is agreement and even harmony. So influence by demonstrating how your idea is helping to develop consensus or how others have already agreed with it. • Amiables are keen to get on with people and for people to get on with them. So spend some time building a trusting relationship and show a genuine interest in them with some interested questioning and listening. • The occasional favour will go a long way to build the appreciation of an amiable and they will be more likely to to reciprocate at some stage.

INFLUENCING DIFFERENT PSYCHOLOGIES

Observing and listening to people will help you identify which is his or her most likely personality style, based on this model. While the breadth of human diversity cannot possibly be characterised in just four styles, this model provides some practical guidance to practise different influencing techniques. And while a very simplified view of personality and influencing styles, it is one that is hopefully straightforward enough for you to try.

Apart from personality, there are other descriptors of our psychology upon which to base preferences and influencing techniques. For example, there are models for learning styles,[10] information encoding styles (e.g. the NLP VARK model)[11] and even right-brain/left-brain dominance.[12]

It is also worth noting the contribution made to influencing by your personal impact. If you want people to take you seriously as a professional, you have to look like one. This is not an advert for uniforms and the stifling of individuality, but more of a reminder that people make judgements about others in a very short period of time: about seven seconds. In that brief window, conscious and subconscious conclusions are being drawn from the evidence presented – i.e. how you look and what you are wearing. So while some of us are keen to express our individuality in the clothes we wear and how we wear them, it is worth pausing to check in the mirror if we are conveying an image upon which we are happy to be judged.

SUMMARY

It is evident from our interviewees that influencing is essential in any high-performance environment. As with any skill, it can be mastered with an understanding and practice of the constituent techniques, practice that for most of us will be life-long.

This chapter has sought to explain the key components of influencing, particularly trust and credibility, reason and logic as well as empathy and rapport. While this builds on some of the skills covered in previous chapters, great influencing will come about only when all of these skills are harmoniously combined in an effortless manner. That takes practice, a lot of practice. But it is worth the effort.

Above all, those who are influential without resorting to power and authority hold a strong belief in what they are trying to achieve. They have developed this belief from a rational and objective assessment of both the evidence and the potential. All of our interviewees demonstrate this and firmly believe that in order to be convincing, you first need to be convinced yourself.

CASE STUDY: WORKING IN A TEAM

NIGEL MITCHELL

Head of Nutrition British Cycling/Team Sky

FIG. 7.1 Nigel Mitchell

What does the legacy of the London 2012 Olympic and Paralympic Games mean to you? Maybe it is about the performance of Team GB and the way this continues to inspire young GB athletes towards the podia of future Games? Or is the legacy closer to home in that the nation now has expertise, structure and service standards within coaching, sports science and sports medicine that are second to none across the world?

There was certainly a great deal of planning[1] and, indeed, controversy about what a London 2012 legacy actually meant. In practice, there are many great examples of the London 2012 legacy and perhaps the most significant in terms of performance sports nutrition is the legacy created by Nigel Mitchell.

Almost as soon as London was awarded the 2012 Games, Nigel set out on his mission to improve the delivery of performance nutrition services to the UK's elite athletes. The legacy that Nigel created was twofold. Firstly, he led a substantial upgrade in the quality, focus and performance impact of nutritional support to elite athletes. In addition, Nigel recruited, trained and inspired a legion of young sports nutritionists, who are among the most influential across Olympic, Paralympic and professional sports in the UK today. That is a significant impact and legacy for one person to achieve in such a demanding environment, although Nigel would never claim this for himself. Indeed, Nigel was at pains to point out several times during our interview that he was motivated by the desire to help others, rather than to seek his own rewards. But don't mistake this for false modesty, because by his own acknowledgement, Nigel is not devoid of an ego and he will certainly pursue his aims and ambition with his trademark strident enthusiasm. He is no pushover and he seizes the chance when he sees it:

It was a fantastic opportunity, as it was in the English Institute of Sport (EIS) plan to develop nutritional services at some stage anyway. I was about at the right time to try and influence the process that was starting at the EIS. I was quite fortunate that the timing was right. The sports were incredibly receptive when we showed them the benefits of the service. We'd changed the focus from not just looking at the idea of healthy eating but actually looking at what we do that actually influences performance. So by putting the concept of performance first, that helped the sports to understand. Once we convinced sports that they needed this type of nutrition service, we needed to go out and recruit a group of young people and train them to deliver it.

Nigel remains a mentor to many of this group, and he values the role of acting as a sounding board and trusted advisor to those with a growth mindset. He knows first-hand how difficult it can be sometimes when you have the drive, but not necessarily the means or opportunity, to realise an ambition. Growing up in a mining village near Barnsley, Nigel went to a school where the expectations set for the pupils were not too stretching:

At quite an early age in my life, there was a big focus on sport and food. I got interested in nutrition at 14, 15. It was at that time that I decided what I wanted to be, a leader in sports nutrition. But I didn't know how to do it obviously, because the career guidance that I got at school was: 'Which pit are you going to go down?' People at school also told me that I would never achieve anything.

Nigel's parents thought otherwise, and that strong vote of confidence and belief in Nigel helped him to overcome the challenges of dyslexia. But parents can only give so much encouragement, so what is it about Nigel that helped him achieve against the odds?

Me, being driven and stubborn. When people are saying to me, 'you can't do this', I'm going to go and do it.

Luckily for sports nutrition in the UK, one of the results of this mindset was that Nigel passed sufficient exams to seek an alternative career path to working down the pits, firstly in horticulture, and then on to his passion, nutrition, studying for a degree at the University of North London. But Nigel being Nigel, he did not wait to study within the formal structure of a degree to learn about nutrition; he was much more interested in the practical application of nutrition to sport nutrition, so he got on with it.

> Even during my A-levels, I was already looking at advising athletes. I was fortunate because I mixed in a circle of some very good high-performing athletes who were friends of mine.

FIRST-HAND VIEW

Within the emerging discipline of applied sports nutrition, Nigel's work has undoubtedly shaped how the service is structured today within elite sport in the UK. Nigel has constantly challenged best practice, where other practitioners may be content to keep with the status quo. I received mentoring from Nigel and I have always admired his level of professional ethics and integrity. Those he has mentored hold him in highest regard, and ... he is noted to have carefully created an environment to allow younger practitioners to develop.

James Collins
Director of Performance Nutrition and Arsenal FC nutritionist

While he admits he might not have had a high level of ability at that stage, Nigel was confident and curious about evidence-based interventions. He wanted to gain some experience of techniques in that area. But due to the lack of opportunities within elite sport at that time, Nigel decided to gain clinical experience as a dietician at the Northern General Hospital in Sheffield. He then moved to the Royal Hallamshire Hospital, where he could further his knowledge and gain more training in research methods. After a few years, Nigel moved into the role of researcher/dietician in palliative care at the University of Sheffield, while also completing his MSc. Not only was this a formative opportunity for Nigel, it also provided him with his first real mentor:

> Working in palliative care changed my philosophy and it changed my attitude. Up until then, it had been all about me. It had been 'What am I going to get out of this, what can I do?' But working in that environment made me realise that if you focus on doing a really good job for other people, then that will reflect well on you. So rather than thinking, 'If I do this, how do I look, what do I get out of it?', you think about others ... you change your true belief that you are there to help other people and you're not there for yourself. That has been my philosophy since then. So when I work with athletes or if I'm mentoring someone, I 100 per cent put their welfare needs before what I believe mine are.

And I believe that by doing that, I do a really good job for them. As a consequence of doing that good job, that then reflects on me. Working in palliative care put things in perspective for me.

At the time Nigel was working in palliative care, he was also still very much driven to work in elite sport, and to that end he persuaded the NHS to pay for him to do the then sports nutrition foundation course. From here he took the initiative to work more formally in sport by contacting the course leader for the master's in sports science at Sheffield Hallam University. At that time, the course didn't include sports nutrition, but Nigel persuaded them that they should cover this, ending up as a lecturer in sports and exercise nutrition at Sheffield Hallam while maintaining his clinical palliative care work. He managed to continue this challenging dual role for 18 months before he made the jump to work full-time in sport.

It wasn't long before Nigel's contacts at British Cycling asked him to help one of the physiologists there with the development of their nutrition skills. It soon became apparent that what British Cycling needed was the direct input of a nutritionist, and Nigel was only too happy to oblige. The relationship grew over the years prior to the Athens Olympic Games in 2004, after which the sports science scene changed significantly as new funding came on stream in readiness for 2012 and a home Olympic Games.

Following the Athens Games, Nigel was asked by the EIS to audit and report on sport nutrition services to elite sport in England. Nigel's audit found that athletes and coaches believed that diet and nutrition were important for training, health, performance and overall well-being. The question that the sports, coaches and athletes had was about the effective delivery of nutrition services. From his own experience working with cycling and boxing, Nigel presented how a successful nutrition service could be developed and delivered. This was based on his model of combining knowledge of nutrition with delivery skills and an in-depth knowledge of the sport in question. This struck a particular chord with his line manager, an ex-athlete who supported his approach of delivery to make a performance impact. The EIS, UK Sport and sports were persuaded and Nigel joined the organisation full-time as lead performance nutritionist for the northern region in 2005, with a remit to convince sports of his vision and to recruit and train the next generation of applied practitioners.

Less easy to convince about this last area were some members of the British Dietetic Association, who were protective of their role and somewhat hostile. Nigel needed all the resolve, conviction and persuasiveness he could muster to overcome some fairly strong attacks.

I was suggesting a model that actually undermined the professional body. The model I presented was one that was skills-, knowledge- and attitude-based, not one that was qualifications-based. For years this group of people had been banging on that to deliver nutrition in sport, you had to be a dietician. I presented saying, 'well actually, to deliver nutrition in professional sports you need *dietetic skills*', which were different.

Nigel stood his ground. He knew that he had considerable credibility as a practitioner: he worked clinically, had an academic profile and worked in elite sport. His critics, by contrast, were not working clinically, were not academically active and didn't work in elite sport. That meant they marginalised themselves. This was compounded when you consider that the greater influence on the debate was from those who were providing the funding: UK Sport. UK Sport had conducted its own review of nutrition service delivery to elite sport in the UK and had the will to do something different, in this case backing Nigel's approach.

As well as the logic and evidence behind his position, what else did Nigel do to persuade others to back him?

> I have an ability to put a certain level of energy and passion across. That really comes from having true belief. That comes from my palliative care experience … putting the outcome that you want to get first and not your own glory. It was about having real conviction in what I wanted to do, which was to set up an effective professional practice.

At that time Nigel was keen to challenge accepted dogma, which he saw as largely based on laboratory studies and not strongly applicable to the real world of elite sport. However, he certainly doesn't shun the benefits of a well-designed study and seeks to validate his work in on-going research collaborations:

> We want to know, 'How does this work within our environment?' So it is very important to me personally that I am constantly involved with academic projects that help to validate some of the work that we do in the field.

With that level of rigour, how does Nigel persuade athletes to follow his advice?

> Firstly, I don't tell anybody to do anything. Secondly, the people that I work with are all wanting the best performances for themselves. So they will do anything that we put forward that looks reasonable. The thing we have to be careful about then is that we protect the athlete. Many athletes are, in fact, very vulnerable, so we have to protect them first of all.

Nigel pays particular attention to the protection of the athlete during his mentoring work.

> I would be horrified if one of the people were to Twitter about their work with a named athlete. That's a good way to lose friends, but unfortunately people sometimes believe that they are beyond or better than where they are actually at. I try to get my mentees to believe that it is the work that they do for other people that is important, and [that] it is not necessarily about promoting themselves. We've all got big egos; working in this environment, people do have big egos. But it is not just saying the words [about prioritising other people over yourself], it is truly believing it and doing the best job that you can.

FIRST-HAND VIEW

Nigel is a key member of our athlete support teams, and his performance within the team is fitting for the world-class environment within which we operate. Nigel has the extensive knowledge required to ensure each athlete's individual plan, and needs, are met as required at all times. Nigel also develops the individual relationships required when working at the top end, and modifies his working techniques as necessary to suit each specific individual.

Grant White
British Cycling National BMX Coach

So apart from the willingness and ability to put other people first, what other qualities does Nigel believe can help people succeed in this environment?

What I've looked for in people is passion; commitment and interest obviously has got to be there. The commitment means that people don't necessarily have to give their whole life to it, but they are prepared to work in a way that is effective in elite sport. To work in elite sport, it doesn't matter what your contract says, it is not a nine-to-five job.

How would Nigel identify these qualities in someone?

One of the qualities I have looked for has been for people who have done additional things while they have been doing their degrees. Who's put themselves out to go and work with the local hockey club, who's put themselves out to support people doing 'Ride Across America' or something like that? They're the people that distinguish themselves. The people that we've brought through like that have excelled themselves, and the ones that didn't do much of that are actually pretty stagnant. The interns that I was involved in recruiting, when they were doing their degrees they spent as much time trying to deliver some sort of support as they spent studying. These are the people that are now flying.

That appears as though you would need a great deal of energy?

Well, these guys are prepared to put 24 hours into 12 hours. Often they'll have full-time jobs and do extra work on top of that, not for the money but because they are interested. It's probably just their personality.

How does Nigel manage his own energy and keep motivated?

I'm very grounded in that the most important thing for me in my life is my family. I've never put my career above my family. Spending time with my wife and kids is very important. Now it is a demanding job with big travel commitments, so time with them does get compromised.

While Nigel recognises that work-life balance is not a very helpful term in the elite sport arena, he also acknowledges that it is important to maintain your overall energy and well-being.

This environment is a high burnout environment, so you have to maintain your focus. You have team stress and individual stress. There are examples where practitioners have become aggressive, isolated themselves and effectively become dysfunctional. The responsibility for this is on the management, and the critical element here is to be very clear about the role expected of them in the situation. You can have really good practitioners and because they haven't understood what is required of them … their behaviour has been very stressed.

What advice does Nigel have for practitioners experiencing the pressure of elite sport, particularly at training camps or competitions?

One of the things that I always try to do is to be invisible with a small 'i'. So be there to do things, but not get in the way, because it's easy to get in the way. But if you're not there, if you're really invisible, that will be the time that you're required; and if you're not available to deliver, that will be when all the scrutiny is on you.

It's the same across Olympic/Paralympic and professional sport; the environment is the same. When the pressure is really, really on, then the environment becomes dysfunctional. You have to understand that actually that is quite normal sometimes, not all the time, but it can become normal. You have to recognise that if people are behaving in an aggressive way, not that that is excusable, but that it needs to be dealt with at another time.

As well as Nigel's own values, some of his approach to managing the pressure of working for British Cycling and Team Sky is influenced by Steve Peters.[2] Peters advocates a 'Happy Ants' model, which describes people working as a team, accepting and overcoming obstacles with a positive attitude. The 'happy ant' doesn't fret, but chooses their role and executes it in a focused and proactive manner. It's a model that helps to reduce emotional reactions under pressure. Says Nigel: 'We're very lucky here to have Steve, who helps us manage that emotional side and enables us to tease out what is unfair behaviour and what is just tough – down to stress rather than anything else.'

One of the side effects of stress in such environments is the blow that can be dealt to your confidence when someone has a go at you, even though it originates from their stress rather than because of anything you have or have not said or done. How does Nigel maintain a healthy level of confidence?

FIG. 7.2   Nigel Mitchell works for British Cycling

My conviction and confidence is evidence-based. Sometimes you can be challenged and when you look at the evidence again you realise that you were wrong. You have to be prepared to acknowledge that at times. But the main thing is to use evidence either at an evidence or service delivery level. Having a sense of perspective is important, so when you have been challenged or criticised it helps to remember what is really important in your life.

Nigel is keen to conclude our conversation with a positive message drawn from his own experience:

So many students who study sports science want to work in elite sport. There are so few opportunities, but they are real opportunities, so why not you? If they are prepared to make the investment of hard work, there are the opportunities for them there. Somebody has got to do it, so it may as well be them if they really want to do it.

CHAPTER 7

WORKING IN A TEAM

For most of us, as for Nigel Mitchell, one of the most rewarding life experiences you can have is to be an effective member of a successful team. The enjoyment and satisfaction that result from being a member of a team extends, for most, to our working lives. All of our interviewees freely described themselves and their work in the context of being part of a team and were quick to qualify any personal successes with credit to other members of their team. For example, Ali Rose talks about the importance of teams in her work with Dame Kelly Holmes (see page 75), as does Paul Brice when he talks about a team under pressure to rehabilitate Jessica Ennis (see pages 62–63). Our interviewees are also in turn frequently credited for being great team players – as Sarah Hardman is by physiotherapist Joanne Elphinston (see page 96).

A definition of a team is when a number of people cooperate towards a common goal or outcome. Within a team, each individual is able to make a distinct contribution to the shared objective. When teams work well, they not only deliver greater success than individuals can achieve alone but also deliver success over and above the sum of the individual skill sets – very like high-achieving sporting teams. But when teams are dysfunctional, they can seize defeat from the jaws of victory, cause chaotic inertia and even bring about the collapse of whole organisations, again just like sporting teams who fail despite being packed with 'superstar' individual players. Try the exercise in the box 'Success and failure' to capture your understanding of factors that contribute to successful teams.

IN THE BEGINNING

Teams work well when each member brings some form of technical ability to the table, but a team needs more than composite technical skills to be successful. In this chapter we'll explore what it takes, apart from technical excellence, to work effectively in a team.

An effective team commits to outcomes that individuals cannot achieve alone. It also has a clear sense of purpose, and team members manage the challenges of their relationships honestly and openly.

In a sporting context, the performance of any elite athlete or team is more and more dependent on the team behind them. In fact, it is difficult to think of any athlete or team who reaches the top of their sport without such support. When a successful athlete is interviewed, you'll often hear them give thanks and credit to their coach and support team. The team behind elite athletes in the UK is most often comprised of their coach, various specialists in sports science and medicine and potentially related disciplines such as technology, weather and equipment design, together with

SUCCESS AND FAILURE

To understand the success and failure of teams, you probably need look no further than your own observations and experience. Maybe you are or have been a member of sports team, or maybe you are coaching a team, or maybe you are working in a multidisciplinary team that supports athletes. As you reflect back on that experience, identify what conditions made those teams work so well and what were the factors that compromised the team's performance.

Factors that make teams work well

_____

_____

_____

_____

_____

_____

_____

_____

Factors that compromise teams

_____

_____

_____

_____

_____

_____

_____

_____

Keep these lists in mind as you read through the chapter. They will also be useful for another exercise proposed towards the end of the chapter.

management support from their national governing body. Not to forget the crucial team of nearest and dearest that provide help, love and patience during the athlete's long graft towards the podium. With all these good intentions, it can all get very crowded and confusing as to who is doing what and why. The athlete (and sometimes the coach) can be left feeling overwhelmed by all this support and their performance will ultimately suffer.

So one of the first points about teams is: what is the defining purpose and is everyone working clearly towards that?

A team supports an athlete's endeavour well when there is a clear and joint purpose to that team. Even though the aim is very apparent (i.e. to win medals), these teams often have a fluid membership and rapidly changing objectives. So those who work successfully in these teams are very clear about their contributions and intentions, yet also very flexible in the extent of their involvement.

A DEDICATED TEAM MEMBER IS PREPARED TO SIT ON THE BENCH

Sometimes you have to accept that you can't add anything significant to the improvement of an athlete's performance or recovery at a particular time. That is quite hard to swallow when you believe that your excellent coaching or sports science skills are exactly what the athlete needs. Usually a coach will decide which applied practitioner contributions are the priority, so you may be tempted to use all of your influencing skills to persuade him or her to adopt your particular intervention. However, the effective practitioner will consider the bigger picture and how their proposal fits into the overall support that the athlete needs at that time. Sometimes they will even conclude that their own intervention is not a priority right at that time and say so. In doing so, they will earn the trust and respect of the coach and fellow practitioners very quickly. It is a judgement call, but the corollary is that a good practitioner will also push hard for his or her intervention to be adopted when they believe that it is necessary, even though the coach and their colleagues do not initially support the proposal. The stories of Dave Clark, Nigel Mitchell and Paul Brice are good examples of this (see pages 18–26, pages 110–117 and pages 55–64 respectively).

Often, teams are not formed through an explicit process: they just come together. As a team forms, or when new members join a team, there is often a process whereby team members assess their fellow team members in terms of skills and behaviours: most of us are keen to know something about who we are working with, what they are capable of and how they behave, particularly under pressure. As the team evolves, there are often some challenges to ascertain who will be the most influential and who will provide leadership. When a team is sufficiently gelled so that it can have open and honest conversations, it is then ready to deliver the kind of performance that will exceed any that could be achieved by individuals alone. This process is often referred to as the 'forming, storming, norming, performing' process.[3] While this is a classic model of team formation, it is not linear and doesn't describe all of the factors behind the creation of a successful team. Those critical factors are the team development process and the team behaviours.

GETTING THE RIGHT PROCESS

A team can be a complex arrangement, even when it is trying to achieve a simple objective. The complexity can escalate when there are specialist jobs to be done, especially if those jobs need coordinating. This is especially true of the teams that come together to support athletes at major games and championships. At these times there are many roles, each of which can be interconnected and interdependent. In other words, many people are trying to achieve a common objective – i.e. to help the

FIG. 7.3 Teams are complex, but the rewards are worth it

athlete perform at their best – but doing so in different ways. Success in this environment needs a huge amount of planning and coordination to make sure that each team member has a clear and distinctive remit. Additional to that, team members have to ensure that they do not get in each other's way and also that key tasks are not left undone in the confusion of who is responsible for what. All that is before you add in the effect of those unpredictable events that are bound to happen at any major championships, plus the perceived added stress of the event itself. At these times, even with the best of intentions, the pressure of the competition environment can cause people to behave in volatile and sometimes unhelpful ways. (More of that in Chapter 9.)

In the lead-up to the Beijing and London Olympic and Paralympic Games, Team GB and ParalympicsGB managed these risks with planning of a military precision and scale. The principles they deployed are described below and are the same that apply to any team striving to perform at their best under pressure.

Purpose and vision

The first place to start is with a vision or a mission that everyone is involved in developing and can sign up to: simple to understand and a beacon of clarity that people can rally to when times get confusing or tough.

Who is in charge?

Excellent teams thrive on excellent leadership. While there is no one type of leader or leadership style that correlates with outstanding team performance, there are some leadership characteristics that promote team excellence. In particular, successful team leaders will listen to and engage individual team members. Team leaders have a fundamental role in cultivating trust between members and creating a culture that enables the team to be courageous and take calculated risks without fear of blame and recrimination. An effective team leader is able to be directive when necessary in order to achieve progress. But they also combine this approach with the skilful coaching of team members in order to encourage learning and creativity.

Values and behaviours

The importance of individual values as a guide to behaviour was covered in Chapter 2. What is important for the individual is no less important for the team. Except that it can be far more challenging to develop team values to which everyone agrees, along with the related behaviours. However, successful teams spend the time to develop shared values because they know that when the pressure is on, the team needs the compass that those values provide to help them decide how to react to unpredictable and chaotic situations. For example, this rock-solid foundation is vital when your team finds itself in dispute with the championship organisers or international federation over a questionable ruling or judgement against your team. Do you react in an emotive and possibly irrational way as you are pummelled by the tension of the match? Or do you look to your deeply held values to guide you to a calm, rational and strategic decision for how to rise to the challenge?

Team values and agreed behaviours are no good unless they are translated into action. They must guide how team members treat each other, especially during disagreements and possible conflict. With shared values, individual team members can hold themselves and each other accountable to their team behaviours, rather than criticise each other as people. This helps to build trust and dissipate possible frictions.

Roles and responsibilities

If you were a member of a team, you would probably want to know why you are on the team and what you are supposed to be doing. You may not be surprised that this is one of the most common reasons why teams flounder: people don't know what they are supposed to be doing, or just as importantly, not doing. So, we are often tempted to make it up and contribute where we see fit. Until someone comes along and ask us indignantly what on earth we think we are doing by 'interfering' in that way!

Well-functioning teams such as British Cycling ensure that each person has a distinct role with clear responsibilities attached. The really good teams capture all the roles and responsibilities in a document that communicates to people what needs to be done by whom and when. The excellent teams take that one stage further and develop a contingency plan, such that if one team member is incapacitated for some reason, other team members know which one of them has to step in and take responsibility for the gaps. The interview with Chris Price (see pages 180–188) provides a good example of this, when he talks about what happened when the head coach was ill at the Vancouver 2010 Games.

As well as the technical roles people take within teams, there is also a school of thought that people also take on behavioural roles within teams. This largely emanates from the work of Belbin, who described nine role preferences that covered three categories of action-, people- and thought-oriented behaviour.[4] The theory of team behaviour proposes that we default to preferred behaviour in teams, and that successful teams have a balance of individuals across the nine behaviours. While it can be useful to think about this model when forming teams, role identity in this way is only one of the many success factors for high-performing teams.

Keep talking

Communication between team members is often taken for granted. But how often does a lack of communication result in false assumptions, misunderstandings, errors and arguments? In any high-performance environment, it is the ability of team members to keep themselves informed and to keep others in the loop that makes the difference between a job half-done and a winning performance. Deirdre Angella is credited by Chris Price for making sure this happened with the team behind Amy Williams' gold medal in Vancouver 2010 – making sure the team kept communicating and everyone knew what they needed to know (see pages 187-188). Professional teams rarely take communication for granted and instigate a process to support the spread of knowledge and insight through the team. Good communication during a team effort also has the additional benefit of raising morale, motivation and performance.

If you are not measuring, you are just practising

Some teams have a very obvious performance outcome, such as a medal at a world championship, Olympic or Paralympic Games. But all teams need some way to measure progress along the way. In fact, high-performance teams will generally focus on getting the process right, rather than paying too much attention to the outcome. The outcome is important, but rigorous and measured processes are needed in order to achieve that. So once a team vision or outcome is agreed, excellent performance is more about the process that the team implements and the measures that it adopts along the way.

A little bit of recognition goes a long way

If people are recognised and rewarded for their efforts and good work, this is often done on an individual rather than team basis. Yet none of us can make significant contributions without the involvement of others, usually in teams. So recognising and rewarding the achievements of teams would make sense, but how often does this happen in practice? In terms of motivating a team to push themselves beyond even their own expectations, a little recognition can go a long way indeed. Not that the high-performing teams in the elite sport world seek that. Indeed, quite the opposite, as most work quietly, confidently and humbly to help their athletes achieve outstanding performance – *humility* is a word often associated with our interviewees. However, recognition goes a long way to boost morale and it doesn't cost much to tell a team that they are doing a great job when they deserve it.

GETTING THE RIGHT FOCUS

The above process for establishing and developing a team can be very useful, but Lencioni[5] offers a simple and powerful model that identifies what makes a team really succeed. It identifies the human factors behind why teams fail or succeed and is summarised in Figure 7.4.

By reversing Lencioni's five dysfunctions of a team, it is possible to describe the attributes of a successful team. This is a team that:

1. fosters trust amongst its members;
2. has the courage to engage with positive conflict;
3. willingly commits to the purpose and vision;
4. holds itself and its team members accountable;
5. focuses its attention and effort on the achievement of results.

As we have explored in previous chapters, trust is a combination of perceived competence and intention. In the context of teams, trust is essential for a team to be creative and to take risks in order to achieve something out of the ordinary. A team can build trust between its members when they acknowledge where the strengths and weaknesses are in terms of their individual and collective competence. Providing honest, open and constructive feedback to each other is the key to raising competence and building trust. Trust will also be fostered by team members being explicit about their intention to give freely of their expertise to the team for the benefit of the shared purpose or outcome, rather than for their own individual advantage.

Any team that seeks to be lively, interesting and creative will end up in conflict: anyone who cares will argue his or her case with vigour and determination, and that can upset some people. But in such cases, it is always helpful to look behind the argument to see the intention. If the intention is one of honest debate to find a better solution, that productive conflict is not only worthwhile but also necessary to generate solutions which help athletes make it onto the podium. So fostering passionate

FIG. 7.4   The five dysfunctions of a team

Source: P. Lencioni, *Five Dysfunctions of a Team* (Jossey Bass, 2002)

debate within teams about key issues is key to high-performance. That doesn't always have to involve conflict, but effective teams are not afraid to hold forthright conversations that others may misconstrue as conflict. The nature of conflict will be explored in more detail in the next chapter, but for now it is worth emphasising that productive conflict can be positive and that the avoidance of conflict can result in a compromise which will deny a team's true potential.

While team commitment can be established at the beginning of the process, it is worthwhile refreshing this every now and then so that all members can rally around any revised common objectives. Holding yourself and each other accountable within a team is the best way to ensure that standards are maintained and key deadlines and deliverables are met.

Finally, the team's attention to results may seem an obvious focus for its efforts, but many a team is distracted along the way. Team effectiveness can be increased when there are process goals as well as outcome goals. As discussed earlier, many teams pay attention to getting the process right, confident that excellent results will follow.

The positive behaviours that deliver team success are implicit in the Lencioni model. An approach to team relationships that takes account of these behaviours will more likely generate the success to which teams aspire, providing the process elements covered in the previous section have been addressed. Try the exercise in the box 'Taking responsibility in a team' to see how you apply this model to strengthening your team.

TAKING RESPONSIBILITY IN A TEAM

Complete the form below to help you build a plan for how you can contribute further to your team's development.

	My behaviours that contribute to this are:	Behaviours I can work on to improve this are:
Build trust		
Foster passionate debate about key issues		
Build commitment		
Hold accountable		
Focus on results		

Compare your responses with those you provided for the exercise in the box 'Success and failure'. There may be some interesting factors, in common or in contrast, which can help you build your own model of team performance.

SUMMARY

Interdisciplinary teams remain the most efficient and effective method of getting athletes and teams on the podium. With the athlete at the centre, the coach can orchestrate an interdisciplinary team that can increase the athlete's training effectiveness and competition performance. In order for that team to work well, there needs to be a clear process of defining the purpose, roles, responsibilities, outcomes and measures of success.

It takes effort, patience, creativity and sometimes grief to work in a team, but that is all worth it when you consider what teamwork can achieve.

CASE STUDY: MANAGING WORKING RELATIONSHIPS

DEIRDRE ANGELLA

Sports psychologist

FIG. 8.1 Deirdre Angella

When asked to describe what it takes to succeed in the highly challenging world of elite sport, one of the words that people often use alongside passion is *energy*. It is true that you do need a great deal of energy to survive and, indeed, perform under the rigours of elite sport, but would you recognise it in someone when you saw it? In Deirdre (De) Angella you certainly would; De has enough personal energy to power the floodlights of the London 2012 stadium. Just speaking to De gives you an energy boost, and you can't help but return the favour by raising some extra enthusiasm you might have struggled to find otherwise. Not to say that De doesn't have the other qualities you need to succeed: the passion, commitment, conviction and resilience that are the hallmarks of the achievers in the GB high-performance sport system. In De's early sporting career as a competitive skier, she learned a lot about the energy required to win and how to manage this effectively during competition. De competed internationally from the age of 12 and at 16 headed to the United States on an academic ski scholarship, a sport in which her father had been a professional instructor.

While in Vermont, De's coach not only helped her develop her technical skills and race tactics, but also helped De to realise how much of her performance was down to what was going on in her own head. Even though she didn't fully grasp it at the time, De acknowledges that she would have benefited from some formal sports psychology input into her skiing. However, De does remember experiencing the mental state of *flow*; this is the mental state 'in which people are so involved in an activity that nothing else seems to matter; the experience itself is so enjoyable that people do it even at great cost, for the sheer state of doing it'.[1] One vivid example came during the first slalom of her final race season, and was perhaps an early understanding of the importance of mental preparation. It led to a growing realisation about what De wanted to do at the end of her skiing career, which unfortunately came about sooner than planned as a result of sustaining substantial knee damage during a downhill race.

> For all sorts of reasons, it was very traumatic. I know now that it was a transition period and it was about loss. When something that massive in your life is gone and nobody actually really thought to talk to you – and you've not thought to talk to yourself – about what the ending will mean ... It was one of those times in my life when I've had a powerful physical response to an emotion, that kind of moment when something has been so important and you know it's all over.
>
> I was quite clear that I wanted to be a sports psychologist. I could see the need for it and I hadn't had that help, so I wanted to see if I could do it. I had no idea how I was going to be a sports psychologist, but psychology seemed a good place to start.

FIRST-HAND VIEW

What makes De a world-class practitioner? The two words that spring to my mind are *thorough* and *meticulous*! Working as part of a multidiscipline team De leaves no stone unturned in preparing a coach or athlete for training, competition, and life and behaviour in general. I certainly recognise De as a leader in the way that we deliver our services to sport and ultimately how we focus our attention on impacting on performance.

Alex Natera
Strength and conditioning coach

So De went to study psychology at Aberdeen University and followed that with a master's in sports science with the focus on sports psychology at Manchester Metropolitan University. Despite the paucity of jobs at the time, De was determined to become an applied practitioner; the academic side of things was less appealing:

It is awe-inspiring to listen to real specialists talk about their area of expertise, but for me I knew where my strengths were, and that was working with people. For me, research wasn't what I wanted from sports psychology: I wanted to work with coaches and athletes.

De's first applied job came soon after she finished at Manchester, when she went to work at the Welsh Institute of Sport (WIS). Here De spent most of her time with swimming, judo and bowls. It was a busy time, which culminated in the 2002 Commonwealth Games in Manchester, where she was appointed HQ Sports Psychologist for Wales.

It was an amazing experience. It was hard graft and emotionally such hard work. It was my first experience of the emotions of those around being totally ratcheted up. It was very much like a pressure cooker situation and watching peoples' behaviour – people that you had known for two years – literally changing overnight! Was I prepared? Yes, in that I took it all in my stride, I was quite level. I was fortunate (as it wasn't planned) that a colleague and I did mini debriefs with one another, which helped to keep perspective. But it wasn't until afterwards that I realised that I was absolutely wrung-out. There was no let-up in three weeks, but overall Manchester was a good experience.

The experience demonstrated the benefits of preparation to De:

I didn't have crisis management situations with swimming, judo or bowls, but there was crisis management to be done with other sports. This was due to the lack of preparation for athletes, coaches and sports; specifically to manage individual performance in a multi-sport, major competition environment. A lot of teams didn't have the support coming into the Games; they just didn't have the funding at that stage. People made mistakes, and I wonder whether they would have been made if they had been better prepared. Of course, once a small mistake is made, in that environment it really snowballs.

But can you realistically prepare for unforeseen events at a major Games?

I can't remember how specific I was back then about what I am about to say, but this is where I am now and I suspect I must have been on this track to have my current perspective: in terms of psychology it is very much about the resources the person has and how they are helped to find a structure and a way of perceiving themselves so that whatever gets thrown at them, whatever scenario arises, they can cope and stay task focused. I get what people mean when they say, 'You don't really know what it is going to be like until you're in it'. But I also believe strongly the environment will be as it will be. A lot of preparation can be done in terms of routines: there are some basics that don't change. For the challenges which do present, it's about awareness and responding in a rational, flexible, self-helping way to whatever happens. One change which does occur is people's perceptions and focus. Accepting the uncontrollables and knowing how to be solution focused is part of being prepared. So can you be prepared? Yes. It goes for support staff as well: you need to know beforehand where to direct focus [to know what your role is]: the right thing at the right time. When you register that you are distracted, it is clear where to refocus.

In our discussion around preparing for the pressure of the Games environment, we explore the importance of self-awareness in the development of coping skills. Where does De's self-awareness come from?

I'm very aware of my own self-talk, I naturally think through options. I've always had good cognitive and kinaesthetic self-awareness. I know much of my awareness comes from how my dad coached me and taught me. I think, although he didn't realise it, he was actually a very good psychologist. I suppose a lot of the learned psychology skills I have come from him, although he wouldn't have put labels on them.

Can younger people accelerate the development of their self-awareness?

The easy answer is 'yes'. This said, there are challenges. It can be developed if an individual or team understand what self-awareness is, how important a skill it is and [if] the benefit can be demonstrated to them. Initially much of it is to do with self-questioning and debriefing, having some key questions to ask themselves, which then direct focus. Skills-based awareness, such as mindfulness, is very important as a method of learning to be present in the moment [performance is disrupted by past or future focus]. The coaching environment can be structured to facilitate self-awareness: as with any skill it needs persistent practice.

In the context of the pressure of a competition or training camp environment, what is important about self-awareness?

It's about being able to notice the difference between being task-focused or emotion-focused and then having the composure to manage oneself effectively; having an understanding of the difference between healthy negative emotions and unhealthy negative emotions. Unhealthy negative emotions left unnoticed or unmanaged hijack and undermine performance. Having the awareness to experience emotion and maintain or regain a task focus is what makes self-awareness so valuable.

Self-awareness is about noticing patterns of behaviour: we tend to respond consistently to similar stimulus. Knowing what the triggers are, having this knowledge about one's self provides the basis for choosing a performance-enhancing response under pressure.

Apart from good self-awareness, what practical techniques does De have for managing herself during times of pressure, especially after her experience of feeling wrung-out after the Manchester Commonwealth Games?

On camps and in competitions, I am really strict about taking timeout for myself. Agreeing that upfront [with the team] is important. I feel the pressure to be constantly there all the time, the same pressure that everybody else feels. But I am aware that it is not healthy for me and that if I am not healthy (if I haven't had enough sleep, if I am not eating right or if I haven't had the chance to turn my brain off), then when it does come to it, I am not able to respond as well as I could.

It is about taking care of the basics: hydration, nutrition and social support. We're no different from athletes; you can't always get 'social support' in sport environments so you need to be able to access it outside the work environment when immersed with the sport. It's not rocket science, but much of it comes back to self-awareness.

However, the reality is that not everybody is particularly good at looking after themselves in these environments.

One of the challenges I have in sport environments is that some managers and coaches can talk a good game about taking timeout, but can actually be really rubbish at doing it! Then they wonder why they've got such short fuses and you end up picking up the communication pieces because somebody's 'lost it' over something incredibly trivial. The trivial instance may have been dealt with if the coach's lack of hydration wasn't contributing to a sore head!

Even when there is agreement about recovery strategies and preparation for how best to work with each other under pressure, there can still be challenges.

There can still be angst. So, even if the support team have agreed when individuals will be 'off the grid', people still get angsty. You can take those reactions personally – that people may perceive you as not working hard enough – alternatively you can choose to maintain the agreed plan and 'role model' effective self-management.

Overall, the Manchester Commonwealth Games was an enjoyable and valuable experience for De. Subsequently, with an eye on progression, De sought a management role and was offered the post of sports science manager at the West of Scotland Institute of Sport. It was an interesting challenge, managing a mixture of applied and research staff, but while De enjoyed the leadership responsibility it also reinforced her primary interest of working directly with coaches and athletes.

FIG. 8.2 Effective consultation can occur anywhere – De supporting an athlete

Providing direction to the team proved valuable experience for when De returned to a more applied role with the English Institute of Sport (EIS) working with the support teams for winter sports.

> Psychology is better delivered when you can draw on nutrition, draw on strength and conditioning, draw on physiotherapy. If all those aspects aren't in place, if an athlete is 'broken', it doesn't matter how good they are psychology-wise, they can't compete. Often the simplest way to solve a lot of potential performance issues or challenges with managing mental factors is to have consistency in training supported by the other sport science and sports medicine disciplines.

However, working effectively within a team requires building relationships, and that territory can require a vulnerability, as you often need to trust people you may not know that well:

> In terms of building relationships, it is about respect and trust. Building respect is about shared projects, a shared purpose and everybody making a contribution to what will make a performance difference. Trust comes from being able to share information and knowing that it will be used appropriately to best meet the needs of athletes, coaches and national governing bodies. Being open in a

multidisciplinary environment is a risk, but whatever job I have started I have come into it with an open approach. I've been willing to share and have been upfront, honest and rational that psychology is only part of the puzzle. You need to have trust and respect to be able to have the necessary upfront conversations. That makes a massive difference.

That is the way it also works with coaches: they need to trust that you are going to be honest and upfront with them. Sometimes, from a psychology point of view, that can be a challenge because there are things that athletes don't want shared. If I keep a coach out of the loop on something, I normally know that they know already. Coaches know everything! And what they don't know, they've got a pretty good idea about. It is a difficult area to manage because coaches can get angry when they think they are kept out of the loop. This can be managed by you building trust with the coach: if they trust you, they will trust you to tell them what they need to know. Part of the job is knowing what is important, what to share and what to 'hold'.

De's interdisciplinary inclination has borne out well in a recent athlete rehabilitation case:

As a support team (psychology, strength and conditioning, nutrition, physiotherapy, doctor and sports massage), we were given control by the coach to manage this athlete [back to training and competition]. The coach is involved and oversees the work. As an intervention and the way it has worked, we couldn't be hoping for anything more. The athlete has a level of self-awareness and is engaged in a way that they have abdicated responsibility to the support team. We work from a plan that I have largely managed. The processes are there, the performances are there and the outcome is happening. It could all change tomorrow, but you proceed in good faith and do all you can, and it's exciting when it works. There's a team of us all working together and it is working for the athlete [and coach].

I've pushed very hard for a lot of the processes and there are things that I have not compromised on this time around. We've done the no-compromise approach and I've been comfortable with it being like that because it is with the athlete's permission. The athlete has been healthy for six months now and although so much could happen between now and 2012, a medal is achievable.

Guiding this approach is a philosophy about creating independence in the athlete. In this case, the athlete's independence and responsibility has been developed to a level where they are willing and confident about delegating much of that back to the support team. The athlete is fully bought into the process, because they have complete trust in the coach and support team to devise and implement a plan to get them back to full competitive health. What does this reveal about De's own practice philosophy or guiding principle?

Principally, the athlete or the coach have the resources. I am there to help them find out how better they can use their resources, how they can be more effective. Part of the job is then to identify the gaps which compromise effectiveness, help them understand what their blind spots are, to provide the catalyst for the individual to be at their most resourceful when it matters.

It's about creating independence in an athlete and them being responsible for themselves. It can be a risk when athletes find their own resourcefulness; you then have to accept that they may sometimes make decisions that are counterproductive to performance. Fundamentally, I am not the person who has to train, compete or deliver in that moment, so everything I do and everything I structure needs to be about that athlete being wholly self-sufficient. I do feel very strongly about that.

FIRST-HAND VIEW

De is a practitioner with integrity, an honest, direct and candid approach, who will always give you a straight answer; communicating in a manner that is concise, constructive and focused towards the objectives in hand. She is a colleague whose opinion is sought when there are difficult conversations to be had that are going to evoke emotions, challenge individual's perceptions and draw people out of their comfort zones.

Nathan Lewis
EIS Senior Performance Nutritionist

However, as discussed above, there are situations where a self-resourceful athlete may choose to abdicate responsibility back to the coach or sports scientist. In addition, some coaches prefer to keep more control and a self-resourceful athlete may find themselves at odds with that approach. So what are De's reflections on how to reconcile these potentially disparate positions?

I think that it is borne out of athlete choice and self-awareness, in that the athlete is in a position to choose what is best for them. The informed choice [of abdicating responsibility back to the coach] may seem to be a bit of a contradiction, but the athlete has chosen that as the way they want things to work. The athlete is still ultimately responsible for winning the medal. It's not the coach or the practitioner who is going to win the medal. To have that kind of trust in your support team is magic.

How would De manage the situation if the coach tended to be more autocratic with their athletes and was not particularly interested in athletes asserting their self-responsibility?

Coaches can be very autocratic. However, in my experience there is always an element of the coach which recognises the athlete needs to do certain things for themselves. The conflict between coaches and athletes arises when the boundaries are unclear about what the athlete is responsible for and what the coach is responsible for. I am quite upfront with coaches about this now. I work with them to improve their communication with the athlete and with what they can change in order to have communication at critical moments.

However, I genuinely believe that most coaches want athletes to be responsible. When they do come across as autocratic, they tend to do it for the right reasons. I will tell the coach when I don't agree with them, but ultimately the coach is the boss. This can be a challenge for sports science and sports medicine, because we come in with our theoretically driven principles. Sometimes we may think we know best, but ultimately it is the coach's call. As long as it is not compromising ethical boundaries or safety, then it is definitely the coach's call.

This sounds as if it could head into the territory of challenge and conflict, not always the most comfortable turf for a young practitioner.

One of the toughest things that you do when you're younger is to challenge older, more experienced, more senior coaches and performance directors. You have to be comfortable with being told 'no'. It doesn't get any easier! Sometimes it makes sense to chip away at these things and sometimes you have to come at it head-on, depending on the relationship with the coach, what it is about, the time of year and what the priorities are. You put your point across and a lot of the time you have to agree to disagree and say, 'right, we do it your way'. It depends on the situation and the sport; you need to know the ins and outs of your sport. It's the difference between the art and science of coaching. The coaches have a lot of science behind the coaching and I have to also trust their art.

Working relationships with coaches are essential for young practitioners to nurture. They seem to require a great deal of trust-building and a certain amount of risk, as well as a willingness to make your point understood when necessary. It is very hard to do that without a level of energy that sustains conviction and engages positively with others. De has plenty of energy, but also recognises that such vigour needs a foundation of composure and serenity:

The reality of making sports science and sports medicine work is people being passionate, knowledgeable, willing to share and cooperate in a team taking collective responsibility. It is also about using your and the team's resources to maintain a healthy perspective.

CHAPTER 8

MANAGING WORKING RELATIONSHIPS

Like it or not, achieving meaningful success in any high-performance environment is largely down to high-quality working relationships, something evident from the interview with Deirdre (De) Angella. Being the most knowledgeable, technically skilled coach or practitioner in the world gets you so far. But to be successful on a sustainable and world-class basis, you have to be able to build and foster effective working relationships. As Jurg Gotz says: 'Talking about qualifications of service providers, you can have the best physiologist, best psychologist … [but] if they cannot create rapport with an athlete and his/her coach, this will not go anywhere, not a chance, full stop.'

When things go wrong in a high-performance environment, it is usually due to some form of breakdown in the quality, openness and communication in our working relationships, leading to conflict. Conflict managed well can be a source of creativity, more robust decision-making and greater performance. Managed badly, and conflict produces quite the opposite, as well as strained relationships, stress and even sabotage. It can be very tempting to blame others when we are in conflict with them, but however uncomfortable it may be, it is worth starting with an honest examination of our own contributions to the situation. One of the more corrosive contributions that we can unwittingly make to the development of difficult situations and conflict is our own silence. Remaining silent when difficult conversations need to be had is certainly easier and more comfortable in the short term. However, the courage to hold ourselves and others accountable will drive performance to the heights needed in the toughest working environments.

THE COMPLEXITY OF WORKING RELATIONSHIPS

Working relationships in elite sport can be very complex and sometimes confusing, especially when they become intertwined with personal ones. Working relationships are an intricate mix of function, respect, friendliness, power and emotion.

Personal friendships can easily take root in the reality of the communal environment of elite sport. Whether you are a coach, practitioner or manager in elite sport, you get to spend a great deal of time with those working with you. Almost every day during the training and competitive season, you will work intensely with athletes in order to help them deliver their performances under pressure; you will share their good times and their bad ones. You will get to know the athletes, coaches and your fellow support staff well, sometimes very well. Add to that the passion, proximity and pressure generated by travelling to training camps and competitions together, where you are cocooned in what can sometimes feel like an alternative reality. You then get to know each other very well indeed, sometimes too well. This can be hazardous and confusing territory for less experienced practitioners and coaches. (For a cautionary tale, read the stories detailing the falling-out between Tiger Woods and his ex-caddy, Steve Williams, the man at whose wedding Woods was best man.) Paradox rules: on the one hand, you need to build relationships with athletes and other staff in order to be effective in your work and, hopefully, enjoy it. On the other hand, building too friendly a relationship can lead to unease about your motives, and unreasonable expectations being placed upon you, which in turn can lead to conflict or feelings of betrayal. Personal friendship often involves confidential loyalty and when a colleague's expectation of friendship-based loyalty is mutually exclusive to your professional obligations, there will be problems.

Another differentiation between professional and personal relationships is power. Although it may be uncomfortable to acknowledge for some, most working relationships operate within the context of the power that one person holds over the other. There may not be an explicit or continuous power, but there will be a subtle, perhaps temporary, power imbalance that significantly alters the expectations and behaviours of one or both people. Genuine personal friendships, on the other hand, are usually devoid of a power component. Or, at least, they should be if they are to be meaningful and fulfilling.

Personal friendships are based on choice, whereas professional relationships are based on the necessity of getting the work done. Not all of us can choose our work colleagues, but then again we don't have to like someone to work well with them, as witnessed in many top sports teams.

Our interviewees are very aware of the difficult balance to be struck between professional and personal relationships. Paul Brice talks about the importance of professional and personal boundaries to his work and particularly how that helps him build and maintain trust (see pages 59–60). Jared Deacon also talks about the change in relationships as he moved from being a fellow athlete to a coach: he remains friends with the athletes but he is very clear about his role as their coach:

> I never socialised with the athletes I worked with professionally. We are friendly enough, but there are certain ways I need to work when I have the coach's shirt on.

Pete Cunningham refers to the expectations he had of his practitioner team in Team GB Sailing. Pete managed to cultivate an environment in his team of professional relationships with athletes and coaches based upon respect, rather than the need to be liked (see page 43).

This professionalism extends into the social arena. When success is delivered, surely it is good for people to celebrate?

> If the sailors want to go out for a few beers, then let them go and do their own thing. There are enough support staff and coaches for the practitioners to go out for a beer with. That professional line between support staff and the athletes is very important.

The message from Pete and our other interviewees was that professional and personal relationships are certainly not mutually exclusive, but that the undesirable consequences of muddling the two usually include trouble. Katherine Grainger, multiple Olympic medallist, describes Sarah Hardman as a practitioner who is able to get the balance right between professional and personal relationships.

> ... one of the special things that Sarah exhibits is genuine care and concern for the athletes – she sees us all as individuals and will try to help in any way she can to make our lives a little bit easier. She doesn't just ask how our training is going but she also takes a moment to ask how we are doing, she understands that how we are feeling can impact on our performance. She displays respect for what we do every day and that makes a big difference to athletes that work with her.

Sarah Hardman is clearly able to be very friendly with the rowers, without compromising the respect they have for her and her professionalism.

Overall then, it appears wiser to start with a focus on developing the professional relationship. If appropriate, the personal friendship will follow.

GOOD INTENTIONS ARE NOT ENOUGH

Most coaches have a genuine intention of building purposeful and productive working relationships with practitioners. It is also, hopefully, of little surprise that most practitioners are keen to work well with and get on well with coaches. So you might expect a deafening harmony between coaches and practitioners across the UK high-performance system. Indeed, we can think of many cases where that is true. However, as no doubt with other countries, there are some pockets of interdisciplinary tension within some UK Olympic and Paralympic sports. This probably exists within professional sport as well, as the causes seem to be generic: miscommunication, misunderstanding and mistrust.

However uncomfortable it is to acknowledge, we are all prone to making stereotypical judgements about groups to which we do not belong, and coaches and practitioners are no different here. This means that good intentions are put at risk of being scuppered by judgements about other groups or, indeed, individuals. These assumptions thrive in the absence of the good communication that governs effective working relationships. The resultant lack of trust compromises high performance, which can be achieved only when good intentions are translated into open communication within honest relationships. That is often easier said than done, yet many coaches and practitioners mange to turn their good intentions into very effective working relationships by investing the time to listen curiously and attentively to each other.

FIXING WORKING RELATIONSHIPS THAT COULD BE BETTER

There are some usual suspects blamed for working relationships that are suboptimal, dysfunctional and possibly in conflict. The suspects tend to be 'the other person's difficult personality' and 'the other person's lack of competence'. If you want to resolve the situation and make the working relationship better, fretting about the other person's personality won't help. Doing so misses the crucial point that it takes at least two people to form a poor working relationship. In any case, the other person may be of the opinion that our own personality may not be helping matters. For example, you may see a colleague as egotistical and overconfident, while he or she may see you as superficial and passive. Both views may be completely off the mark, or they may both hold some home truths. So where does that leave this difficult situation? Most likely in a place that is hard to come back from, since criticising personality quickly becomes personal, and that is a sure way to develop even more intransigent positions.

The road to returning to a positive relationship starts by addressing the lack of trust that exists. Whether you trust someone or not is largely built on your perception of his or her intentions and competence. If there are questions about intention and competence in a working relationship, it will not progress. These need to be sorted out, and yet doing so is for many an uncomfortable experience. It requires first the willingness to invest time and effort in resolving the situation, then some honest conversations and some two-way feedback. Pete Cunningham talks about the power of some frank honesty to help a team perform (see page 42).

The honest conversation should explore the intentions of both parties. In the majority of situations, it turns out that intentions on both sides are well-meaning, but it helps to clarify this. Once that is established, an atmosphere of trust can start to develop. At this stage, it can be helpful to provide feedback to each other on the behaviours that help and hinder the working relationship. Providing and receiving feedback can be an uncomfortable process for some, but it need not be and is also an essential activity in high-performance working relationships. One simple model that helps to frame good feedback is the AID approach (see the box 'A simple model for providing feedback', page 15).

Generally, when providing constructive feedback, it is better to describe behaviours that are missing, rather than those that are perceived as wrong. However, even using a model and a positive focus, providing feedback can feel uncomfortable for both parties. (Think for a moment how you would feel if you had to give feedback to a coach that their behaviour came across as rude or arrogant.) To help minimise this, it is useful to prepare for the feedback discussion in advance, possibly with some notes and certainly with some reflection on how you might react to any feedback you may receive. With a good level of self-awareness and reflection, there shouldn't be too many surprises. However difficult it may be, providing and receiving feedback is a feature of high-performance.

FIG. 8.3 Trust is critical to podium success

WHEN THINGS GO WRONG

It is, however, inevitable and indeed desirable that sometimes conflict breaks out. After all, if you really care about something, aren't you prepared to argue to the hilt for it? The interviews with Nigel Mitchell and Danny Kerry provide great examples of 'the system' being better for conflict (see pages 113–114 and pages 205–206 respectively). People will have different views about how to approach issues and challenges, and there is much to be learned from exploring those differences with an open mind. With that approach, not all conflict is harmful to working relationships. Indeed, conflict can prove to be energising and reinvigorating. When handled well, it leads to better quality work and more open, honest and trusting work relationships.

Conflict managed badly can be very damaging and can often arise from many small instances of silence, rather than a single reckless outburst. Conversations left unsaid, in the relative ease of silence about a particular issue, often result in a slow-cooking stew of resentment and mistrust. The lack of trust destroys goodwill and cooperation, which undermines the risk-taking culture needed in elite sport.

While conflict can often arise because of unclear roles and responsibilities, our behaviour is often a significant contributing factor. Understanding our behaviour during conflict, and recognising how to manage this, can help us get the most out of the situation. There are many theoretical models that can help with this, so we'll illustrate this with one, the Thomas–Kilmann model.[2]

THE FIVE CONFLICT BEHAVIOURS IN THE THOMAS–KILMANN MODEL

Accommodate	When you want to cooperate and are willing to put aside your needs and desires as well as acquiesce to the other person's demands. This is also described as the 'You lose, they win' scenario.
Avoid	When you are neither cooperating nor asserting your needs and desires. This is when the danger of silence can occur as difficult conversations remain unsaid and conflict is left unresolved. This is also described as the 'You lose, they lose' scenario.
Compete	When you seek to realise your needs and desires over those of the other person. This is also described as the 'You win, they lose' scenario.
Compromise	When both people resolve the conflict quickly by agreeing to 'meet in the middle'. Each person concedes some ground on their position, but neither side is satisfied that their needs and wants are fulfilled. This is also described as the 'You lose, they lose' scenario.
Collaborate	When both people seek to resolve the issue with a solution that both believe is best for the problem. It may take some time to reach that situation, but both people are concerned for a mutual goal and the quality of their working relationship. This is also described as the 'You win, they win' scenario.

The five styles can also be differentiated according to the concern that each person has for the goal and the relationship, as shown in Figure 8.4. Each of the five behaviour styles is appropriate under different circumstances. Flexing between these styles enables us to be more in control of our behaviours and more effective at managing different types of conflict. The box 'Conflict management strategies' provides some considerations as to when these different styles are appropriate.

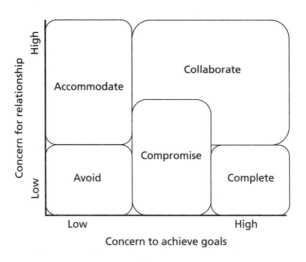

FIG. 8.4 Conflict management styles according to concern for the goal and the relationship

CONFLICT MANAGEMENT STRATEGIES

Accommodate	When the outcome of the conflict is actually of low concern for you, this style will help. It is also appropriate if you are more concerned with building the working relationship with the other person. Caution should be taken to avoid appearing as weak and acquiescing, rather than cooperative. So it is worth letting the other person know that you have given up something important in order to help resolve the conflict.
Avoid	Not all battles are worth fighting and some conflicts resolve themselves anyway as greater issues emerge in other areas. So avoidance can be useful, especially if you are unprepared for the situation. When conflict takes you by surprise, it can be better to buy some time. It is worth temporarily avoiding the discussion until you have more information, or a better insight into what resolution you can accept.

Compete	Clearly, this style works best when there can be only one winner. When you are not too concerned about the relationship and the goal is very important, then you need to compete. Competing is not a negative strategy in this context. But it is worth managing the temptation to compete on every occasion, in order to pick the right battles.
Compromise	When the conflict is marginal to the key issues and both sides are willing to yield their positions, compromise is a useful strategy. Compromise is a risky approach when the issue is significant. In that situation, compromise is counterproductive and the issue remains unresolved to both parties full satisfaction.
Collaborate	When the issue is important, collaboration is the most effective conflict management strategy. But collaboration can happen only when trust is present in the relationship. With that trust, information can more easily be shared to understand the other person's position. This takes time and energy, so the collaboration style works best when you have time and is not helpful when a quick resolution is required. The collaboration means that one person may have to set aside their priorities as they accept that the other person's information and analysis are stronger. Collaboration is different from compromise. Both parties are highly concerned about the goal and the relationship, such that the best goal is achieved and the relationship is preserved, if not strengthened.

CONFLICT STRATEGIES

Think about difficult situations or conflicts in which you have been involved. Alternatively, you may be facing a difficult situation and could think about applying this model to that.

Describe the situation below and then, using the boxes 'The five conflict behaviours in the Thomas–Kilmann model' and 'Conflict management strategies' as your guides, assess the pros and cons of each conflict management style.

Situation 1

Description		
	Pros	Cons
Accommodate		
Avoid		
Complete		
Compromise		
Collaborate		

Situation 2

Description		
	Pros	Cons
Accommodate		
Avoid		
Complete		
Compromise		
Collaborate		

SUMMARY

Taking personal responsibility for the quality of working relationships is one of the keys to success in the high-performance sport environment. Getting on effectively with those we work with not only determines our success, it also provides a significant amount of our job satisfaction.[3] The quality of working relationships also correlates with the level of perceived pressure and stress that we are under. Apart from these important considerations, time and time again we have heard coaches and senior practitioners comment that performance, problem-solving and creativity all arise when people relate and work well with each other. For example, one of the senior practitioners we have worked with over the last eight years is very clear that when sports complain about the service delivery of a practitioner, it is not regarding any deficit in their technical skills. Rather it is about the practitioner's ability to communicate and build relationships with coaches and athletes.

For many people, some of their working relationships evolve into the most important friendships in their lives, yet sometimes the blurring between professional and personal relationships can cause confusion and sorrow.

Difficulties in working relationships often originate from a lack of trust as a result of confusion about the other person's role, responsibilities or intentions. While the first two may be difficult to clarify, intention should be open to understanding and challenge if necessary. If you want to develop an understanding of another person's position and to build trust once intentions are clarified and accepted, seeking and providing feedback is the key tool to help you.

There is much to be gained in terms of quality of work and creativity when conflict is managed well. Managing conflict well means addressing the behaviours we use when seeking resolution. Once working relationships are going well, we shouldn't take them for granted. All relationships need nurturing, and showing appreciation can reinforce the quality of that relationship. If you work well with someone, you are likely to trust him or her so that they can become a very useful source of feedback. Actively seeking feedback from that source on appropriate occasions can help you to develop your skills even further.

CASE STUDY: PERFORMANCE UNDER PRESSURE

NIK DIAPER

Head of Sport Science and Sport Medicine (Paralympic Sports),
English Institute of Sport

FIG. 9.1 Nik Diaper

What do you do when you find out that you are not, in world terms, as good an athlete as you hoped to be? In the case of Nik Diaper, this ultimately led to his current position as Head of Sport Science and Sport Medicine (Paralympic Sports) at the English Institute of Sport (EIS). It's a post he holds despite being, at the time of writing, only 30 years old, an unusually young age for such a position. Just as with elite athletes, however, Nik is a clear example of exceptional talent in the right environment achieving success in a much quicker timeframe.

Nik spent his early years in Kenya, a country he represented as a swimmer at the Commonwealth Games. Living in Kenya gave Nik an interest in animals and wildlife, and this is where he first thought he wanted to focus his career. After finishing his A-levels, Nik took went to train full-time in the United States for six months. For a high achiever, the sudden shift from being a big fish in a little pond to a little fish in a big pond took some coming to terms with, as Nik now readily admits. It did, however, get him thinking more about performance and why others were so much better than him.

From small beginnings, such thoughts led to Alsager in England and a place to read sports science at Manchester Metropolitan University (MMU). Still at MMU, and while doing his master's, he was approached by Dr Vicky Tolfrey to work with the Great Britain wheelchair tennis team. Despite this being a sport he had never heard of, and without having any knowledge of Paralympic sport, Nik grabbed the chance and spent the next two years supporting the athletes in the laboratory and at training camps.

Looking back, Nik now sees this period of his life as the hardest he has ever worked. He was doing his MSc full-time, as well as putting in 18 hours a week in the sports hall and working with wheelchair tennis.

> I remember thinking 'I have no excuse, I just have to do it, I have what it takes to do it, to get everything done, balance my time, etc.'; it was a good time but a hard time.

This approach has served Nik well throughout his career so far. He acknowledges that he has always had an organised work ethic, something he felt he needed 'to overcome not being gifted academically and therefore having to work very, very hard'. Nik also has a deep level of appreciation for the opportunity provided him by his parents. Growing up in Kenya, he had seen under-privilege on a daily basis, and as an international student his parents paid higher university fees, and they had worked hard to save for this.

The hard work certainly paid off, for when Nik was halfway through his MSc he found out that Wheelchair Tennis wanted to take him as an accredited scientist to the 2004 Paralympic Games; his MSc study on cooling strategies for wheelchair athletes had been the final selling point. A familiar situation saw Nik once again managing his energy and resilience as, in quick succession, he handed in his completed dissertation, had an interview for an intern position with the EIS (which was successful) and got on the aeroplane to Athens.

The Athens Paralympics was not only an exciting period for Nik, it was also a seminal moment for British Wheelchair Tennis, the team winning gold and silver medals just when the sport received full medal status for the first time. For Nik the six weeks away presented a series of challenges that he admits he was not prepared for:

> The length of time you were away from family and living out of a suitcase – at the time I still thought it was a glamorous profession to be involved with, I soon realised it was not. How hard you have to work behind the scenes doing things that athletes never see and take for granted and rarely thank you for. Not that we do it for the praise, but you do have to take your own self-satisfaction for it. Being away from home and loved ones was difficult, I did not think I would find it as hard as I did. In particular there were two incidents which brought home to me the pressures of the environment.

The first occasion gave Nik a forceful reminder that athletes are people and that 'you need to understand the person to understand the athlete'. In this case it was being asked to support one of the player who, two days before they were due to compete, had a complete breakdown. Nik admits this breakdown caught him completely off-guard, frightened him even. At the time no one was sure that the athlete would be able to compete. Given the pressured environment of a Paralympic Games, Nik recalls being quite upset that no one had informed him that a failed suicide attempt was the reason this athlete was in a wheelchair

> It was an uncomfortable time for me, one which gave me a big slap in the face given how well things had been going up to that time. I was quite frightened to begin with, never having seen anything similar happen before.

FIRST-HAND VIEW

The majority of my work with Nik has been associated with his roles in identifying talented athletes. He has always listened carefully to my requirements, identified the main parameters and applied logic to discern if an athlete might be who we are looking for. As a person, my trust in Nik extends to his straight talking and honest approach in all dealings. In the sporting world, which is populous with highly competitive individuals, this integrity is something that I place a very high value on and believe is the main reason I have found the opportunity to work with Nik both productive and enjoyable.

Tom Dyson
Lead Coach, Adaptive Boats GB Rowing Team

Uncomfortable in this new situation, Nik found himself having to carry out roles that he had not expected, to support the player, at the time thinking 'it is not what I signed up to do'. Perhaps not, but as Nik was learning fast and at a young age: if it helps performance, then it becomes part of the job!

If that challenge was not enough, the player that Nik was sharing a room with began to open up in a way that he had not expected given the athlete's usual confident, direct demeanour and apparent resistance to buy into the GB programme. Despite the athlete's views, there was mutual respect between the two and this led to Nik being in a privileged position, where the athlete began to confide in him as a way of coping with the pressure that the athlete felt. He began to see a side of the athlete that was very different to what had previously been revealed.

> It was fascinating to see the athlete as the person, not just necessarily the athlete, and how nervous they actually were going into the Games despite being a medal favourite. I found myself being opened up to in a way I did not expect, and remember thinking I am in a very privileged position here, and the best thing I

can do is to just listen to what they have to say, and not pass judgement or take sides.

This was further re-enforcement for Nik that athletes are first and foremost human beings and need to be treated as such. But perhaps more importantly for Nik, it also brought the realisation of the benefit of being prepared and flexible enough to do what is required when away at major events. To finish the story: in one of his proudest moments, Nik found himself leaning over to hand the athlete the Union Jack flag when he won the final.

Nik's return from Athens saw him go straight into his new position as an intern in the EIS on the Fast-Track Practitioner Programme, a one-year programme run by UK Sport, which is designed to fast-track the development of practitioners who demonstrated the potential for employment within the UK high-performance system. On the back of the Athens experience, Nik admits:

> I went into the role thinking I was nearly there in terms of the finished product and probably with hindsight a little overconfident in my own ability. I got a sharp realisation that I did not know much in the grand scheme of things.

Nik's EIS manager was Dr Greg Whyte, at the time head of sports science. In Greg, Nik had a

> ... fascinating character as a mentor and someone that I knew I could learn from. We got on well right from the start. I liked Greg's style, his apparent carefree attitude and his willingness to say things as they were, whoever he was talking to. On top of which, his depth and breath of physiology knowledge was immense; at the time, Greg was the man to be around and many of the young practitioners had a great deal of respect for him.

While an intern, Nik discovered that he had a natural ability which would hold him in good stead in the future – that of reflection. He now knows he is a very reflective person, engaging naturally in real-time and post-event reflective practice. It was a skill that he had to draw on heavily when, after applying for and not getting a job within one of the foremost Olympic sports in the country, he was told by the head of sports science, 'I liked you, but the performance director felt you were too arrogant for the post'. Nik recalls:

> That was like a slap in the face for me, and I disagreed with it at the time, but looking back I can see where it came from.

Surprised, Nik had to accept that this was the perception, and he reflected on why he had given that impression. The scientist in him meant he wanted to validate the comment, so he did just that, asking those whose opinions he valued if they saw the same thing. They told him: 'Yes, you are confident in your ability but not arrogant.' Nik expands:

Of course there is a very fine line between being confident, overconfident and arrogant and I kind of had to look at myself and think, 'Why did I give that impression?' I had been holding my ground on something I said and I'm not usually one to back down on something I feel strongly about. But I had to take the feedback on board and do something about it. It was a harsh, but well-learnt lesson, reinforcing the importance of thinking about your first impression and I am more aware when meeting someone for the first time of some of the things that might make them think that. Now I am no less confident and I will still say what I want, hold my ground and not back down. But I am more aware of my own personal style and preferences and how I need to adjust these depending on a particular situation or style preference of others.

FIRST-HAND VIEW

Nik has a very strong quality in that he is able to listen carefully and fully understand the needs of the athletes and coaches. He fully absorbs himself into the project he is working on and therefore is able to give you constructive and helpful advice that not only is proven in lab-based work, but can also more importantly be transferred into a real-world situation. From a coach's point of view, having a practitioner that you fully trust and who supports you in your efforts to help athletes achieve their goals is invaluable.

Jayne Ellis
Paralympic Coach, Great Britain Cycling Team

After his year as an intern, Nik accepted a role as performance profiler working with Paralympic sports, a position he admits he first took with some reluctance: 'I was not going to apply, to avoid being pigeonholed as "the Paralympic guy", but there was not much else out there at the time and I was persuaded to.' Once in the role, Nik found

… in effect a blank piece of paper, it was a new role that was a partnership between the British Paralympic Association [BPA, now Paralympics GB] and the EIS. I soon found I just had to get out and do things, it was my chance to create a name for myself, and working with the six sports on the BPA managed sport programme I managed to start to build my reputation.

Nik goes on: 'I built my bridges by being out and about at training camps and was able to build links and rapport with coaches, with no agenda other than trying to help them and knowing that other than wheelchair tennis, I did not know much about Paralympic sport and needed to learn fast.'

Sports and coaches can be notoriously difficult to change and influence, so how did Nik go about this?

Eighty per cent were very open to my ideas, perhaps because I took the time to understand the demands of the sport and learn from athletes and coaches before offering my thoughts. My aim was to add and build rather than do things differently – I would certainly never respond to someone else's idea by saying, 'That's a rubbish idea, it will never work,' for example. Rather, I would say, 'That's a brilliant idea, let's talk further and develop it'.

If the 2004 Paralympic Games had been for Nik about hands-on work with the athletes, for 2008 and Beijing his role was much more strategic, focusing on the heat and acclimatisation strategies to be used by the athletes. This gave him an insight into just how much work and logistical planning is required to ensure success in taking a team to the Olympic or Paralympic Games. The Games themselves were another exhilarating yet challenging experience, Nik's role being primarily at the pre-Games holding camp in Hong Kong, where he was in charge of the monitoring of the athletes, a role that kept him incredibly busy. From here he went straight on to the Games in Beijing to gather performance intelligence data and footage on other nations for the BPA. This was another long stint, but one for which he was not a fully accredited member of Team GB, so he felt slightly removed from the real action:

For me it was a strange experience compared to being accredited in Athens; you don't really feel part of it when you don't have accreditation and are based outside of the athletes' village. It's hard to explain, but you lose some of the sense of identity of being part of the team, and access to venues and facilities is incredibly difficult without accreditation. In that respect, it allowed me to see the other side and how difficult it is to perform your duties without accreditation.

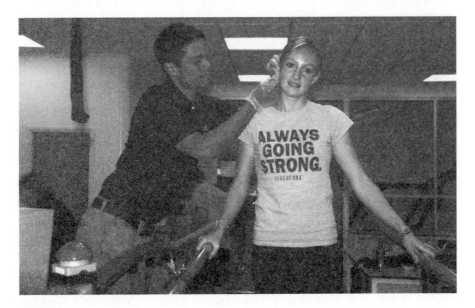

FIG. 9.2 Nik Diaper

This, of course, is for many practitioners the likely scenario at a major Games, having a key role but supporting from the outside, As Nik goes on to say:

> Not having it [accreditation] does not make your role any less important, but it can be an extremely emotive issue for some people.

One thing, however, he had learnt from four years before was to put in place better self-management, for even the most resilient of people still need their own time. For Beijing, Nik made sure that he built in timeout when he could do his own thing and escape momentarily from the 'madness', which in his case often meant going for a swim. In addition, the team at the holding camp had a policy of allowing an afternoon off every four days. Given that working days are often 12–15 hours long in this environment, this was crucial to ensure that staff were able to maintain their performance for the required duration.

Any excitement from the Paralympic team's success in 2008, when they finished second overall in the medal table, was quickly doused on returning to the UK, to find that strategic funding decisions meant he was facing redundancy. This was not something Nik saw coming. The experience was a sobering interruption in what had been, to date, a smooth upward-moving career.

With redundancy looming, Nik started looking and thinking about his future. He wanted to stay in the applied side of sport, but now extremely disillusioned, he felt that working abroad or pursuing a different career altogether were options. Instead, a move to the UK Sport talent team became available. In contrast to a few years before, Nik decided to retain a Paralympic focus, an area where he was fast being seen as an expert. From a very pragmatic point, he also knew that it was within the Paralympic sports that he could have the most impact and make the biggest difference.

Nik was appointed Senior Talent Scientist at UK Sport in April 2009. Six months into the job, he admits, the challenge became clear:

> I was having to operate at a practitioner level as well as at a strategic level within two different organisations and across eight different sports with the expectation that I would produce Paralympic medals within a two-year period and with only my position dedicated to this task. At times it felt overwhelming and I began to lose confidence in my ability to deliver what I had set out to do.

Something needed to change, as the stress of continual 15-hour days led to him suffering from colds and coughs. It was now that Nik had to act in a way that many struggle with – namely, being able to have difficult conversations while remaining objective and honest with those that he reported to

> I had to be sure that my emotional responses were not clouding my judgement of the situation, and present facts rather than emotion.'

These experiences certainly helped Nik to learn about himself and to know and develop his own management style, something critical in his current role – head of sports science and sports medicine for Paralympic sport in the EIS. At the time of our interview, Nik had been in post for two months, and for the first time in his working life found himself in a position where he has inherited a role as opposed to developed it from scratch. Given Nik's journey to date, you could say that the role ismade for him. It may be, but it is still one in which Nik foresees some battles ahead. When asked about his likely approach to these, he thought for a while and replied:

FIRST-HAND VIEW

What Nik does extremely well is deliver professionalism. He is able to blend into a multitude of environments, teams and hierarchical strata and impress. But this does not come by chance. In the years that I have known Nik, supported him and challenged him, one aspect is consistently constant – his preparation. He ponders a communication, the wording of an email – whether it is better to meet or speak over the phone. On the other side, when things do not go well, whether it is something he or others could do better, he feels the effect profoundly – reflecting extensively on learning and finding a way to perform at a higher level next time.

Steve Ingham
EIS Head of Physiology

I've developed a great deal as a person over the past few years and I'm more aware of my strengths and weaknesses. I think flexibility of style and approach will be critical in my role and I can only be flexible if I know what my own preferences are. I like to think that I've developed some strong relationships over the years and perhaps due to my own multicultural background I seem to be good at judging situations and personalities. I think that it's important to take people with you – whatever the journey may be.

How, then, as a relatively young head of service will he go about influencing people? This, Nik admits, was one of the greatest challenges when he was on the fast-track Practitioner Development Programme, where he found there were few opportunities for him to get his teeth into and practice his influencing tools.

I am not particularly sure how well I do it, and I am sure I could do it better, but influencing is very much part of the role I now have. I started to have to do a lot of it in my previous role, writing strategy, making a case for funding, but it was an area that to begin with I found difficult, just trying to conceptualise it.

He continues:

The higher up you get, the more people will take pot shots at you and the more you start to develop critics. I used to be afraid of making mistakes, but I've learned to accept that they are a part of life – particularly how you respond once you've made one. The greatest mistake is not to recognise and learn from your mistakes.

CHAPTER 9
PERFORMANCE UNDER PRESSURE

You often hear athletes talking of being 'in the zone' and performing at their peak, but as a coach or support practitioner, what are you like when you are at your best? How well can you maintain your focus and energy when you are under pressure? In those circumstances, how well do you manage yourself so that you do not become too stressed?

Read the interviews in this book, and you will develop a sense of the importance of being able to perform under pressure. None of our interviewees would have made it to where they are now without being able to anticipate, manage, perform well in and actively recover from very pressurised situations.

Up to this point in the book, we have looked at progressive skills, from being able to understand and manage ourselves, through to being able to build and sustain effective working relationships. As well as technical excellence, these skills form the essential toolkit for high-performance success. But the real litmus test of excellence is how well you are able to maintain those skills in highly pressured situations. For some, when they are under stress those skills evaporate very quickly and they revert to reactive, emotional and impetuous behaviours that undermine their effectiveness and that of their team.[1] Which is challenging, because elite sport is all about pressure.

Pressure, that is, to perform when it matters, often in front of passionate crowds and with status and money at stake; a challenge that permeates from the athletes through to the coaches, to the practitioners and to the whole support team. Firstly, there are the obvious pressures associated with the acute and intense expectations of the big competitions. Then there is also the background pressure associated with the demands of very busy jobs in a fast-changing environment as practitioners' time and energy are concentrated on helping athletes prepare for their peak performances at key championships and Games. Pressure builds on top of that demand when people sense that they don't have the level of control over their work they would like. This is particularly evident when there are changes to the system, processes, organisation or leadership, which occur frequently in an environment characterised by fast-moving targets and which are exacerbated by decisions made in the heat of the moment in response to an unexpected poor performance. People can also feel under pressure when working relationships are awkward and the prospect of conflict is close by, as discussed in the previous chapter. In essence, there are many pressures that can lead to stress in a high-performance environment, some of which are self-inflicted by our low self-awareness of when we are chronically stressed. However, the question is not how we avoid stress; rather, it is about how we take control of our reactions to it and recover from it.

As has been seen, it is the people who can manage stress well that are highly valued in the elite sport system. For example, Alex Natera, strength and conditioning coach,

English Institute of Sport, says of one of our interviewees, Deirdre (De) Angella: 'Additionally, in the high pressured occasions and environments that we work in, when stress levels are literally through the roof, the cool, controlled demeanour of De is a great assurance to all working with her.'

In this chapter, we will look further at the causes of pressure, with a view to understanding how you can manage these positively to increase your capacity to perform under pressure.

PRESSURE, PRESSURE EVERYWHERE

It is a fact of life that for that many people in the world of elite sport, good pressure is the spice of life. Indeed, for all our interviewees, their careers continue to be peppered with the pressure of exciting challenges, together with the inevitable highs and lows that come with winning and losing.

If you are drawn to this world, you are likely to be the type of person who actively seeks pressure in their endeavours. In doing so, there will be a risk of becoming overwhelmed and stressed. But if you can take control of your reactions to pressure, the resulting sense of achievement and even euphoria can be quite intoxicating. In any case, if you strive for success in a high-performance environment, experiencing pressure is part of the deal. As an illustration of this, check back towards the end of the interview with Paul Brice, when he talks about his realisation that the job is all about pressure (see page 63). In this environment, it is difficult and possibly counterproductive to avoid pressure. Reassuringly for most people, the more they successfully manage pressure, the more able they are to sustain their performance under yet more pressure. We'll look at some techniques for managing pressure in the next section. Before that, it is useful to understand the sources of pressure in the high-performance environment.

External pressure

The obvious place to start is the ultimate pressure cooker of the Olympic and Paralympic Games. Four intense years of training, pain and sacrifice all boil down to that moment of truth in the crucible that is the track, pool, court or pitch. The world watches, and everyone feels the expectation and the scrutiny. Anticipation of success is enough to launch the stress response to take-off velocity, while for some it is the fear of failure which sends that stress reaction into the stratosphere. The athletes who earn their place on the podium are often the ones with the mental toughness to focus on the process of their skill and not get too distracted by the potential outcome. They are the ones who perform better under the pressure of competition than in training, as opposed to collapsing under the force of it. Through it all, stress is infectious, so those around the athlete, including the coaches and practitioners, are exposed to wave after wave of stress. Add to that their own pressure reactions, and you can get an idea of how stress levels can spiral out of control very quickly.

FIG. 9.3 Pressure comes from within as well as external challenges

It is hard to anticipate all of the pressures at a major Games or championships. In his interview, Danny Kerry provides a good illustration of this when he talks about his first experience as a head coach at the Olympic Games in Beijing (see page 201). Rather than try to prepare for every possible situation at a major Games, there is actually more to be gained from preparing personal coping strategies for when unexpected events do occur. In that way, you can be best prepared, as Deirdre Angella explained a third of the way through her interview (see pages 129–130).

There are, of course, other pressure environments, notably training camps and even some tough training sessions. At these times, it is useful to remember that other people also get stressed, and you may end up on the sharp end of their reaction to pressure. For an example, read the part of interview with Sarah Hardman where she recalls how a stressed coach reacted to her (see page 95). Perhaps that experience has helped Sarah develop an effective approach to managing her own pressure and supporting others when they are under pressure – as acknowledged by Katherine Grainger, three-times Olympic Silver medallist (see page 100).

Another time when many people feel the pressure is when an athlete is injured, where there is often an urgency to help them rehabilitate back to the world competitive stage. The story of Jessica Ennis's injury in 2008 provides some insight into the pressures that individuals and teams can experience, as described in the interviews with Paul Brice and Alison Rose (see pages 62–63 and 80).

Outside of these situations, there is often a substantial amount of pressure that people experience in their everyday jobs. For example, one area that has been under intense expectations and scrutiny in recent years is that of Talent Identification (TID). You may recall the public face of this activity in such media campaigns as 'Sporting Giants' and 'From Pitch to Podium', whereby potentially elite athletes are identified for fast-track development into target sports. Nik Diaper worked in this area for a while and described in his interview the personal cost that high levels of chronic pressure can exact (see pages 152).

Pressure from within

When identifying the major pressures that we face, we must inevitably look to ourselves at some stage: our own emotional and behavioural drivers of pressure. The truth is that not all people experience harmful stress reactions when they are under pressure. Many people are able to maintain a focused attention and an energy that enables them to cope with a substantial volume of work with a high level of responsibility. What often differentiates these people from those who experience stress is their level of self-awareness and their ability to manage those characteristics of their emotions and behaviours that can be counterproductive.

There are many models of personality and working style that can help us develop an insight into our own behaviour when we are under pressure or in stress.[2] For illustrative purposes, we'll refer to just one model of working styles here, the Transactional Analysis (TA) model, developed by Eric Berne.[3] In this model, the working styles are summarised as five approaches: being perfect, being strong, trying hard, pleasing others and being in a hurry. These styles or drivers of our behaviours can be very effective when we are aware of them and in control of them. However, if we are operating on autopilot (i.e. the drivers are operating subconsciously), we can remain unaware as to when these useful drives actually start to work against us. For example, being perfect can be a successful strategy when you want to produce work to a consistently high and accurate standard. However, if someone with this driver experiences a stress reaction to pressure, they can become too demanding of themselves, sometimes emotionally beating themselves up for not being perfect or good enough. That just adds more pressure, which usually makes the situation far worse.

FIG. 9.4 Recovery is a critical part of performance

MANAGING PRESSURE

Managing pressure is about managing the sources of pressure. A starting point is to take control of our workload. That is likely to mean some good old-fashioned prioritisation of our work, according to the importance and urgency of the tasks on our 'To do' list. With the addition of some focused attention, most of us can increase our productivity substantially. Sometimes, however, there will be too much work piling up, so it is worth negotiating with your boss to reduce the volume or even delegating some of your workload to a willing colleague. Taking control of our work in this way goes a long way to reducing the perception of pressure. But many of us still get stressed about issues outside of our control, such as system changes and even other people's personalities. There is little to be gained by getting anxious over issues we can't control and more to be gained by focusing on that which is within our control. 'Control the controllable' is a well-known saying in elite sport. One area where you can do this is to take responsibility for your workload. That may involve a challenging conversation with your manager or a coach, but it is more likely to bring about a workable solution.

If uncertainty is a source of our stress reaction, then it is sensible to reduce the uncertainty as much as possible. Within the work environment, the common areas of uncertainty are roles and relationships. If we are unclear about our role and the consequent vague expectations upon us, seeking some answers to that from our boss or others can help to clarify where our focus should be. As a result, we are far less likely to experience a stress reaction. During times of change, there is often great uncertainty, as referred to by Nik and Sarah in their interviews. Again, how stressed we become about this is determined by our ability to focus on our immediate job, rather than to be distracted and possibly distressed by the events going on around us, over which we have no control over anyway.

Perceived lack of support is another source of stress: if you don't think that your boss is backing you as much as she or he could, there is a risk that you will feel isolated and even vulnerable. That one can be difficult to solve, but expressing those concerns to your boss can at least register the concern and enable an agreement to be reached where more support could be given.

PREVENTING PRESSURE TURNING INTO STRESS

Pressure is more likely to cause stress when our self-awareness declines and we stop looking after ourselves. Low self-awareness means that we miss the early warning signs that are there for us to notice: those subtle changes in the way we think, the way we feel and the way we behave.

When pressure builds into a stress reaction, many of us experience these early warning signs, such as a feeling of being overwhelmed and an anxiety or even preoccupation about a particular work issue. This is a different experience to feeling passionate and engaged about a work challenge, which is good pressure. But when

BEING 'IN TUNE' WITH YOUR EARLY WARNING SIGNS OF STRESS

One of the key strategies in avoiding excessive stress is to be self-aware, such that you know what mental state you are in. Are you 'in the zone' with a focused, efficient and creative approach to your work, or are you just getting through the day in an unstructured, inefficient and somewhat dejected manner? If it is the latter, it could be a stress reaction. Deirdre Angella reiterates the importance of self-awareness when it comes to managing pressure (see page 130).

So that you can develop your own early warning system, identify your own signs of stress from the list below.

When I was last under pressure, I:

- Felt irritable
- Felt tension in the neck and shoulders
- Had low energy
- Didn't sleep well
- Found it difficult to concentrate
- Started to doubt my own ability
- Was preoccupied with thinking about things I couldn't fix
- Couldn't relax
- Withdrew from socialising with friends
- Didn't do as much outside of work
- Had stomach reactions and pains
- Worried a lot
- Felt moody more that usual
- Had negative thoughts
- Felt drained
- Felt disillusioned

Which of these do you recognise about yourself? These signs are not exclusive to stress and may be due to other emotional issues, but they are a useful guide to how we are feeling compared to normal. If you notice a change or significant deterioration, you may be moving into a stress reaction. Knowing your early warning signs can help you more easily take control of a stress reaction with some immediate remedies.

being passionate about an issue leads to excessive rumination and declining focus on other important matters in our lives, that is more likely to be due to stress. As stress builds, many experience fatigue and an energy decline, which is exaggerated by disturbed sleep as the severity of stress grows. When the ability to concentrate on one issue at a time fails us and we become incapable of relaxing, we are very stressed indeed. In his interview, Jared Deacon refers to a strong stress reaction that he experienced, when a number of pressures coalesced and impeded his performance on the track (see page 4). It is an interesting example not only of how far someone is prepared to push themselves, but also of how our self-awareness can dip when we are under pressure. At the end of Chapter 2 we also referred to the risk of burnout. Burnout is a related condition to stress, so it is important to avoid becoming overly stressed, as this can take an individual into quite a vulnerable state.

Several of our interviewees talked about how they managed to maintain their energy and performance so that they didn't experience harmful stress. For example, Sarah Hardman talked about the importance of taking 'downtime' during the frenetic demands of being at major competitions (see page 97). Deirdre Angella also described her strategy for maintaining her focus and energy in camps and Games environments (see page 131). For De, it is as much about getting the basics right as anything else. The basics for effective energy management and stress reduction are regular quality exercise, nutrition, hydration and sleep.[4] On top of that, it is useful to have some support, someone you can talk to about the pressures you are experiencing. That other person can provide a very useful sounding-board and bring to your attention if you are looking run-down and stressed.

Keeping a sense of perspective is another successful strategy for some of our interviewees. Nigel Mitchell provided a good example of this in his interview when he described what keeps him 'grounded' (see pages 115–116). As Nigel says, keeping your focus helps, and if you can maintain a sense of humour throughout the long days, then you might well be helping the team. This approach gets noticed, as illustrated by what Dr David Gorrod, Team Physician to GB Sailing, says about Dr Pete Cunningham: 'When we go to major events such as the Olympics, he is to be seen testing urines at 7 a.m. and mixing the sports drinks at 11 p.m. and never loses his sense of humour.'

SUMMARY

The successful people in elite sport are able to perform consistently under pressure. If they feel any stress, they take the responsibility upon themselves to manage that. After all, if you don't take control of the pressure and stress you are under, it is likely to take control of you.

Being under pressure is one of those situations where strong self-awareness pays dividends. If you are aware of your positive and negative reactions to pressure, you can take more control. However, if you find yourself gradually worn down and moving towards stress or even burnout, maybe your self-awareness hasn't been as sharp as it could be.

Most of us have some early warning signs that tell us we are moving from 'being in the zone' of good pressure to being overwhelmed by bad pressure. There are some steps that we can take to keep ourselves performing well during intense and busy times, particularly around managing the demands on our time and being clear about the role and responsibilities that we should focus on.

As you are reading this book, you probably already have an interest and probably a good amount of knowledge about coaching and/or sports science and medicine. Which means that you probably know how to look after yourself both physically and mentally to keep at the top of your game as often as possible. The challenge of a career in elite sport is to translate that knowledge and practice into a sustainable plan for looking after yourself for acute peaks and extended periods of high pressure.

CASE STUDY: INSPIRE TO EXCELLENCE

JURG GOTZ

Canoe Slalom Olympic Podium Programme – Head Coach

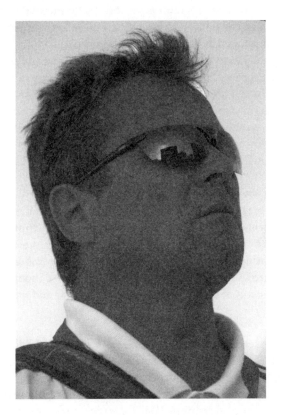

FIG. 10.1 Jurg Gotz

In the development of young people, there is much debate about the relative strengths of nature versus nurture. As is shown with a number of our interviewees, our parents can be powerful catalysts and role models. None more so, however, than Jurg Gotz, who was inspired to excellence by his father. Now in his role as Head Coach Olympic Programme Canoe Slalom for GB Canoeing, he himself plays a similar, patriarchal role with the coaches and athletes on his programme.

Jurg, as might be imagined by his name, is not British but Swiss. He followed in his father's footsteps as a white water paddler of some note: 'I was born on the river, he was a white water paddler, so I basically grew up on the banks of the river, and I did not stay on the banks for very long.' He competed for the national team between 1974 and 1984, including at four World Championships between 1977 and 1983; at that time, canoe slalom was not an Olympic discipline.

Unusually, perhaps, for an elite athlete, Jurg started coaching in his club, ultimately taking over the role from his dad, who had been Jurg's primary coach. He was also still competing and working as a primary school teacher. A PE degree at university followed for Jurg, during which time he was still teaching at a secondary school near Berne and coaching canoe slalom. Teaching of some sort beckoned as the way forward for Jurg, but for a decision that was to change his life course. Canoe slalom was admitted on to the Olympic programme for the 1992 Games in Barcelona. A move that suddenly elevated the status and funding available to the sport, its coaches and athletes, with Olympic medals now the ultimate end goal.

How much this decision has influenced Jurg's life is perhaps best demonstrated by the fact that 1 February 2011 marked the 20th anniversary of him working as a full-time coach. His is a life which has been one of frequent short-term contracts and limited long-term stability in employment – as is true for many working in the high-performance system. But there is much more to life than that, and in common with all high-performing coaches, Jurg's passion and excitement in bringing the best out of others, whether athletes or coaches, is infectious, even after 20 years on the job.

Nowhere is this more so than when we meet him at the Lee Valley White Water Centre, site of the 2012 Olympic Games Canoe Slalom competition and home to the elite squad of the British Canoe Slalom team. On a traditional British spring day, Jurg talks with passion about his life's course and how coaching, like teaching, is all about working with and bringing the best out of others. This is especially true when working with people who are so intrinsically motivated that it is less about motivating them and having to use energy to do this, and more about helping and supporting them. He expands:

> The switch from teaching to coaching came naturally. I would not put myself in the selfish category, so it was not a case of moving from selfish to selfless, although I did in later years come across someone who told me I was very arrogant as an athlete and I was very shocked. But is *arrogant* selfish? Probably not, so I would not perceive myself. Well, I was more easy-going, wanting people to feel nice and to avoid conflict. So it was never me, me, me…
>
> But as a coach you still need to be able to fight a corner. It might be just you and one athlete, but you fight to get that athlete into the team, and do so over dead bodies if needed. Selfish to selfless is a bit of a cliché; as a coach you still need to have two elbows if possible. The thing is, as a coach your contribution to the end result is somewhat different. Out in the start pool, Athlete X, even if on your team, is out there on his/her own, you cannot do any more than just watch. And it is more than that ex-athletes struggle with because it is not you anymore or even an extended arm of you. Which means you have to find out what makes the person tick and define the support strategy accordingly.

Finding the right support strategy is not easy, especially at the beginning of your career as a coach. Jurg explains:

When you start as a coach, you only have one tool, and that is what you did yourself, what worked for you, it is the tool that you apply to others. If you are lucky, and it is down to pure luck, that tool just fits, but that is very unlikely. You need to develop other tools to click with different athletes.

Coming from a teaching background, Jurg had a couple more tools in his armoury than most when he started, ones that are just as critical when working with elite athletes as they are with young people: communication skills, questioning and feedback, and understanding individual differences. He still had much to learn, however. And learning was happening on a daily basis, as from 1991 to 2000 he was a full-time coach for the Swiss national team, a role he combined from 1993 with that of performance director for the Olympic disciplines. These were embryonic days for performance sport, and while Jurg started to build a support team around him, these were mainly volunteers.

High-performing people by their very nature push themselves hard, and for some this can have adverse personal effects. In Jurg's case, a combination of work and personal issues led to health problems and him leaving his position after the 2000 Olympic Games; taking time out to, in his words, 'get back up again'. As he notes,

When things like this happen, you can either learn and stand up or not learn and stay down. I decided to learn.

Another thread common to our interviewees emerges – that of opportunity and timing. Having lost out at interview for a coaching position with the British team, Jurg was offered an alternative technical coaching role by the performance director, John Anderson, in October 2001. The day after accepting this, another offer came through: to work for a TV company as a journalist. A man true to his word, he stuck with the British role, a decision for which many British paddlers and coaches have much to be grateful.

FIRST-HAND VIEW

What he has that fits in so well is the respect he has earned from athletes, coaches, volunteers, management, both within GB and internationally. Personable, warm, always interested in the individual and not one to stand around and wait for things to happen, Jurg has a generous nature while at the same time [he is] quite firm about the ground rules he works to. It takes talent and skill to raise the bar, to lift expectations, to kick compromise into touch, and Jurg regularly exhibits these.

John MacLeod
Canoe manager, London 2012

Following the Athens Olympic Games, Jurg was appointed head coach in 2005, at the time a very hands-on role, directly coaching athletes. Jurg was, however, very clear that the size of the sport meant that to really build a world-class system would need a head coach who did not have direct athlete involvement. After the 2008 Olympic Games, this was the role that Jurg moved into, and his remit now is one of influencing the athletes indirectly via coaching the coaches and putting in place the correct support structures and technicalities.

To this end he set up a class coaching system after Beijing, using four technical coaches across the disciplines in the senior programme and a similar model for the development athletes. While this might sound like a sensible decision, it was one that took 28 days of discussion to bring about and which still does not always sit comfortably with others, as Jurg explains:

> We had one athlete who wanted a different coach to the one assigned to him via the class system we had adopted, and while this again took a lot of time in discussion and consultation we are working to make that happen, and I am heavily involved on a day-to-day basis in ensuring this does by providing additional support to the coach in question.
>
> I do not set the [daily training] plans now. Either the coach or the athlete does; I turn up for the session, which has been set, I give my pairs of hands, eyes and ears and experience to support an athlete and his technical coach. Over the year, therefore, I have quite a lot of time with the athletes, but I am not leading their programmes.
>
> My philosophy is one of high athlete ownership, which creates a unique and exciting way of working, which is a product of many years' experience. You do, however, still get some super-selfish coaches who want to hold their cards very close to their chest and end up having to pull out, as they cannot cope with it. In our programme we do not hold the cards close to our chest, we share knowledge and experiences. That way, we can tap into the power of more brains using the coaching and support team as a whole.

Jurg continues:

> ... athletes are on their own at the start line. However, the result is a product of team effort behind the athlete; the coach is, in effect, the '12th man on the pitch'.

It is at this point that Jurg reveals that, while he was inspired onto his life path by his father, he now has a very different philosophy to him, his father being 'an old-style coach, a very directive, telling coach as opposed to a questioning coach'. Jurg's way, on the other hand, feels part of him and has been developed consciously over the years. Something boosted, like all good coaches, by making sure he does not slack on his own professional development. Most recently he has taken an executive coaching course, which he feels 'has added a layer of consciousness, something I always had but now understand better'.

FIG. 10.2 Jurg Gotz

What, then, caused Jurg to move from his father's approach to coaching? For this, we need to wind back to Jurg's earlier years, when, in return for Jurg doing translation at international meetings, the German head coach took him under his wing. (Jurg speaks French, German, English and Spanish.) Jurg reflected how, in 1986, when translating at an international canoe slalom coaching conference, his language ability gave him the chance to learn everything that was going on and to see how other coaches worked, how they ticked and did things. Something that continued as his reputation as a translator grew.

Once he was appointed as a technical coach to Britain, Jurg found that for the first time he did not have other roles to focus on (and here he starts to list psychologist, bus driver, masseur, analyst, team manager ...), which is something that he is very grateful for. The change came about as a result of Jurg wanting to focus on his job and apply what he thought was right. He had started in the role when the British programme had a significant budget for the first time, and structures were only just being put in place to cope with this change.

When he began, he introduced the 'round table' where decisions are made together with athletes and staff from sport science – the strength and conditioning, physiotherapy, technical coach, sports science officer and athlete all sitting together. This was something he originally saw the strengths in and encouraged. However, with time the system grew, and after 10 years the development team required a big 'oval table' to avoid the danger of overcomplicating things and losing direction.

Now, with the approach of openness and empowerment, canoe slalom has adopted the Steve Peters model of putting the athlete at the centre to drive their own programme. The old 'round table' has become the individual Athlete Development Team (ADT). Each ADT is now made up of the athlete, his/her technical coach and whatever other support is needed, with this group meeting as the Athlete Development Meetings (ADM) with the head coach and performance director. In practice, this means the number of people at the meetings range from five to 10. This does not mean there is no role for the coaches. Quite the opposite, as often the athlete will delegate responsibility to the coach and the technical coach remains the key figure, but it enables experts to be pulled in as required. It is perhaps the ultimate end goal of the accepted coaching continuum whereby the role of the coach on an elite-level changes from telling to facilitating.

FIRST-HAND VIEW

I have worked with Jurg for over 10 years; when the going gets tough, you can always rely on Jurg to step up to the front line beside you, no matter how difficult the situation becomes.

The best individual coaches are absolutely outstanding at operating one-to-one with their athletes, but Jurg's skills as a head coach are much wider. His high level of emotional intelligence and people skills mean that he is outstanding at understanding people and knowing how best to communicate with each to get buy-in. He is a great believer in consultation and goes further than the extra mile to ensure that he gets the appropriate feedback to ensure the right outcome.

John Anderson
GB Canoeing Performance Director

The difference is that Jurg starts from the end goal – namely, that 'it is the athlete that drives the boat down the river'. This is introduced to the athletes when they are on the development programme and while Jurg admits not all athletes will ultimately get to that level, that does not stop them from aspiring to do so. This philosophy, of course, calls for great coaches, ones who can adapt their tools and approach depending on the individual athlete and their requirements at any one time. If great coaches are needed, what, in Jurg's mind, makes a great coach?

A number of things. Curiosity. Work ethic – being a good coach requires lots of repetitions, putting the work in, being hungry to learn and hungry to work and perseverance. I can see athletes who did not have the best technical talent but they succeeded because they had hunger, curiosity and worth ethic; coaches need the same. They must be experts in communicating and being able [to deal] with humans, whether athlete or stakeholder; you cannot have the wrong person at the round table.

And it is here that Jurg now focuses his efforts, helping develop his team's interpersonal skills. As might be expected from him, this does not mean trying to develop 'mini Jurgs'; rather, it is bringing in external experts to challenge his team, helping them to grow and develop the high level of self-awareness so evident in Jurg himself. For it is continued growth that is important to Jurg:

I have spent my life on a slow-track course, not a fast-track one. A slow track gives you more time to learn and gain experience. I struggle to say what my approach has been over the last 10 years, as it has never been the same, it is always growing.

Asked about key developments for him, Jurg picks up on conflict, supporting the view that, contrary to what might at first seem logical, conflict is good, and that sport, of course, is conflict. What is needed is to be able to have open conflict that is not personal. Jurg expands:

You have to revisit roles and responsibilities all the time. Ninety-five per cent of conflict is based on differences regarding roles and responsibilities, so rules should be set up but also revisited and you must make sure that people who will be governed by them can also contribute to the rules.

Conflict should be open, not via chat rooms, which means dealing with difficult conversations is key. Can you, for example, say to someone, 'I don't agree', being open and transparent, face to face. That is something that we are probably not good at, that culture where it is OK to disagree still needs some more work; we can disagree and we need to disagree. You need a foundation of trust to both have the time to listen and then at times agree to disagree. You need to be able to say what you think, and not say yes when you want to say no.

Now displaying his passion, Jurg continues:

As a coach you need to ask yourself 'Who are you?', 'What are your values?', 'What are your beliefs?' Because some of these are very deep-rooted, but they will help you answer the next question: 'What are you as a coach?' And is there symmetry between the three? Sometimes you need to go through conflict with yourself to find out who you really are, and that can be uncomfortable – finding and knowing yourself. But the more you know about yourself and how you tick, the more you can decide if you are the right coach and have the right tools to work with a particular athlete, and that takes time and experience.

What does Jurg think about the concept of fast-tracking versus experience and the hard-earned ability to take the knocks along the way? While agreeing that fast-tracking is possible if you are hungry and curious, Jurg also uses the following analogy:

> You have just finished school, so are you a teacher now? Well, 100 per cent of the answers are no. Now you have been an athlete for 10 years and you have just finished, are you a coach now? Well, probably 50 per cent or more will say, 'of course I can be a coach now'. And what would you apply as a coach? What you have just been through yourself. So in terms of a toolbox, it is no more than what you have just lived one-to-one yourself.

And while you can learn and acquire what it takes to be a coach and do so very fast, that requires strong self-awareness, as Jurg notes. His role is

> ... ultimately to support the athlete make the boat go faster, but what is the intervention that we [the coach and athlete] will make to do this? If you only have one tool, then that is the only one you can apply and you might be lucky and it works. You may then have a group of five athletes, and only one tool for all. Well, I do not want to answer the question, answer it yourself and apply a bit of logic. On the other hand, the more you know about yourself, the more you might realise that you are the wrong coach for that athlete, because they need a different tool.

Who, then, in particular, inspired Jurg? For the answer to that you have to go back to his early days and the German national head coach who took him under his wing in return for Jurg's translation skills. Here the answer may seem surprising as, after a short time thinking, Jurg goes on:

> Strangely enough, the way he operated is not the way I operate. He was the 'I am right' person, but at the same time was full of logic, his judgement was based on a huge amount of experience. He could not always put all the reasons behind his decisions, but he was right, and he was successful. So this influenced me, the amount of experience he had, the amount of data and knowledge he had: that influenced me. He impressed me more on the knowledge and technical side of things. In terms of soft skills, I think athletes were absolutely the centre of attention. His programme was athlete-centred and knowing him well now, under that rough skin was a soft touch, one who listened to and observed his athletes. His level of detailed knowledge of his athletes plus his experience was what impressed me.

And that, of course, is the advantage of a slow-track development – experience that is critical, more particularly, experience that you learn by doing it yourself or observing and learning from others, soaking up knowledge from others.

After nearly two hours, it is time for Jurg to go back to the water, but as a head coach, what final advice would he have for young aspiring support practitioners?

Talking about qualifications of service providers, you can have the best physiologist, best psychologist … if they cannot create rapport with an athlete and his/her coach, this will not go anywhere, not a chance, full stop.

CHAPTER 10

INSPIRE TO EXCELLENCE

When did you first fall in love with sport? What was the event or situation that caused you to feel that emotion? Did watching the sheer skill and supremacy of an elite athlete's winning performance capture your imagination and make you ask, 'How can I achieve something like that?' Or was the power of team spirit awakened in you as you first kicked a ball around with the other kids in the street?

Whatever the case, it is most likely the power of inspiration caused you to fall in love with sport. That inspiration may have changed over the years as you have carved out and advanced your career. But there is still likely to be some emotional stimulus that causes you to dedicate your time and energy to the pursuit of your own excellence within sport, to make the difference that you know you can make. That inspiration is quite different from motivation. Motivation, as we discussed in Chapter 3, is the process that helps us achieve our goals. Most athletes, coaches and practitioners in the world of elite sport are very self-motivated, although it always helps to have someone else supplement that with a little encouragement now and then. Inspiration, on the other hand, goes beyond motivation by awakening and tapping into an emotional need that reveals a goal that holds deeper individual meaning for us. This may be a simplistic differentiation, but motivation is more about the head and inspiration is more about the heart.

Inspiration is at the heart of elite sport. It is impossible to get the uplifting and sometimes irrational dedication required to succeed in this environment without the ambition, passion and sheer hard work that inspiration generates. Inspiration is the

WHO OR WHAT INSPIRES YOU?

So what are your sources of inspiration and how visible are they in your work? Often inspiration comes from the moment, those great sporting moments that you remember for a lifetime. Those moments are built on sheer hard work, a great deal of commitment and some talent. Often the people who have overcome adversity or performed beyond even their own wildest expectations inspire us the most. Equally, many of us are moved and inspired when we witness the sporting performances that arise from sacrifice and are against all odds.

It is worth reflecting on this for a while, as being very clear about your source(s) of inspiration can help you find the motivation to keep going when things get tough. Think about the people who inspire you and what it is about them or what they did that inspires you.

force that drives you to success, even when you don't think you have the talent, as illustrated by Jared Deacon in our first case study (see page 4).

Inspiration is also the factor that many people believe won the Olympic and Paralympic Games for London in 2012. When Lord Coe and his team went to pitch the London bid to the IOC in Singapore in July 2005, their key message was about the power of inspiration. The bid team made a promise to the IOC that the London 2012 Games would 'reach young people all around the world and connect them to the inspirational power of the Games so they are inspired to choose sport'. Keeping true to this promise has seen projects inspire young people to participate and lead sport in many parts in the world. From 'Swim Safe' initiatives that have not only helped to save the lives of children in flood-prone Bangladesh but also engaged them with sport, to community links projects such as the one that saw a group of deprived East London children learn how to play hockey with the GB and England men's hockey squad. Paraphrasing the inspirational American football coach, Vince Lombardi:[1] 'for those children a dream was inspired which gave them a greater sense of purpose and direction'.

As with motivation, inspiration benefits from occasional refreshment. This can come from anywhere, so it helps to be open to a wide range of people and their stories. As well as needing your own sources of inspiration, it is likely that very soon, if not already, you will need to be inspiring others in your work. That is because high-performance sport systems in many countries work in a matrix format, rather than a command and control one. A matrix format is one where people work on a project or goal together for a while and then move on to the next project or goal. In high-performance sport, coaches and applied practitioners can work for different organisations, yet work together to support the same athlete or team. They work together for the same outcome, but may not report to the same boss. In such a system, authority and meticulous management may get you compliance from others, but it is the skill with which you inspire people that will encourage them to commit their talents and energy. The difference between the two may appear on paper to be marginal, but the difference in potential performance gain is substantial.

This chapter reviews the key skills that will help you build and consolidate your ability to lead others through inspiration. If you have read the previous chapters, you will realise that the skills covered become more complex as the book progresses. The ability to inspire is no exception, in that it is a composite of many other skills. For example, you can best inspire others when you authentically believe in the cause yourself. This takes considerable self-awareness, clear values, the ability to get your message across passionately, as well as the knowledge of how to influence others. All of these are skills that we have covered in previous chapters, but this chapter explores how you can use these to strengthen your ability to inspire.

INSPIRATION IS LEADERSHIP

The ability to inspire is a key leadership skill. Inspiring leaders cause people to take action that both satisfies their needs and at the same time achieves something the leader wants. For many who study leadership, it is the key competency.[2] When leaders get it right, inspiration is a powerful tool with which to generate and focus the energy of the people they are leading. However, not many leaders use inspiration to get the best out of their teams – perhaps because it is actually quite difficult to be inspiring, certainly on a repeatable and regular basis. But probably more because it is easier for leaders to motivate rather than inspire. Often that motivation is based upon an element of transaction, such as a reward for completing a goal or even a sanction for failing to do so. However, as we have discussed previously, most people who choose a career in high-performance sport are self-motivated, so extrinsic motivation techniques don't add a great deal to their performance. Motivation in this context is more about getting people to comply, rather than enthusing them to achieve what even they may have thought of as impossible. Intrinsic motivation, as we discussed in Chapter 3, is very personal. Such motivation is in response to an individual's values, and therefore leaders have little impact in creating it. A leader can help someone express that motivation by creating the right environment for them to perform well. A leader can also help to awaken a dormant motive, for example by setting some challenge. But the most effective leaders know that they can achieve more through inspiring than by trying to motivate an individual who is self-motivated anyway.

Jurg Gotz is a good example of a leader who knows the difference between inspiring and motivating the people he leads and others around him. Those who have worked with Jurg often comment about the discreet way he builds and strengthens the belief you have in your own potential. Even though English is not his mother tongue, his command and subtle use of the language to generate a picture of what is possible, is certainly part of his inspirational toolkit. But more than that, it is Jurg's ability to

FIG. 10.3 Inspiration in action

articulate an emotional meaning for each person that causes the individual to raise or consolidate his or her aspirations. Says Paul Ratcliffe, Canoe Slalom K1 coach and Olympic silver medallist:

> Having the ability to allow people to grow and evolve in their own way is one of the best ways that I could describe Jurg as a coach. He has a great ability to allow people to search out the answers while guiding in a non-directive way.

An inspiring leader builds confidence in the people she or he leads. From that confidence, greater commitment and performances can be achieved. The inspirational leader is quite different to an autocratic and even a charismatic one. While both the latter styles of leadership may be effective in particular circumstances, an authentic and inspiring leader is more likely to stimulate extraordinary and sustainable determination in others.[3] There are many such leaders across the UK high-performance sport system, an example being Nigel Mitchell and the selfless encouragement that he gave the many nutritionists he has mentored. James Collins, director of Performance Nutrition and Arsenal FC nutritionist, says: 'I received mentoring from Nigel as part of the UK Sport Fast-Track Practitioner Programme and I have always admired his level of professional ethics and integrity.'

INSPIRATIONAL TECHNIQUES

Being inspirational works when you yourself have full conviction in your proposal, when your intentions are genuine, when you are being authentic and, finally, when you are confident. That takes some doing. But those who are able to understand and be true to their values and the related mission are the ones who are most plausible when trying to inspire others. The paradox is that truly inspirational people seem not to be trying to inspire others: people take inspiration from their words and actions alone. In reality, many are in the business of engaging people to buy their vision, and put effort behind it. Which is why inspirational techniques are useful in the workplace, whether you are leading a project, a team, a sport, an institution or a governing body.

In order to strengthen our inspirational skills, we need to be able to identify the contributing techniques (as described in the box 'Inspiring – a natural process') and then practise them. From a very reductionist perspective, inspiration is the ability to use words, ideas and actions to create an emotional connection and enthusiasm towards a goal or outcome.

When people are inspired, they act more on feelings than on logic. Logic can motivate, but emotion can inspire. Great sporting performances require both.

That is why the deconstruction of inspiration skills starts with providing people with a vision of what could be, in order to ignite their collective imagination and give life to their goals. An inspirational vision connects with peoples' values and sense of purpose. That vision could also offer a higher or alternative sense of purpose, as long as it resonates with peoples' deeply held values. A deeply held value to which it can be appropriate to appeal is a sense of justice or equity. In high-performance sport, many coaches and applied practitioners hold strong values around performance, dedication, commitment, humility and teamwork.

INSPIRING – A NATURAL PROCESS

Here is a quick checklist to provide some focus for the process of inspiring others. Try not to get too reductionist or obvious about inspiring, though. Those who are most inspirational appear not to be trying to inspire: they just *are* inspirational!

- Have conviction in yourself and your purpose
- Appeal to the values that you have in common with the people you are trying to inspire
- Remember that people need to trust you
- Have a vision and, in so doing, bring the future into the present
- Create a group sense of ownership of the challenge
- Reduce doubt by demonstrating that you believe in the people you are trying to inspire and that you trust their abilities
- Choose and use positive words and symbols
- Persuade by illustrating a pathway to success.

You can bring your vision to life by talking about the future in the present tense, as Martin Luther King did so movingly in his 'I have a dream' speech. By doing so, you add inspirational clout to your message. Not that you have to lead one of the most important civil rights movements of all time in order to be inspirational, but similar inspirational techniques can be applied when you are trying to encourage others. Creating a picture in someone's mind as to what great could look like can help stimulate him or her to create their own goals related to that picture, and therefore buy into your vision. In painting that picture, language is key. We talked about the power of positive language when we covered influencing skills in Chapter 6 (see pages 105–106) and the same principles apply in inspiration. Taking that one stage further would be to consider using symbols when you are looking to inspire. Symbols can stimulate people both emotionally and cognitively. For example, just showing people a picture of a light bulb (a symbol that for many communicates the notion of 'idea') can trigger insights and ideas for them.[4] Closer to home, the world of elite sport is strewn with symbols –medals, podia, mountains and the Olympic rings, to name just a few. It may be rather a cliché to use these symbols, but you could use or create other symbols that support your inspirational effort.

Sometimes it is helpful to indicate a pathway to success in order to minimise doubt that may be present. However, inspiration is not about providing all the answers. Inspiration works best when there is an unknown and an uncertainty, one that enables people to feel they are part of the solution. Inspiration is even more powerful when it connects people with each other and energises them towards a common

FIG. 10.4 Inspiration is all about what could be

undertaking. So appealing to a collective need and offering a joint sense of purpose can ratchet up your ability to inspire. The added advantage of inspiring with a collective purpose is that it reduces doubt as more people sign up to the vision and feel a common ownership. Especially if you can link that vision to a group or team's collective values and sense of righteousness (see Chapter 7).

Part of that removal of doubt is helping people to believe in themselves and their capabilities when they are challenged or under pressure. Our interviewees have demonstrated this ability throughout their careers. Each one of them has sought to help the people that work for them develop their sense of self-efficacy[5] so that they can achieve more than they might have thought possible.

As well as the above techniques, the prerequisites we have covered elsewhere, such as the building of trust (see Chapters 6, 7 and 8), are critical. You can't inspire people if they don't trust you. You may be able to coerce them or use some form of power over them in order to get them to comply, but they won't do more than what is necessary and will probably begrudge you and your actions as a result.

If you want to inspire and gain loyalty when you are in a leadership position, you must also create the culture that enables people to be inspired. Shared values are a starting point for a positive culture. If you are leading a project or an interdisciplinary team, developing those values together will lay the foundation for your inspirational efforts. With a consensus around these values, you are in a better position to relate your inspirational message to how people's actions can uphold those values.

The inspirational techniques that we have covered will probably not be conceptually new for you, or indeed alien to your own skill set. Identifying the underlying techniques runs the risk of turning inspiration into a science, though it is actually at its best when practised as a spontaneous art. So while it is important to maintain your authenticity by allowing your natural inspirational self to take prominence, understanding the principles involved will help to enhance your skills further.

SUMMARY

We all have the potential to inspire and empower others. In doing so, it is helpful to understand our own sources of inspiration and to be open to further varied and possibly unusual sources of inspiration.

It is hard to imagine being successful within high-performance sport without the inspiration that breathes life into the challenging goals and demands of that environment. Perhaps that is why so many people are drawn to work in elite sport, because it is so inspirational. From the immense efforts of potential Olympic and Paralympic athletes, through to the quiet humility of the coaches and practitioners that support them, there is plenty to be inspired about.

Inspiration is highly emotional and personal, so it can be an incredibly powerful tool when seeking to spur people and teams towards extraordinary efforts. The greatest inspirers use their craft thoughtfully and selflessly, towards a purpose that is worthy and necessary.

But there doesn't have to be a grand cause or movement to call upon our inspirational skills. Inspiration has a positive role to play at the project, team and organisational levels as well. By decoding the riddle of inspiration into its constituent skills, it is possible to understand and develop our own unique and authentic powers of inspiration.

CASE STUDY: MAKING CHANGE HAPPEN

CHRIS PRICE

Head of Physiotherapy, English Institute of Sport

FIG. 11.1 Chris Price

On the Whistler sliding centre track at the Vancouver Winter Olympics in 2010, Amy Williams won gold in the skeleton event. She did so by setting two track records in three runs, eventually winning by a margin of 0.56 seconds. All of this against the backdrop of the horrific death of Georgian luge competitor Nodar Kumaritashvili a few days before on the same track. While not taking any of the credit away from Amy, one of the key people behind her success was physiotherapist Chris Price.

Responsibility and pressure? Perhaps, or perhaps not if you have previously worked in a trauma unit where decisions about life and death are an everyday reality. As with Jurg Gotz, Alison Rose and Dave Clark, there is much to favour some 'slow track' life experiences to help you cope with the perceived pressures of sport.

And sport was always where Chris Price wanted to be, not as an athlete but as a physiotherapist – 'ever since I can remember'. Chris's childhood was immersed in cricket: his mother worked at Edgbaston and both parents were avid fans. As a youngster, Chris spent many hours watching the then England and Warwickshire physiotherapist Bernard Thomas warm up the team prior to matches. Chris decided that this was what he wanted to do when he grew up.

In common with many of our interviewees, Chris describes himself as 'playing sport but not well' (cricket in his case), although he did trial for Warwickshire as a junior. He admits, however, to lacking the deep motivation required to commit to playing cricket a high standard; instead preferring to enjoy the game and the people within it. Away from cricket, Chris made his O- and A-level choices to support his goal of being a physiotherapist. It was not until a few years later when studying at university, as one of only two men on a course with 23 women, that he realised he was a slight oddity – namely, a man in what was then a female-dominated profession.

Undeterred, he graduated, and while sport was an option and a passion, he made a conscious decision to go and explore other areas of the profession. A decision that, although he did not realise it at the time, would provide him with the foundation that was to be so useful in later years. Working within the NHS, Chris spent time working in cardiothoracic surgery, neurosurgery, general medicine, care of the elderly, intensive care and orthopaedics.

His desire for challenge still undiminished, he moved to California to work as a physical therapist, expanding his portfolio of experience still further, working in orthopaedics, open heart surgery and drug rehabilitation and with young people. When asked why, his answer is simple:

> To explore, to see a different culture and way of working. I learnt a lot, especially about myself, about creating relationships and the importance of current friends and family. It taught me how to survive on my own 12,000 miles away in a different place.

Chris goes on:

> I am naturally quite introverted and very comfortable in my own company. While I will happily mingle, I am happy not being in the spotlight. When I first started having to do presentations, it was 'Oh God, here I go'. Now, I accept them and am more comfortable with them. Even still, if I am preparing a presentation I will still go through it 10–15 times to know that I understood the brief, write a couple of drafts, sense-check it with someone, then run through and a final rejig to make sure it gives the message I want it to give.

By 1993 Chris had moved back to the UK and was working in Edinburgh with firmer ideas of what he wanted to do longer term. A third common trait amongst those we interviewed now emerges, that of risk-taking. Something Chris was not averse to doing as he had returned from America with nothing lined up. Rather, he looked for options, ending up working in a hospital in Livingston where he mixed working in community paediatrics with some musculoskeletal sports injuries work.

A fourth and final commonality follows, that of luck or chance leading to greater things. In Chris's case it was a chat with the renowned sports injury consultant Donald McLeod, at the time chief medical officer for the Scottish Rugby Union, and one of the early pioneers in the developing specialism of sports and exercise medicine. As a result, Chris started to work at the sports injuries clinic run by Donald and colleagues John Wilson and Ken MacKenzie at St Johns Hospital.

Working alongside them started to peak my interest in musculoskeletal sports injury problems and while my interest peaked, I also realised that I did not know that much about them. I therefore started doing more work for the Scottish Rugby Union at a private clinic and other sports. Donald McLeod in particular was fascinating to observe and had he a mass of knowledge built up over time. He to me exemplified the point made by Syed in his book *Bounce*,[1] of taking the time to become an expert, gaining experience over time, making a few mistakes and reflecting on them and over time building up that pool of excellence. It was now that I started to make a conscious decision about where I wanted to be.

Reflecting on his somewhat twisting career path Chris says,

I wanted to avoid 'I am a man in physiotherapy, therefore I go into sport,' and I am very glad that I had that broad experience. In the sporting arena if you get smacked in the chest you need that depth to be able to understand the relevant anatomy and physiology and be able to use a stethoscope to listen to the chest if you need to. It makes me a better physiotherapist, having been in trauma and neurosurgery. Personally I think it is important for physiotherapists to get a full grounding across the NHS disciplines before going into sport.

FIRST-HAND VIEW

Chris played a significant role in moving our sport in its infancy in sports medicine, which assisted us in being one of the most successful Olympic winter sports in Great Britain. His professionalism and knowledge in providing the highest level of physiotherapy added massive value to all athletes, who were able to focus purely on their preparation and performance. In addition, Chris assisted in building up a solid sport science and sports medicine structure and helped to link all interacting disciplines, which resulted in strengthening our programme and enabled it to grow and develop to where it is today. If I would paint a picture of Chris, it would be that of 'professionalism' combined with high values and standards, who takes ownership of his actions.

Andreas Schmid
Head of Technical Development, British Skeleton

He goes on to explain:

> For example, ITU (Intensive Therapy Unit) has a great team ethos, you have loads of people all trying to sort out one person, it was an early experience of functioning in a team. This was important as well as the grounding of knowledge. I am therefore very keen for physiotherapists to have worked in the NHS, I really do value the breath of experience that brings.

By 1995 Chris had started to formulate what he wanted to achieve, and it was very much Olympics-focused. When asked why this was so, he replied,

> Why the Olympics? On reflection I wonder whether I was the right personality to work in rugby and football and be successful. For me, a bit like athletes really, the Olympics are the pinnacle.

Chris's next steps towards his goal saw him move to work at a BUPA hospital that had a strong sports injuries connection within its physiotherapy department. Here he gained experience working with a range of sports: rugby, soccer, track and field, and ice dance. But while this was giving him a wide breath of experience, he started to question whether it was leading him to where he wanted to go – the Olympic Games. When in the late 1990s Chris applied to both the British Olympic Association and to British Cycling and did not get an interview, he knew it was time to change. He decided that he needed to go back to university to study sports physiotherapy and to get some more experience working with top-level athletes.

Chris was, as he puts it, seven-eighths of the way to going to Saudi Arabia, to work for a year to save some money and fund a course in Australia, when fate intervened. He had come to the conclusion that, despite loving his job and working with great people who were very knowledgeable, it was not going to get him to where he wanted

FIRST-HAND VIEW

Chris's calm and assured approach reassures the athletes he works with and makes everyone around him feel at ease. This has been most evident during times of stress and pressure at or immediately prior to major events when Chris's presence and assured approach to work has helped everyone feel more confident and in control. Chris's thoughtful and reflective approach to developing and delivering high-performance athletes means that he contributes to all elements of the programme and has often been responsible for identifying significant ways in which it can be developed and improved beyond injury risk reduction and management.

Simon Timson
Head of the England Development Programme/Science and Medicine
England and Wales Cricket Board

to be. He had resigned from his post in Scotland and was doing contract work while waiting for his visa when he received a phone call from Bath University. At the time Chris had no idea about Bath, the university or its drive for sporting excellence. As he now knows, the university physiotherapist had just resigned and Bath was introduced to Chris by a physiotherapy agency.

The rest, as they say, is history. Chris went to Bath, staying on beyond the initial six-week contract. The English Institute of Sport (EIS) was formed, and when Bath became one of the EIS regional sites, Chris started working for the EIS full-time. At the time of our interview, he had become head of physiotherapy for the organisation. What, then, of Chris's initial aim to work for the Olympics? He smiles:

> When I set that goal, the EIS did not exist. The EIS vision is to be the world's leading provider of sports science and sport medicine services and that really resonates with me. One of my personal values is to be the best I can be, so excellence really resonates closely with me.

What of Chris's other personal values?

> A personal value is massively about empowering people around me, and to draw out the best from other people, and to provide them with opportunities and experiences which allow them to develop in the way in which they want to develop.

We ask Chris to expand further on what being a leader means to him:

> Being a good leader or manager is about getting to the nitty-gritty of what people actually want, by observing, listening, discussion, to understand what drives them. Once you have worked this out, you can then match what the team needs with what the individual needs. The best leaders are those that understand the task and understand their people – what does the team need, what do you need, is this going to answer our task? The best leaders that I have had are very good at understanding what the task is and are also very good and understanding their people. They have the ability to listen, to really listen and to understand, to summarise the information and to ask good questions to get to the heart of the matter.

As for himself:

> I believe I am practising these skills and slowly getting better at reading people. I have a degree of emotional intelligence and actively focus on trying to work out what people need. 'Is it more directing or less directing?', for example. Or to be guiding in the outcome; for example, 'this is what I want to happen, off you go'. For me it seems to roughly work on a continuum linked to experience, although there are still times when you have to say to relatively senior people 'This is the way it is going to be' or to give a framework to

relatively junior ones and let them go off and use their skills. It's situational leadership and I think I am getting better at matching the style and approach to the task!

At this point Chris explains a deeper reasoning behind his earlier stint in America:

My introversion is driven by self-reliance. Going to America meant that I had to spend three to four months building a new life, where I did not know anyone and had to try to create relationships. This definitely helped breed self-reliance and toughing it out. The leadership role I am now in means I have had to consciously leave my introversion behind. Some people might be quite surprised that I am quite introverted, I do not fit the traditional model of leadership, which is 'this is the way it is going to be'. But then when I look around me, the good leaders I see do not follow that trend. When I first stepped into the role (as national physiotherapy lead) I was conscious that I now oversaw 60 people and that I needed to seek out and build relationships with a large number of people, something that was not an overly natural process for me. But having done that I am now in a position where I do not have to consciously think about that. Has it made me a different person? Probably outwardly, but the inner values remain the same.

On having leadership responsibility, Chris continues:

I have had poor managers, ones who would one day be up and the next they would be down. Ones who when they were stressed, you did not want to be around. My current role has strengthened my view that good leadership hugely directs and dictates people's enjoyment of work. A good leader and manager can flex their style between 'This is the task, this is what I want you to do' and giving you the flexibility to find your own way to achieve it. Poor leaders are ones who are divorced from what is happening on the ground and have no ability to communicate with the team and do not know how to and have no ability to relate to their staff. They can still be a lovely person, but do the staff feel they can go to them with problems? I was very introverted, but I have worked hard and found a way around this. I continually like to know and check what is happening on the ground and using that to gauge if things are going well. That is really important for me to know, even if I am not the one who can solve it.

So what type of people would work well with Chris as someone who is fair, democratic and has a fair degree of humility?

Yes, I think I am all those things, but in being democratic, I am also having to learn to fanny around less, giving greater clarity regarding goal, outcome and timelines. While it is therefore good to be fair, humble and democratic; if people leave feeling, 'Well, what was that all about?', then that is a waste of time.

FIG. 11.2 Chris and Amy Williams, the latter on the way to Olympic gold

FIRST-HAND VIEW

One particular incident that sticks in my mind happened about a year before the Vancouver Olympics. Chris and I were together one evening, after a evening sliding session, in the dark at the lakeside near to the ice track in Koenigssee, Germany. We had to break the ice covering the surface of the lake in order for me to stand in the freezing water for two minutes as part of my regular recovery routine. None of the other athletes wanted to do it – no surprise! As he stood there with his stopwatch, Chris was giving me words of encouragement and keeping me focused on what I was doing and why I was doing it, while I stood there shivering! He said something like: 'When you are standing on that podium in Whistler, you will think back to times like this and be grateful that the discomfort and effort were all worthwhile.' I have never forgotten that, it sums up Chris. He is totally committed to each athlete and knows how to bring out the best in each of them.

Amy Williams
Olympic gold medallist

What else does he value?

What else I really value from my senior staff is innovative ideas. I would say that I am squarely in left-brain thinking; I am incredibly logical and methodical and very analytical. My creative juices do not flow, so I have a couple of staff who are more right-brain thinking, asking different questions, which I value hugely. And I do not like 'yes' people – if people think I am talking rubbish, I would like to think that they would tell me so.

There is no greater time than an Olympic Games to require clear and directive leadership. Chris also notes that it is a time for honest reflection:

It is about understanding your own strengths and weaknesses and acknowledging, 'if I am not so good at that and there is someone over there who is, then I can switch my ego off and align behind whoever is best for a particular role'. Within the skeleton programme, we had role clarity, which developed over time with frequent practice. There was clarity about 'this is what you do, and also this is what you do not do'.

As Chris talks, it is obvious that much thought had gone into the programme, with a group of different personalities all coming together around Chris, the 'introverted coordinator'. What was key, however, was that they were all there to win a gold medal, each member aiming to be the best they can be at what they do.

High-performing teams are never easy beasts, as Chris notes:

It was not all rosy and all wonderful. We did have to stop and have a sense-check 12–18 months out from the Games: 'How are we communicating and functioning as a team?' De [Deirdre Angella, see pages 127–135] did a lot of work with the team on personalities and how best to communicate with each other, and while it did not change how we worked with each other, the primary thing for me was to know when to back down, i.e. recognising when to back off in a group who are in each others' pockets six months of the year.[2] De worked with us on basic principles so that, for example, 'when you see this, you can communicate with me and you can communicate with me in this way'. Another example was to be positive and be all about performance. For me it was 'I do not mind' as I was the coordinator and did not mind when people came to me.

Going into the Games, the team benefited significantly from this teamwork, building prior trust, respect and meticulous planning:

In Vancouver on the second day of training, Micky, the head coach, was ill. We had previously agreed that if you were ill you not only said so but you also moved out, so that is what Micky did, he took himself out of the team. Because of the prior planning, everyone knew what their new role was to make sure all the gaps were covered, and we all shifted seamlessly.

History records that the outcome was successful.

What about Chris's time at the Games: how did he cope personally being a man who loves the outdoors and finds his release in running, walking and cycling?

In Vancouver, we did not have built-in time to exercise. However, we did spend a lot of time carrying kit and equipment to and from the track. Understanding the Olympic environment is key and having been to Turin (the 2006 Winter Olympics) really helped me cope with Vancouver – for example, there was one colleague who was not chilled while we waited for the 30-minute delay to start times. He was like I had been four years before; pacing up and down all the time. For me because of the planning and preparation done before Vancouver, I was more chilled and calmer.

CHAPTER 11
MAKING CHANGE HAPPEN

From when William Temple first put the dimples on a golf ball in 1908, via Greg Lemond's 1989 Tour de France victory with aero-bars and through to the polyurethane panels on swimsuits at the Beijing Games in 2008, elite sport thrives and indeed depends on innovation. Athletes, coaches and whole sporting systems find that they have to keep innovating just to maintain their current competitive position. This 'Red Queen effect'[3] means that the leading Olympic and Paralympic nations are in an innovation arms race to develop and introduce even the smallest of advances that will keep them competitive (as, of course, are the sports technology and clothing suppliers). As one very well-known successful performance director often says: 'If we stand still, others will beat us.'

But it is not only sports technology and equipment that are fertile areas for innovation. Athletic techniques, coaching techniques, sports science and medicine, and talent identification are all areas of continuous improvement. In terms of athletic technique, you have probably heard of the Fosbury flop, the 'back-first' technique introduced by Dick Fosbury, which revolutionized the high jump and won him gold at the 1968 Olympic Games in Mexico City. But have you heard of the shot put cartwheel technique? While it was certainly innovative, it was also questionably advantageous, possibly amusing and probably dangerous. The technique, as with so many others, has not survived the rigorous challenge of becoming the accepted gold standard. One more recent innovation that did was the use of the dolphin kick in swimming, frequently described as swimming's fifth stroke; what started out as seemingly unusual behaviour by one swimmer is now 'must do' if you want to be successful. As you can imagine, many other innovations fail to make it to the world stage of elite sport. It is, after all, a competitive world, even for innovations. Most innovations are culled early on as either impractical, unwieldy, or simply because they offer no performance advantage. In addition, if they are perceived to give too much of a competitive advantage, distorting the event from human endeavour, or are dangerous, the international governing bodies may ban them (such as polyurethane in swimsuits from 2010 and tri bars in cycling road races).

This chapter explores some of the processes and techniques that can help you both to innovate and, more importantly, to successfully introduce change into the services you provide. We'll first look at techniques that can help the innovation process and then we'll describe a change model to help you plan the introduction of your innovation. The difference between *innovation* and *change* may seem academic, but for our purposes here *innovation* occurs when you have a problem or opportunity that you think will have a positive outcome, though you cannot be completely sure. *Change*, on the other hand, occurs when you have a clear outcome in mind and the challenge is to identify the tasks and processes that will help to introduce that change.

FIG. 11.3 Elite sport thrives on innovation

Before we start, it is worth bearing in mind the crucial principle that operates before innovation and change are even contemplated: get the basics right first. Unless the core performance factors of coaching, athlete fitness (including being injury-free) and skill are in place, the impact of most innovations will be unfeasible or unsustainable. The really good coaches and applied practitioners spend substantial time understanding and developing the basics of their profession and service. Next, they take those basics to the world-class level. Then they innovate.

BEING INNOVATIVE

Innovation doesn't have to be restricted to the headline advances of sports technology and athlete equipment. Arguably, just as much impactful innovation can be credited to the everyday improvements made within the coaching and applied practitioner arenas. Our interviewees value such innovation. See, for example, Chris Price's discussion above of his innovative 'right-brained' senior staff, compensating for his own logical, analytical 'left-brain thinking' (see page 187).

Others provide examples of their own work to illustrate this point. Dave Clark explains how he introduced a change to the cyclists' squatting technique in the gym, which contributed a positive performance impact (see page 25). Dave also revealed the innovation he made to the canoeists' gym work when he highlighted how they could more closely replicate the full roster of the paddler's propulsive move. In his interview, Paul Brice explained how he developed and introduced his 'critical determinants of performance' (CDP) model (see page 62). That innovation is now widely used in athletics as an assessment, training and recovery tool. Alison Rose uses innovation on a near daily basis in order to fix chronic and complex problems, drawing on related techniques such as Pilates as well as her own visualisation skills to help design interventions that will lead to improvement or help prevent injury. Ali also comments how much she learns from her athletes, reinforcing the point that athletes are an important source of innovation.

Nigel Mitchell risked professional isolation in order to achieve buy-in to his innovative approach to performance nutrition. It helps that Nigel's default attitude is one of curiosity and determination to constantly improve, as is recognised by many in the elite sport system. James Collins, director of Performance Nutrition and Arsenal FC nutritionist says

> Nigel has always been a leader. He has constantly challenged best practice, where other practitioners may be content to keep with the status quo, which has ultimately lead to the growth of the discipline.

Although the performance advantage of our interviewees' innovations may have been obvious to them, none were easy to introduce. There is often resistance to change, even when the rationale for doing so is strong. An example of this is the story told by Alison Rose about getting the Olympic diving coach, Adrian (Ady) Hinchliffe, to buy into her innovative proposals (see page 79). Ady now says of Ali: 'It was not long before I knew I had found a keeper in a team we have been working hard to develop in British Diving for the High-performance Training Centre.'

TECHNIQUES

Many people consider that 'being innovative' is more of an attitude than a process. Indeed, innovation is also often held as an individual and organisational value.[4] Here it is worth noting that a scientific training can sometimes dampen an individual's innovative tendency. The reductionism of the scientific method can lead people to focus too narrowly, seek solutions too quickly, and be uncomfortable with some techniques such as brainstorming. Whereas innovation is all about 'What could be?', the scientific approach is more comfortable with 'What is'.

However, there are some techniques that can help to foster an innovative attitude: curiosity; abstracting; brainstorming; exploring; experimentation; assessing and reasoning. Before we discuss some of these techniques in more detail, it should be noted that they do not form a linear process, as innovation rarely happens in straight lines.

For some, being curious is a natural attitude, but for the rest of us it is also a technique that can be developed. Many of our interviewees are simply curious about so many areas. They are constantly exploring and asking themselves and others the question 'Why do we do it like this and not like that?' Just a quick read of the interviews with Alison Rose (see pages 74–83), Dave Clark (see pages 18–26), Jurg Gotz (see pages 163–171), Paul Brice (see pages 55–64) and Danny Kerry (see pages 198–206) will give you an idea of how successful people often have a strong curiosity. They are senior coaches and practitioners who are known for their curiosity and their ability to ask really incisive questions. Asking questions fairly early on in the innovative process can help to provide some focus and to save time. Questions that need to be asked include 'What is the performance parameter that we are trying to impact?' and 'Are there other more important determinants of performance that we should be investigating?' That early focus is essential when time and money are finite, although it is also important not to close down curiosity and lines of investigation too early.

Abstracting is a useful technique in the innovation process. It involves a sharp observation and analysis of all the factors that contribute to a performance and then reduces them to the critical ones, as illustrated by Paul Brice's CDP model (see page 79). This is likely to be an iterative process as you identify key factors, their relationships and patterns. By discovering the critical factors, you reveal the opportunities where innovation is likely to make the biggest impact. With that direction, a creative phase to generate ideas and possible solutions can follow, often achieved with some form of brainstorming exercise, during which all the ideas are collected together, however wild and silly they may seem. The time to narrow these down comes later; what is most important at the first stage is capturing everyone's ideas. An evidence-based approach to exploring and experimenting can then help to assess which solutions stand up to the competitive environment and which ones will potentially yield a reliable performance gain.

On a day-to-day basis, innovation can be as simple as doing something that someone else is doing, but better. This is often how the small increments in the quality of your service or process can provide the marginal gains that help an athlete reach the podium. You don't actually have to reinvent the wheel to make a performance impact. Alternatively, innovation can be about applying what someone else does in another sport or arena to your work. This is fertile ground for innovation. That is why there is a great deal of emphasis on sharing knowledge and understanding across sports within the UK and other national elite sport systems. This sharing is also encouraged within the coaching and sports science domains, as these professionals are well placed to introduce techniques from one sport to another.

THE CHANGE PROCESS

Most innovations do not reach the field of play, let alone offer a clear-cut contribution to the sheer hard work and talent apparent in an athlete's performance. But the marginal gains of those few innovations that do evolve into best practice are worth the casualties of the hundreds that falter prematurely. But even those are not failures: their development provides useful understanding as to what did not work and why, as well as a valuable experiential process for the innovator.

Many innovations do not make it past the pilot stage because there is considerable resistance to their introduction. While it is true that elite sport is culturally less content with the status quo than many other sectors, there is reluctance to take risks with sporting performances that are believed to be working well. This is particularly evident in the last year of the Olympic and Paralympic cycles, as sports seek to minimise the potential risks associated with unproven innovations.

Being innovative is admirable, but making change happen as a result of that innovation is impressive. Thomas Edison once said that 'Genius is 1 per cent inspiration, 99 per cent perspiration', a warning well worth considering if you want to inspire an actual change in a product, service or process. Making change happen can be the 99 per cent hard graft. When you are looking to introduce your change successfully, it is often helpful to use a model of change as a guide to the key steps involved. Using such a process can also help to minimise some of that graft. As there are so many models of change available, we'll select one that has been useful for people working in elite sport.

That model is Kotter's eight-stage process:[5]

- Stage One in this model is to establish a sense of urgency. The premise being that significant change happens only when there is a real need to take advantage of an opportunity or to solve a problem. Otherwise, people often accept the status quo either through complacency or because of concern about the risk of change.
- Stage Two is to gather the right team behind the change you are seeking to make. The right people in terms of the skills, motivation and influence to drive the change through. As we discussed in Chapter 7, this team can work best when the members trust each other and they have an emotional commitment to the change (as also discussed in the previous chapter).
- Stage Three is to create a positive vision of how the service or process will be after the change as well as the performance impact that will make. Again, this principle has links to the previous chapter on inspiring others.
- Stage Four is to communicate with all interested parties to get buy-in. Paul Brice talked about the importance of this stage when he was rolling out his CDP model.
- Stage Five is to convert buy-in to action, as Paul Brice's launch of his CDP model also illustrates. This stage is all about enabling people to benefit from the change you are proposing. Paul gained wider use of his model by seeking scrutiny from experienced coaches. Once those coaches were persuaded of the model's benefits, they became users of the model: support was converted into action.
- For Stage Six, achieving quick-wins is the key focus. This is because creating momentum behind any change initiative is vital to its early acceptance and eventual success. So it is important to communicate the success of those quick wins in order to build confidence behind the change.
- Stages Seven and Eight are respectively about continuing that momentum and making the change stick. Successful changes are achieved when people are persuaded by both the logic and the emotional appeal of realising opportunities or avoiding dangers. When the process introduced by the change become routine, you know you have achieved a substantial element of your change goal.

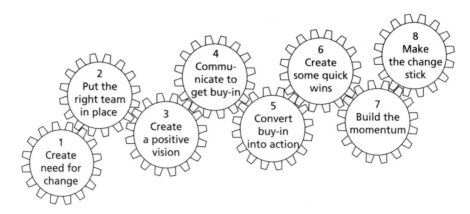

FIG. 11.4 Kotter's eight-stage process of change

The above change model may have been designed more with large-scale process and organisational changes in mind, but many of the stages are relevant for even small changes that we wish to make when trying to support the athlete or sport. Achieving successful change is first about understanding what performance benefit would be brought by the change. With that clear message established, it is then sensible to plan both the stages of introduction and a communication strategy. Knowing whom you have to persuade and how to persuade them will make introducing your change much easier and more successful (see Chapter 6). When the change is underway, it is important to communicate early progress to all those involved and affected, in order to build confidence in the process and gain momentum towards a positive outcome. Try the exercise in the box 'Planning change' to help you see how to apply this model to changes that you would like to make.

PLANNING CHANGE

The table below provides a brief description of Kotter's eight stages of change. The example provided is where a coach wants to change the formation of his hockey team from 5–3–2 to 4–4–2, because of recent defeats and a lack of high-quality forwards.

Once you have read through the stages and example, think about changes you might introduce and use the table to plan them with the eight-stage model.

Stage	Example *Hockey team formation change: 5–3–2 to 4–4–2*	Your own plan
1. Create the need for change and add a sense of urgency	Gather some performance analysis of strengths and weaknesses of existing formation. Present the team with some data on the success of the new formation when used by competitors. Raise awareness about the reality of insufficient forwards and the likelihood of further losses if the formation remains the same.	
2. Put the right team in place to support the change	Convince your support coaches of the arguments so that they support you. Give each coach a role in persuading and reassuring the team members of both the need and the opportunity of the change.	
3. Create a positive vision of the benefits of the change	Describe the strengths of each team member and how they have the potential to perform even better with the new formation. Talk about the victories won by other teams using the 4–4–2 formation against your competitors.	
4. Communicate to get buy-in	Talk to as many of the squad as possible to reassure them and demonstrate your belief in their potential within the new formation. Ask supportive squad members to help get other squad members on board.	

Stage	Example *Hockey team formation change: 5–3–2 to 4–4–2*	*Your own plan*
5. Convert buy-in into action	Manage those with concerns sensitively and positively. Persuade them of the benefits. If they are resistant, give them a role in critiquing the new formation, so that they feel part of the change and are not isolated.	
6. Create some 'quick wins' in order to build momentum	Set up some practice sessions that are likely to demonstrate the potential of the new formation. Use the strengths of specific players in the new key positions to show what is possible. Organise a friendly game with a competitor you believe the team have a good chance of winning with the new formation.	
7. Continue the momentum with more changes	Build on success in practice and competition with further positive sessions. Review progress with the team and focus on the positives, while being open and realistic about the challenges.	
8. Make the change stick by reinforcing and communicating the benefits	Keep talking with the team. Make 4–4–2 seem normal to them, but keep the flexibility to change back to 5–3–2 when needed or other formations.	

SUMMARY

Elite sport is changing all of the time, so nobody can afford to stand still. That is why many sports embrace and engage with the ever-changing uncertainty of the competitive landscape. Continuous change is not only the culture, it is also the currency of elite sport. You may recall from the interview with Pete Cunningham (see page 36) the quotation attributed to Albert Einstein on the wall of the RYA Performance Centre in Portland: 'The definition of insanity is doing the same thing over and over again and expecting different results.' This means that the world of elite sport provides some great opportunities for those who are interested in being innovative in their careers and seeking progress through change.

But there is little appetite for innovation for innovation's sake. Before any innovation and consequent change comes a critical stage: getting the basics right. This adage applies equally to our own skills as it does to the more exotic innovations you might see on a yacht or track bike. Raising our basic skills, processes and services to a world-class level provides the necessary foundation for innovation and change.

Innovation for some is a state of mind. Driven by their constant curiosity, they innovate in every sphere of concern and influence that they have. This doesn't preclude the rest of us from realising our creative potential, as there are some proven techniques behind the innovative process, as covered above.

However, innovation is only part of the performance impact story. For an innovation to be successful, it has to be implemented, and that takes change. Meaningful change on any level is not easy, as there is often a cultural and sometimes behavioural resistance to letting go of the status quo. People, teams, systems and organisations need reasons to believe in change, and those reasons aren't always logical. The rational reasons are either associated with taking advantage of a performance opportunity, or reducing the risk of failure of the status quo. The emotional reasons for change are often more important and certainly more complicated. That is why it is important to advocate the potential of change in terms that will engage people with both the logic and the vision. By adopting a change process, such as described in the model above, we are more likely to transform a positive outcome of change from one of chance to one of choice.

DANNY KERRY

Head Coach, GB and England Women's Hockey

FIG. 12.1 Danny Kerry

How can a national team coach be successful when, by his own admission, he struggles to connect and bond with his players, let alone understand what is going on in their heads? That is the question which Danny Kerry found himself asking after the Beijing Olympic Games. Following a disappointing campaign that left Team GB's women's hockey team out of the competition at the group stage, there were bound to be questions raised. There were none tougher than those Danny asked of himself. Through the detailed, and at times painful, review process, Danny came up with answers that involved learning to reach out to the players as people and to pay more attention to what made each of them tick.

Applying the solutions was a great deal more challenging. However, one of the characteristics that his players and colleagues recognise about Danny is his perseverance. That determination, and some radical logistical and cultural changes, led to the team moving from eighth to fourth ranking in the world over the following 24 months. The team then made history in February 2012 by reaching their first final in the Champions Trophy, the sport's third most prestigious event. Kate Walsh, the most-capped GB and England player, said in 2011:[1] 'One of the things we learned from last year's competition was that there's a really fine line between the top teams – the margins are very small.'

How to overcome those margins requires some very precise thinking, and Danny Kerry is a very precise man. Danny chooses his words thoughtfully and with deliberate reflection as we meet within GB Hockey's inner sanctum at Bisham Abbey. Throughout the office, there is a purposeful atmosphere that more than hints at the ambitious and methodical campaign that underpins the friendly and warm welcome given by Danny and his team. But Danny is not a man who indulges in complacent satisfaction. He is too driven and too self-critical to relax before the ultimate prize is won. Even then, you get the impression that the hunger will remain, for by his own admission Danny is a perfectionist. Where did this concoction come from? Well, it can't do much harm to have a sport-loving family with a father who had a love of running and squash, and a brother two years older who showed early promise as a hockey player. Danny's drive and competitive spirit, however, were nurtured outside of the sport so familiar to him now:

> I was a gymnast from the age of four through to 11. I was getting towards the national squads as a youngster. I did an awful lot very young.

If it weren't for his gymnastics coach turning up late one afternoon, hockey might never have known Danny Kerry. For while waiting, Danny was invited to join his brother's hockey practice session. Reflecting on that experience, Danny recalls an early differentiator, a significant theme in Danny's coaching philosophy that we will return to later:

> As a gymnast (in the nascent days of hockey warm-ups), I could do the splits and stick my legs around my head and this impressed the coach who, wanting his young hockey players to embrace the benefits of flexibility, said, 'Look everyone, this is what stretching is about!' I knew I was onto something!

FIRST-HAND VIEW

I have been coached by Danny Kerry since 2005, since when there have been lows and highs on the field. One thing that has never waivered is my belief in Danny and what we do. Danny's meticulous eye spots things that others may not even think about, his thorough and professional approach makes me try and emulate that in my training. You would never have to ask Danny what he wants to achieve; if you work with him you can see it.

Alex Danson
GB Olympic Hockey Team

So Danny's hockey career started with a *Billy Elliot*-style moment that caught the attention of someone who happened to be a national hockey coach. The versatile young gymnast also found hockey appealing: a team game without the presence of superstar egos. While Danny Kerry is not devoid of a healthy ego, he certainly is not the kind of man who needs it to be constantly pampered. He presents as a man who doesn't need to shout about his skills; quite the opposite, he could well be mistaken for the quiet man of hockey.

Danny was certainly not quiet as he ventured onto the pitch. He couldn't afford to be: an early start to Danny's Hockey career meant that at school he honed his skills with players who were a couple of years older, so he had to make his voice heard. And it was here at school that Danny came into contact with the first of a number of key influencers on his life – Ken Gregory, his PE teacher. Like many of the time, Ken gave up his time to support his pupils as well as having 'good values and morals. He was competitive, but a gentleman.'

This environment nourished his competitive spirit and ambition, such that by his early teens he was playing against adult teams. Hours of purposeful practice supplemented many a match playing for Pelicans, Peterborough and Wakefield. Danny joined Southgate at the end of his first year at university, playing alongside some of the GB Olympic medal winners of 1988. This was a professional environment and the one that Danny had been looking for in his drive to play senior international hockey.

By his third year at university, Danny's coaching career started, as he became captain and by default the coach of the men's team. Here he experienced for the first time the leadership conflict between being popular and sticking to his own value system. With time, as the enjoyment of playing declined and the opportunity of a full international cap passed, Danny made the conscious decision to move fully into coaching, in his words to 'prove he could do it'.

What were the early influences on Danny's approach to coaching? One significant influence was the coach who invited Danny to join his brother's hockey session.

> He was very different to anyone I'd ever come across. He was a perfectionist by anyone's standards. He would see things from a very left-field perspective and have a hugely different logic to everybody else. I found that very curious.

In particular, this approach reinforced in Danny the need for sound technique based on knowledge and process.

> His coaching sessions were highly, highly technical. Everything was about precision and practised to the nth degree.

So Danny developed a very analytical methodology to his coaching. Even at that time Danny had a genuine enjoyment of helping people to grow in challenging environments. However, tactics and technique largely won out over people and potential at that stage in Danny's career, and the technical emphasis still permeated the coaching philosophy that Danny took on the plane with him to Beijing in the summer of 2008: 'I was going to defeat the world by knowledge and process.'

Danny's first Olympic Games turned out to be quite a bruising occasion:

In Beijing, my first experience as head coach, I was put through the mill. We had so many things go on. Everyone says these things go on at the Olympic Games and you think, 'Really? Things can't be that bad, surely.' But it was! You name it, everything happened. There are things that I had to handle as a young first-time head coach that you wouldn't wish on your worst enemy.

This is where Danny reflects on the likelihood that knowledge and process, as important as they are, only get you so far, especially when you are under the stress and scrutiny of an Olympic Games. In order to thrive and perform in that pressure-cooker environment, you need to be able to foster your team's hopes, diminish their concerns and inspire them with the right word of encouragement at the right time. And yet, these are the critical skills that can be first to fade when we are under pressure:

I handled the challenges, but the interpersonal skills and self-checking, those things were even more forgotten because I was so involved with the pressure of everything going on.

Things all came to a head at the post-games review:

In my review, I got absolutely hauled over the coals for all the interpersonal relationship side of things. Although it hurt at first, with time and reflection I could appreciate that what I wasn't doing in Beijing was walking out of my room and talking to my staff, the athletes, putting an arm around a shoulder here or there when needed. I was too busy in my room working on the analysis and process, on how to play against Argentina in the next game. As a result, the team and staff saw me as someone who was just driven and not interested in them.

To be fair, the review also concluded that tactically, technically, and with strategic planning and programming, these were all excellent. It is just that they didn't see the people-side of my skills.

Danny accepts that this feedback helped him understand that he needed to broaden his coaching skills:

The feedback hurt, because I really do care about people, although I obviously wasn't showing it and they just weren't seeing it. So I then worked incredibly hard to take and show a real interest in other people. I constantly work on this and realise that it takes a long time to change perception.

Given Danny's analytical inclination, it is not surprising that he took a very purposeful approach to understanding and mastering a range of interpersonal skills. He studied a wide range of material on interpersonal skills, leadership and change. In particular, Danny was drawn to some of the models that describe how different personalities can

FIRST-HAND VIEW

I have been fortunate to work with Danny as his assistant coach since 2005. During that time I have witnessed him grow, not just as a coach and a leader but also as a person. Danny took the team to the Olympic Games in 2008. The results and top six finish would have been deemed a success to most people; however, for Danny they became a watershed and turning point in his coaching career. An intelligent and deep thinker, Danny self-reflected and the resultant changes he has made in his leadership and coaching style has led to the successes the team has enjoyed over the last two years.

Karen Brown
Assistant Coach, GB Women's Hockey

work well with each other. These models confirmed Danny's analytical preference and his comfort zone within the world of match statistics and tactical analysis. No surprises there, but the exercise also helped Danny to better understand the reasons and motivations behind some of his behaviours. He worked out why he felt more comfortable withdrawing from people and into numbers before the team's encounter with Argentina, rather than engaging with the energy and concerns of his own team players. The detachment was intensified by the fact that the majority of those players resided on almost the opposite end of the personality spectrum to Danny. When events were going well, these players were outgoing, positive and fun. However, when the pressure was on, these same players benefited from a more reassuring, nurturing and inclusive style. This style was not naturally within Danny's repertoire. That is not to say he didn't care about each and every player, just that he didn't express it when that reassurance was perhaps needed more than ever.

Matters improved dramatically after applying some of the insights gained. Indeed, with some further studying and help from his team psychologist, Danny developed his 'Golden Thread' strategy. The Golden Thread defined the values, culture and behaviours that all of the women's hockey team, coaches and support staff could buy into. This was essential in developing the self-awareness and openness that enabled the team to be more honest with each other. They had direct and sometimes difficult conversations, knowing that they were all working with the honest intention of getting the most out of each other and the team. Slowly an environment of trust was built, one that successfully translated to the ultimate test of the 70 competitive minutes on pitch.

This focus on the human side of coaching complemented the process and technique elements of Danny's coaching philosophy. Indeed, Danny's coaching philosophy has evolved and continues to evolve from the early influence laid down by the national coach from Danny's early years.

Because he was such a perfectionist in terms of technique, I very much bought into that at a young age. I've come much further away from that now. I'm much more looking for the differentiators and potential in people.

FIG. 12.2 Danny giving the team feedback

Danny's coaching is now just as much concerned with nurturing strengths, as it was with fixing technical weaknesses. Danny extracted some of these key principles from the thresholds and differentiators model, inspired by the work of Daniel Goleman[2] and Malcolm Gladwell.[3] Central to Danny's coaching philosophy is the creation of the practice environment, because that is when most of the skills progression and tactical development is achieved. The practical specificity of each practice session now has a couple of significant components: decision-making and retention.

> I used to have a huge drive on technical detail, but then wondered why it failed in competition. The reality was that it didn't have decision-making built into it, so any technique practised now develops perceptual motor skills and not just motor skills.
>
> The other part of the practice environment is that we want retention, such that what we practice we deliver under match conditions. The way we've gone about that, after the practice we consolidate by asking the athletes specific questions such as 'What did you want to achieve, what actually happened?' We are trying to achieve *cognitive overload* and thereby increase retention. We're trying to make them have the thinking, rather than the coaches have the thinking. We do see now much better retention. So what happens in the practice environment, we do see the athletes carry to the pitch.

Danny summarises the essence of his current coaching philosophy: 'Get the practice environment right and keep on raising the athletes' (and staff's) self-awareness.' Something Danny believes is just as important for the practitioners and coaches that work for him, as it is for his athletes' performance. Danny now has a team of 17 coaching and support staff: he must also lead the team behind the team. This is demonstrated when Danny is recruiting new members to his team, as many of his questions are centred around self-awareness. Danny wants to know how well the practitioner is aware of their own behaviour and attitudes when in the presence of elite athletes. Does the practitioner pay attention to the professional boundaries that need to exist between elite athlete and staff members? As he noted, practitioners who are used to being the 'alpha male' in a group will frequently struggle to succeed in a support-focused role.

Changing the practice environment and helping the whole team to develop self-awareness, have by no means been the only changes Danny has achieved during his tenure with England and GB Hockey. The single biggest change that Danny strived for, stressed and eventually achieved was the centralisation of the women's programme to Bisham Abbey. Having all the squad working in the same training environment on a regular basis was the most important advance in the programme as far as Danny was concerned. So much so, that Danny had been working on this strategy since 2006, well before the Beijing Olympic Games in 2008, because he was convinced that fundamental change was absolutely necessary if the team were to win medals at the highest level:

> In every other Olympic cycle to date, athletes had been distributed all around the country. The fact is that we are judged on our ability to play in a team. And yet the performance practice environment was nothing like that. It was small clusters of people distributed all around the country. Fundamentally we weren't doing stuff as a team, so our level of team understanding on all sorts of levels wasn't where it needed to be in order to win medals.

Beneath the principle of improving team cohesion and performance by working together in one location lay the inescapable fact that the athletes had established lives where they currently lived. Tough choices were needed and Danny knew very early on that this was going to require his leadership skills to be at their best. Remembering Danny's analytical preference, it is not surprising to hear that he did his homework before he took action.

> So I immersed myself in literature, workshops and spoke to experts about change! Armed with that I took a two-prong approach. Firstly, I 'drip-fed' the seed of the idea very early on in 2006 so that people could 'smell it coming'. I got the need to centralise into people's conversations and onto the agenda, so people knew it was coming. I was well aware that it would take time. The initial point was to get them to come round to the idea: what it would mean for them and what it would need for performance? But on a really, really subtle level.
>
> Then in early 2008 I thought that the time was right. We had a heavy programme in 2008, so that the athletes could see the benefits of being together a lot more. The time was ripe to talk about what if we don't change, what are the risks and what are the things that are preventing us from changing.

The second approach was to appeal to the athletes on an aspirational level, of what I believed could be achieved through change. I wanted them to see the benefits beyond Beijing.

While keeping the team focused on the Beijing Games, Danny made it very clear that he would seek to centralise the programme after Beijing. When the decision time came, an interesting challenge arose for Danny, which highlighted for him the importance of creating an environment where people could be honest about their views. The team members had clearly indicated broad support for the centralisation to Danny himself, but the opposite was true when providing feedback to the performance director's post-Beijing review panel. Many of the athletes' contended to the panel that they 'had told the coach what he wanted to hear' when it came to their view on centralisation.

'They don't want it, Danny, they don't want to centralise!' That was the conclusion handed down to Danny by the review panel, one that left him disconcerted if not disappointed. He was disappointed in the implicit value system that permitted one view to be expressed in public and another effectively in private. This reinforced further his determination to create and weave the 'Golden Thread', whereby trust was built in the team based on shared values and the confidence for each team member to 'say it as it is'. Danny wanted to create a team that was more honest about and within itself. Then maybe they could take the joint risks that were necessary to get them on the podium without undermining each other, unwittingly or otherwise.

Despite the initial judgement of the review panel, it was obvious that the review process did not canvass all the athletes' views, only those who had issues with the proposal. A vociferous minority had determined the strategy. So in Danny's view the conclusion didn't represent the breadth of opinion on the matter, but he let the matter rest while he pursued the Golden Thread strategy. As it turned out, in early 2009 the athletes came to Danny and said, 'Where's the centralised programme?' The majority speaking up in this way meant that centralisation could proceed, albeit nearly a year later than needed.

With that green light, Danny set about the centralisation strategy in earnest. Danny focused on providing the vision and gave the athletes the space to air their concerns and thrash out the detail themselves as to how the whole programme could be

FIRST-HAND VIEW

One of Danny's main attributes as I see it is the ability to work on himself and seek advice on areas that he feels needs improvement. That introspection in a balanced way is immensely powerful to the quality of self-reflection and awareness, thus ultimately impacting his influence on performance.

Tom Cross
Sports psychologist

centralised and refined. The manner in which Danny expressed his vision of the change reveals the flexibility of expression he had developed. There was a time when the analytical Danny would have sold the move with facts, data and all the logic he could muster. While the logic didn't disappear, Danny flexed the manner in which he sold his vision by speaking from the heart and used the emotion of 'what could be achieved' to appeal to the more expressive natures of the majority of his athletes. This was authentic and easy for Danny to express to his athletes, because that is actually how he felt about it.

> What use is it aspiring just to be an Olympian? We're funded to win medals. You aspire to medals! Look at the sports that win medals, look at cycling, look at rowing, look at sailing – they all have centralised programmes. And we're a team sport, think of what we could achieve if we were together!

So now the passion and energy of the team is centralised at Bisham Abbey and the sense of cohesion and optimism almost seeps out of the walls of HQ England and GB Hockey. Centralisation and the Golden Thread are starting to produce the podium places and medals that the team are capable of achieving.

CHAPTER 12
TAKING RESPONSIBILITY

As you progress through your career, you may well look back with increasing clarity on the character, skills and experiences that have helped you to reach the heights of your achievements. If you are in a leadership role already, you will no doubt have experienced critical junctures and moments of truth that revealed to you the essential values and motivation that make you the leader you are. Your reflections will most likely show that your self-awareness combined with many of the skills we have covered in this book, will have served you well in delivering to a consistently high standard under some very challenging conditions.

Alternatively, just because you may not yet be in a leadership role, that doesn't mean you haven't displayed leadership qualities. Even as a young coach or applied practitioner, you will have led the delivery of some elements of the programme you are working in. If you haven't done so already, you will probably lead the development or introduction of new coaching techniques or a support intervention at some stage. You will then have to draw on your existing leadership skills, even though you may not have a leadership title or explicit leadership role. For leadership does not develop from having a title or a role, it emanates from the values, behaviour and influence of the individual. That is why everyone can develop and provide leadership. But not everyone chooses to step up to the mark, because while leadership can be very rewarding, it is also highly challenging.

The greatest challenge any leader will face is to take responsibility. Responsibility is about being accountable and answerable for the goals we set, the actions we take to achieve those goals and the choices we make along the way. A leader in any high-performance system and particularly within an elite sport system has to take responsibility for all the decisions taken by themselves and by those in the organisation that they lead. In that sense, leadership is not any easier when targets are met and medals are won, compared to when performances are way down on expectations. Although leaders may not be given credit for the former, they certainly have to take responsibility for the latter. With that principle, performance directors can find themselves in the same situation as football managers and quickly lose the support of their NGB or funding agencies if the athlete results disappoint.

This chapter explores the critical leadership principle of taking responsibility, which applies to both leaders and those who wish to demonstrate leadership potential.

THE RESPONSIBLE LEADER

If you have read through the interviews this book, you will have noted that our interviewees have held themselves answerable in all their endeavours. Some of our interviewees have faced very interesting options, possibly fortuitous for some, but all of them have taken responsibility for the outcomes of the related choices that they made.

For example, Dave Clark uprooted his family on at least two occasions when he pursued roles in other countries. He took responsibility for the possible disruption that this caused for his family and subsequently made it a priority to achieve stability in terms of location and schools as he consolidated his career. Jared Deacon's choice to speak out during a reorganisation put him in direct opposition to his employer (see pages 7–8). But Jared went ahead and took responsibility for his actions, when others kept silent. After the bruising experience of the Beijing Olympic Games, Danny Kerry took responsibility and first of all looked to himself and his own behaviours, rather than blame others (see pages 201–203). Nik Diaper took responsibility for the feedback he received after he was rejected for a job (see pages 149–150). It was challenging feedback to receive, but he took it on board and resolved to change his behaviour so that he came across more as he wanted.

All of the interviewees have displayed a leadership characterised by taking responsibility for everything that they do, however uncomfortable that may have been for them at certain times. They have all talked about times when they have taken responsibility for their goals, actions and choices. Some also described how they take responsibility for how they feel and how they look after themselves, especially under the pressure of major competitive events. Every one of our interviewees gave examples of taking responsibility to initiate significant and calculated change to help their athletes keep ahead of the field. Other people also commented on their ability to take responsibility: Simon Timson (Head of the England Development Programme/Science and Medicine, England and Wales Cricket Board) says of Chris Price:

> He is a clear and decisive decision-maker, a quality that is highly valued by the athletes, coaches and managers Chris works with … This generates confidence in Chris, his work and judgement. He is not afraid to take big decisions and always does so with the very best interests of the athlete and team in mind.

Alex Natera (strength and conditioning coach, English Institute of Sport) says of Deirdre Angella: 'I certainly recognise De as a leader in the way that we deliver our services to sport and ultimately how we focus our attention on impacting on performance.'

Above all, the 12 people featured in this book took responsibility for the direction they chose in life and did not blame others for the decisions they made along the way. The blame game is all too easy in the high-pressure world of elite sport. Reputations, egos and livelihoods are at stake; so many may be tempted to lay the liability of failure at someone else's door. The reality is, however, that allocating blame and achieving excellence are mutually exclusive undertakings. As American Football coach, Lou Holtz put it: 'The man who complains about the way the ball bounces is likely to be the one who dropped it.' Blaming is a defensive exploit, whereas taking responsibility needs proactivity in the key areas described opposite.

THE SEQUENCE OF TAKING RESPONSIBILITY

When a leader accepts responsibility for their actions and those of whom they lead, they send a strong message that they are fully committed to facing the challenges, accepting the duty and ready to account for the successes and failures alike. Figure 12.3 below summarises the key aspects of the sequence of taking responsibility.

FIG. 12.3 Taking responsibility sequence

Start with self

A leader has to take responsibility for his or her own performance, self-awareness and well-being. All of our interviewees talked about the importance of keeping themselves fit and well in order to maintain focus and efficiency of effort. For many, that means being aware of their energy levels and regular active recovery: taking a break every now and then and thereby preventing exhaustion and burnout. This is discussed further with examples from our interviewees in Chapter 9.

Set the vision

A leader is responsible for the development of a vision for their team or organisation. Translating that vision into a team purpose with the accompanying focus, goals and priorities is also the leader's responsibility. Successful leaders realise that while it is important to obtain team engagement in setting these, the responsibility for their achievement ultimately rests with themselves.

Achieve the targets

Leaders are ultimately responsible for achieving the goals or targets that are set on the basis of the vision. There are many examples of leaders in sport, business and politics who don't accept that 'the buck stops here' when results fail even their own expectations. But this is not an argument for wide-scale resignations of leaders who apportion blame elsewhere; rather, it is an invitation to consider the importance of maintaining credibility and the support of those who follow. Most leaders who try to persevere after they fail to take responsibility for the targets they have set, lose the support of their team, their organisation and their stakeholders (e.g. sponsors, funding agencies) far sooner than they realise.

Keep people aware

Leaders also lose support when they avoid responsibility for communicating with their teams about the major issues. Leaders can retain the focus and drive of their teams by proactively and honestly communicating with them about progress, reiterating the purpose of the team and maintaining the morale during challenging periods. Leaders who don't take responsibility for communicating can find that their teams are distracted by speculation and even gossip, with misunderstandings, confusion and conflict not far behind. By providing clarity and reinforcing direction in such situations, leaders demonstrate that they are taking responsibility and not blaming the distraction on their team.

Be a role model

Perhaps the greatest responsibility a leader has is to set an example for those whom they lead. A leader's behaviour is a signal of what is acceptable in the team or organisation's culture. Through his or her values and consequent actions, the leader is the one who offers or withholds implicit or explicit permission for their team's behaviour. In other words, team members can think, 'If the leader can behave like that, so can I' – the alternative, of course, being double standards. In setting an example, effective leaders know that their behaviours actually resonate and intensify through the team's actions. Therefore, the leader's behaviour needs to set a higher standard than that of their team, in order to provide a positive challenge for their team's behaviour. This can cause confusion and difficulty for some coaches and practitioners when they first move into leadership roles. For although they aspire to be a leader, there can be the temptation to act as they did when they were not leading, particularly when it means you are now leading those who were previously friends and colleagues. While maintaining authenticity and consistency in our behaviours is central to successful leadership, leaders have to take more responsibility than that. Very simply, as a leader you cannot behave as 'one of the gang' and expect the continued respect of your team when the difficult times inevitably emerge. Acting as one of the gang can lead to a false impression of friendship, the dangers of which we covered in Chapter 8 (see pages 137–138). While leaders can be friendly with team members, being their friend will result in confusion as loyalties become misplaced or misinterpreted. An effective leader takes responsibility for managing their relationships with team members in a close but professional manner that is consistent to all team members and at all times. It may be a difficult transition if the leader has previously been a friend to the team members, but many people, including our interviewees, are able to combine professional leadership with personal friendship. Jared Deacon reflects on this area in his interview when talking about the change in his relationships with the athletes that he coaches: when he became a professional coach, he maintained professional relationships with his athletes without becoming over-friendly (see page 7).

However, such transitions can sometimes cause a sense of isolation for the leader, one that a successful leader takes responsibility for and manages.

MANAGING ISOLATION

As you progress up the ladder in any organisation, there are fewer people that you can connect with in terms of what it is really like to be in your role. As the saying goes, 'it is lonely at the top'. When Danny Kerry returned from the Beijing Games and had to rebuild the team, he felt a sense of isolation. But he decided to take responsibility for that and sought to connect with other senior and head coaches across the elite sport system (see pages 201–202). Although they may be distant from their team in some important ways, there is no need for any leader to isolate him or herself from reality. Yes, it is easier to make the crucial selection decisions when you are not best friends with key players, but a leader also needs to know what the mood and morale of their team is like. So a difficult balancing act is required between being genuinely supportive, curious and friendly on the one hand, and maintaining a professional relationship on the other. For some, it is easier to keep a distance altogether, even though it runs the risk of excessive insulation from what is really going on in their teams. However, a leader can take responsibility for managing their isolation with these three main approaches.

It is good to share

Connecting with people at the same level as you or higher across different sports can help you to develop a broader perspective. You may not be surprised to hear how many times your challenges are the same challenges faced by people in other sports. Even though your peers may not have the answers for you, it is refreshing to know that you are actually not alone. Pete Cunningham reflected on this point during his interview:

> You tend to get a little isolated … as you go up the tree, there are less people to connect with I am always conscious that we are a little bit isolated. So I try to keep connected and still speak to my original mentors occasionally, such as Tudor Hale. We also have a senior sports science group across the sports, that meets now and then to share information and views.

It is good to talk

Many leaders benefit from having a completely independent advisor, sounding board or mentor – or whatever you want to call them. Essentially, that is someone with

FIG. 12.4 Leadership: determined resolve with humility

whom they can discuss their thoughts; someone who has no vested interest in the outcome of the leader's success or failure, other than to celebrate or commiserate with them. With a mentor, a leader can talk about their nascent ideas before they are sufficiently mature to introduce to peers, managers or their teams. A mentor can also help a leader sense-check their insight into different situations, in order to increase the rigour of their decision-making. Finally, a mentor can help a leader hold themselves to account and take responsibility without the leader being concerned that they are being judged.

As well as having a mentor, a leader can benefit from being a mentor. This is a role which Paul Brice (case study Chapter 4) has recently taken on with two new applied practitioner recruits to UKA.

It is good to appreciate

While a leader should have the self-awareness to recognise the strengths that took them to a leadership role, they should also appreciate the likelihood that other people helped them get there. Not remembering those who helped you on the way up is a great way to generate some reticence and even resentment from those who were supportive of your efforts and loyal to your cause early on in your career. It can then get very lonely, particularly if you hit a bad patch or find you could benefit from additional support. This can be prevented by some simple recognition, appreciation and humility.

We did not select our interviewees for it, but they all turned out to display a considerable humility when they told their individual stories. Without prompting, every interviewee acknowledged the colleagues, friends, leaders and mentors that had helped them in their careers. Some commented that remembering and appreciating the people who had helped them kept them grounded and authentic. Even though all of our interviewees take responsibility in their leadership, they are very different leaders; which supports the contention that there is no one right way to lead. What is important is that the leadership is authentic.

THE AUTHENTIC LEADER

We proposed earlier that a person might have to adapt some aspects of their behaviour when they move into a leadership position or role. That is not to say that leaders should fake behaviours, or wear a mask for their leadership. Rather, it was to point out that successful leaders model the behaviours they want their team to display. That can be achieved by flexing existing behaviours, as opposed to adopting new ones that would not be seen as genuine.

To be an authentic leader is to know and understand yourself as well as your team and to act in ways that are consistent with your fundamental character and the values you hold. Authentic leadership is all about self-awareness, the ability to know when you are being honest, when you are being the 'real you'. That still leaves room for versatile behaviours to influence and inspire people, as long as they are consistent with your values. Some people interpret authentic leadership as being more about the person and less about the leader,[4] inasmuch as it is the integrity of the person from which the leadership qualities of insight, ingenuity and influence arise.

The authentic leader has much in common with the leader that takes responsibility. Foremost is their desire to live their values, which guide their goals, behaviours, choices and decisions every day. Very evident is their lack of need to pretend; they just are who they are and are both comfortable and confident in being so. You will not see any affectations in authentic leaders, as they have an acceptance of who they are. That is not meant to imply they no longer seek to develop themselves – far from it. But authentic leaders are able to be themselves and do not seek to act out their leadership. In any case, that approach requires much less energy and is a good deal more rewarding.

DEFINING YOUR LEADERSHIP QUALITIES

Here is an exercise to help you think about your own authentic leadership qualities.

- Firstly, whom do you consider as authentic leaders? Think about and write down the qualities and traits that make them authentic leaders to you.
- Once you have the list, think about how those qualities and traits match your own.

In our work with coaches and applied practitioners, we help them develop a performance profile of themselves, using criteria such as the qualities they see in leaders that they admire. Often these are qualities and skills that can be developed. So consider creating your own performance profile and include on the criteria the qualities from the list you made above. Then check the rest of the book to read further about developing some of these skills, such as communication, influencing and inspiring.

Authenticity and honesty are close cousins and both help a leader take responsibility for the outcomes of their goals and actions. However, an authentic leader needs to be wise about total honesty, because a leader cannot always be open about everything he or she knows. Such complete and open honesty would be counterproductive in the competitive world of elite sport, where competitive advantage often rests on confidential information.

Authentic leadership means that while the person is the leader, the leader is not necessarily the person. Just because you are a leader at work does not mean that you have to be a leader at home or outside of work. For one thing, work is a different context and those outside of work may not take too kindly to being led all of the time.

SUMMARY

Leadership is difficult work, but it can also be rewarding. If you are interested in leadership, you may be reassured to know that you do not have to be born with specific leadership traits in order to discover your capacity to lead. You can uncover that potential by developing the skills we have covered in this book. When others start to notice those skills in your work, they will recognise the leader in you. While you need the opportunity to lead, it is best not to wait until leadership taps you on the shoulder. Seeking leadership is a great way to bring your leadership skills to life. That doesn't have to be in an explicit leadership role, as elite sport provides many opportunities for coaches and applied practitioners to display leadership in other roles.

The hallmarks of the successful leaders we have interviewed for this book are their willingness to take responsibility and their authenticity. Taking responsibility as a leader means avoiding the blame game and seeking first to understand both successes and failures through the impact of your own vision, goals, choices and behaviours. Responsible leaders communicate proactively with their teams and athletes to minimise misunderstandings and keep their team's efforts on track. In taking leadership responsibility, there is a risk that leaders can become isolated and out of touch with what is really happening on the field of play. But leaders can take responsibility for and seek to minimise that isolation: by keeping themselves connected and challenged by peers and possibly even by a mentor or a trusted colleague.

Leaders who take responsibility stay true to who they really are: they are authentic. As an emerging leader or someone who is already in a leadership position, you will find it much easier and more enjoyable to draw on your self-awareness, character and values as an inspiring and enduring source of your leadership.

NOTES

CHAPTER 1: KNOWING YOURSELF

1. Daniel Coyle proposes that 'ignition' is often required to achieve a motivational state that can sustain you through many hours of deep and purposeful practice. Apart from deep practice and ignition, Coyle suggests that a third factor is needed to realise talent: Master Coaching. Interestingly, Jared was coached from an early age by his elder brother, who would probably have known Jared well enough to challenge him in an effective manner. Coyle, D., *The Talent Code: Greatness Isn't Born, It's Grown* (Bantam Dell, 2009).

2. This principle is explored by Daniel Coyle (ibid.), who talks about 'deep practice', referred to as 'deliberate practice' by other authors. It is also an echo of the principle that 10,000 hours of devoted effort are required to become an expert, as proposed by Anders Erikson ('The Making of an Expert', *Harvard Business Review*, July–August 2007) and popularised by Malcolm Gladwell in his book *Outliers: The Story of Success* (Little Brown and Company, 2008).

3. Church, A. H., 'Managerial Self-Awareness in High-Performing Individuals in Organizations', *Journal of Applied Psychology*, 82(2) (1997), pp. 281–292

4. Rosete, D., and Ciarrochi, J., 'Emotional Intelligence and Its Relationship to Workplace Performance Outcomes of Leadership Effectiveness', *Leadership and Organization Development Journal*, 26(5) (2005), pp. 388–399. Buckingham, M., and Clifton, O., *Now, Discover Your Strengths: How to Develop Your Talents and Those of the People You Manage* (Pocket Books, 2009). Actually, as this latter book argues, it is far more effective to develop your strengths, rather than focus on improving your weaknesses (unless they are 'mission critical').

5. Goleman, D., *Emotional Intelligence: Why It Can Matter More Than IQ* (Bloomsbury, 1996).

6. Bar-On, R., Handley, R., and Fund, S., 'The Impact of Emotional Intelligence on Performance' in Druskat, V., Sala, F., and Mount, G., (eds), *Linking Emotional Intelligence and Performance at Work* (Lawrence Erlbaum, 2006), pp. 3–19. Neale, S., Spencer-Arnell, L., and Wilson, E., *Emotional Intelligence Coaching: Improving Performance for Leaders, Coaches and the Individual* (Kogan Page, 2011).

7. Lupien, S. J., Maheu, F., Tu, M., Fiocco, A., and Schramek, T. E., 'The Effects of Stress and Stress Hormones on Human Cognition', *Brain Cognition* 65(3) (2007), pp. 209–237.

8. Church, A. H., 'Managerial Self-Awareness in High-Performing Individuals in Organizations', *Journal of Applied Psychology*, 82(2) (1997), pp. 281–292.

9. Pease, A., and Pease, B., *The Definitive Guide to Body Language* (Orion, 2004).

10. Lorimer, R. and Jowett, S., 'Empathic Accuracy in Coach–Athlete Dyads Who Participate in Team and Individual Sports', *Psychology of Sport and Exercise*, 10 (2009), pp. 152–158.

11. Scheier, M. F., and Carver, C. S., 'The Self-Consciousness Scale: A Revised Version for Use with General Populations', *Journal of Applied Social Psychology*, 15 (1985), pp. 687–699.

12. Schön, D., *The Reflective Practitioner: How Professionals Think in Action* (Basic Books, 1983).

13. Marchel, C. A., 'Evaluating Reflection and Sociocultural Awareness in Service Learning Classes', *Teaching of Psychology*, 31(2) (2004), pp. 120–123.

14. Butler, R. J., 'Psychological Preparation of Olympic Boxers' in Kremer, J., and Crawford, W., (eds), *The Psychology of Sport: Theory and Practice* (British Psychological Society, 1989), pp. 74–84.
15. Brown, K. W., and Ryan, R. M., 'The Benefits of Being Present: Mindfulness and Its Role in Psychological Well-Being', *Journal of Personality and Social Psychology*, 84(4) (2003), pp. 822–848.

CHAPTER 2: VALUES INTO PRACTICE

1. The combination of deep humility combined with a determined will is referred to as 'Level five leadership' by Jim Collins. It is one of seven characteristics that drive an organisation into higher performance (as deduced by Collins from his research). Collins, J., *Good to Great: Why Some Companies Make the Leap ... and Others Don't* (William Collins, 2001).
2. Massey, M., *The People Puzzle: Understanding Yourself and Others* (Reston, 1979). Massey described three phases of value development: Imprint (up to the age of 7), Modelling (ages 8–14) and Socialisation (ages 15–21).
3. Massey also described Significant Emotional Events (SEEs): ibid.
4. Pomeroy, L., in Edwards, R .B. (ed), *The New Science of Axiological Psychology* (Rodopi, 2005).
5. Lyle, J., *Sports Coaching Concepts: A Framework for Coaches' Behaviour* (Routledge, 2002).
6. Lencioni, P., *Five Dysfunctions of a Team* (Jossey Bass, 2002).
7. EIS values: collaboration; innovation and excellence.
8. **sport**scotland institute of sport values: continuous performance improvement; performance with integrity; individual and collective responsibility; openness and mutual respect; an asset to our nation; innovation; and leading through quality.
9. Rath, T., *Strengths Finder 2.0* (Gallup, 2007). This is a very useful text (with an accompanying online tool), which helps you identify your strengths. The focus is on developing your strengths, rather than on resolving your weaknesses, as that can lead to dissatisfaction and mediocrity.
10. Ofman, D., *Core Qualities: A Gateway to Human Resources* (Scriptum, 2002).

CHAPTER 3: MOTIVATION AND DIGGING DEEP

1. Attributed to Albert Einstein.
2. At the Barcelona 1992 Games, the GB Sailing team won one bronze medal, placing ninth on the sailing medal table. The performance improved at the Atlanta 1996 Games with two silver medals, again placing the team ninth on the Sailing medal table. Performance significantly improved in Sydney 2000, with the team winning three gold medals as well as two silvers, placing them top of the Sailing medal table.
3. Team GB won four gold medals, one silver medal and one bronze medal to lead the medal table at the competition held in Qingdao.
4. Keegan, R., Spray, C., Harwood, C., and Lavallee, D., 'From "Motivational Climate" to "Motivational Atmosphere": A Review of Research Examining the Social and Environmental Influences on Athlete Motivation in Sport' in Geranto, B. D. (ed.), *Sport Psychology* (NovaScience Publications, 2010), pp. 1–55.
5. Vallerand, J., 'Intrinsic and Extrinsic Motivation in Sport', *Encyclopedia of Applied Psychology*, 2 (2004), pp. 427–435.

6. Deci, E. L., and Ryan, R. M., *Intrinsic Motivation and Self-Determination in Human Behavior* (Plenum, 1985). This is a much-cited book in this area.
7. Deci, E., and Ryan, R., (eds), *Handbook of Self-Determination Research* (University of Rochester Press, 2002).
8. Deci, E. L., and Ryan, R. M., 'The "What" and "Why" of Goal Pursuits: Human Needs and the Self-Determination of Behavior', *Psychological Inquiry*, 11 (2000), pp. 227–268.
9. Latham, G. P., and Locke, E. A., 'Self-Regulation through Goal Setting', *Organizational Behaviour and Human Decision Processes*, 50 (1991), pp. 212–247.
10. These are referred to as approach and avoid goals. Elliot, A., 'The Hierarchical Model of Approach–Avoidance Motivation', *Motivation and Emotion*, 30(2) (2006), pp. 111–116.
11. Dweck, C. S., *Mindset: The New Psychology of Success* (Ballantine, 2007). This makes for an interesting read on mindsets and how we can control them to achieve our potential.
12. Pink, D., *Drive: The Surprising Truth about What Motivates Us* (Cannongate Books, 2011). Daniel Pink looks at the motivational drive delivered by a need for mastery, autonomy and purpose.

CHAPTER 5: CONNECTING WITH OTHERS

1. Hallowell, E. M., 'Managing Yourself: What Brain Science Tells Us about How to Excel', *Harvard Business Review*, 88 (2010), pp. 123–129.
2. Pease, A., and Pease, B., *The Definitive Book of Body Language* (Orion Books, 2004).

CHAPTER 6: INFLUENCING OTHERS

1. Areni, C. S., and Sparks, J. R., 'Language Power and Persuasion', *Psychology and Marketing*, 22(6) (2005), pp. 507–525.
2. Areni, C. S., and Sparks, J. R., 'Style Versus Substance: Multiple Roles of Language Power in Persuasion', *Journal of Applied Social Psychology*, 38(1) (2008), pp. 37–60.
3. For further reading in this area, search online for Roger Bailey's work with meta-programmes.
4. Knight, S., *NLP at Work* (Nicholas Brealey Publishing, 2004).
5. Lorimer, R., and Jowett, S., 'Empathic Accuracy in Coach–Athlete Dyads Who Participate in Team and Individual Sports', *Psychology of Sport and Exercise*, 10 (2009), pp. 152–158.
6. Arnold, E., and Underman-Boggs, K., *Interpersonal Relationships: Professional Communication Skills for Nurses*, 5th edn (Saunders, 2007).
7. Pease, A., and Pease, B., *The Definitive Guide to Body Language* (Orion, 2004).
8. You may have come across models such as MBTI (Myers-Briggs), Insights and OCEAN. An interesting read of the OCEAN model is: Barondes, S., *Making Sense of People: Decoding the Mysteries of Personality* (Prentice Hall, 2011).
9. Bolton, R., and Bolton, D., *Personality Styles at Work* (Amacon, 1996).
10. Quite a contentious area with regards to the validity and reliability of learning style models. If you are interested, one example is: Kolb, A. Y., and Kolb, D. A., *The Kolb Learning Style Inventory, Version 3.1*. Technical Specifications (Hay Resources Direct, 2005).
11. The VARK model developed form the work on NLP. Technically, this is a *Representational Systems* model, rather than a *Learning Styles* model – though the two are often conflated. Hawk, T. F., and Shah, A. J. 'Using Learning Style Instruments to Enhance Student Learning', *Sciences Journal of Innovative Education*, 5(1) (2007), pp. 1–19.

12. HBDI (Hermann Brain Dominance Inventory) assesses brain hemispheric processing and further extends this to a metaphor for cognition and learning. However, there is not a strong line of evidence behind the proposed lateralization of cognitive tasks. Indeed modern neuroimaging studies suggest just the opposite. Hines, T., 'The Myth of Right Hemisphere Creativity', *Journal of Creative Behavior*, 25(3) (1991), pp. 223–227.

CHAPTER 7: WORKING IN A TEAM

1. 'Before, During and After: Making the Most of the London 2012 Games', Department for Culture, Media and Sport (DCMS) Legacy Action Plan, June 2008.
2. Peters, S., *The Chimp Paradox: How Our Impulses and Emotions Can Determine Success and Happiness and How We Can Control Them* (Vermillion, 2012). Dr Steve Peters is Team Psychologist to British Cycling and Team Sky.
3. Argyle, M., *The Psychology of Interpersonal Behaviour*, 2nd edn (Pelican, 1972). Argyle proposes four stages in his theory of group dynamics: forming, storming, norming and performing. In the forming stage, members of the group get to know one another by sharing knowledge and ideas. It can be a very lively stage of the process. The storming stage occurs next, when members possibly compete for influence and leadership. Others may be uncomfortable with frank conversations and possibly conflict, so they may withdraw. This is a critical stage for teams, as trust is either won or lost here. The norming stage is when the team settles into an agreed approach and style with the focus on agreement but also, perhaps, compromise. If the team reaches the performing stage, it is working optimally and is best placed to achieve its goals.
4. Belbin, R. M., *Management Teams: Why They Succeed or Fail*, 2nd edn (Elsevier Butterworth-Heinemann, 2004).
5. Lencioni, P., *Five Dysfunctions of a Team* (Jossey Bass, 2002).

CHAPTER 8: MANAGING WORKING RELATIONSHIPS

1. Csikszentmihalyi, M., *Finding Flow: The Psychology of Optimal Experience* (Harper Perennial, 2008).
2. Thomas, K. W., and Kilmann, R. H., *Thomas-Kilmann Conflict Mode Instrument* (Tuxedo, 1974). Another model is Elias Porter's Strength Deployment Inventory, which draws on his theory of 'Relationship Awareness' and the underlying motivational value system that drives our behaviour when things are going well and during conflict. Porter, E. H., *Strength Deployment Inventory* (1971, 1996, Personal Strengths Publishing).
3. Morgeson, F. P., and Humphrey, S. E., 'The Work Design Questionnaire (WDQ): Developing and Validating a Comprehensive Measure for Assessing Job Design and the Nature of Work', *Journal of Applied Psychology*, 91(6) (2007), pp. 1321–1339.

CHAPTER 9: PERFORMANCE UNDER PRESSURE

1. Peters, S., *The Chimp Paradox: How Our Impulses and Emotions Can Determine Success and Happiness and How We Can Control Them* (Vermillion, (2012). Peters is Team Psychologist to British Cycling and Team Sky.
2. These include the personality models Bolton & Bolton, MBTI (Myers-Briggs) and Insights.

3. Berne, E., *Games People Play: The Psychology of Human Relationships* (Penguin, 2010).
4. Loehr, J. and Schwartz, A., *The Power of Full Engagement* (Free Press, Simon & Schuster, 2005).

CHAPTER 10: INSPIRE TO EXCELLENCE

1. Vince Lombardi's son wrote a book about his father and his inspiring leadership qualities: Lombardi Jr, V., *What It Takes to Be No. 1: Vince Lombardi on Leadership* (McGraw-Hill, 2001).
2. Zenger, J. H., Folkman, J., and Edinger, S.K., *The Inspiring Leader: Unlocking the Secrets of How Extraordinary Leaders Motivate* (McGraw-Hill Professional, 2009).
3. George, B., Sims, P., McLean, A., and Mayer, D., 'Discovering Your Authentic Leadership', *Harvard Business Review* (February 2007), pp. 129–138.
4. Slepian, M. L., Weisbuch, M., Rutchick, A. M., Newman, L. S., and Ambady, N., 'Shedding Light on Insight: Priming Bright Ideas', *Journal of Experimental Social Psychology*, 46(4) (2010), pp. 696–700.
5. Bandura, A., *Self-Efficacy: The Exercise of Control* (Freeman, 1997).

CHAPTER 11: MAKING CHANGE HAPPEN

1. Syed, M., *Bounce* (HarperCollins, 2010)
2. During the competitive season, the team are on the road together for up to six months, travelling around the circuit, staying in low-key accommodation, living and working together 24/7.
3. The *Red Queen effect* is the phenomenon whereby you have to keep innovating just to maintain the status quo. The phrase originates from *Alice's Adventures in Wonderland* by Lewis Carroll (Macmillan, 1865):
   'Well, in our country,' said Alice, still panting a little, 'you'd generally get to somewhere else – if you run very fast for a long time, as we've been doing.'
   'A slow sort of country!' said the Queen. 'Now, here, you see, it takes all the running you can do, to keep in the same place. If you want to get somewhere else, you must run at least twice as fast as that!'
4. UK Sport, and its technology partners in conjunction with many national governing bodies, has a track record of researching and developing significant advances in sports and athlete equipment. UK Sport has a dedicated team of research and development professionals. Similarly, the English Institute of Sport has 'innovation' as one of its three core values and invests considerable resources into sports medicine and science innovation.
5. Kotter, J. P., and Cohen, D. S., *The Heart of Change: Real-Life Stories of How People Change Their Organizations* (Harvard Business School Press, 2002). Kotter reprises the same principles in his more recent book: Kotter, J. P., *Our Iceberg Is Melting* (Macmillan Press, 2006).

CHAPTER 12: TAKING RESPONSIBILITY

1. Interview with Kate Walsh by Ben Baker, www.morethanthegames.co.uk, 4 May 2011.
2. Goleman, D., *Working with Emotional Intelligence* (Bloomsbury, 1999).

3. Gladwell, M., *Outliers: The Story of Success* (Penguin, 2009).
4. George, B., Sims, P., McLean, A., and Mayer, D., 'Discovering your Authentic Leadership', *Harvard Business Review* (February 2007), pp. 129–138.

ACKNOWLEDGEMENTS

The authors would like to thank all those who so freely gave their time, expertise and honest reflections when being interviewed. Without you, there literally would be no book. This book also arises from the privilege of being able to work over the years with the many talented coaches, administrators and practitioners within the UK high-performance sport system. We thank all of the leaders, previous participants and mentors on the numerous development programmes we have been involved with over the last 20 years.

Our thanks go to Hester Brierley and colleagues at the English Institute of Sport, staff at **sport**scotland institute of sport and Artemis racing, who helped with photos. Also to Kirsty Schaper and Nick Arcroft at Bloomsbury who have supported and encouraged us with our vision for the book.

Tim Kyndt would also like to thank: Dr John Briffa for his invaluable advice while writing this book; Annette Kyndt, whose courage and devotion to professional excellence have been an inspiration; and Ben Gifford for his enduring support and wise counsel.

Sarah Rowell would also like to thank Andy Peace for his unending support and patience.

Tim Kyndt
Sarah Rowell
www.behindthemedals.com

AFTERWORD

High-performance sport is an impressive showcase of exceptional people doing exceptional things. This is true not only of athletes, but also of coaches and sports-science and medicine practitioners. A career in this field demands not only cutting-edge technical skills and knowledge but also highly developed non-technical skills. In recent years, the UK sports system has maximised the opportunity to invest and develop such people. *Achieving Excellence in High Performance Sport* captures the philosophy, approach and practice – and indeed the fascinating personal stories – of the some of the UK's leading coaches and practitioners. Through a series of case studies, Kyndt and Rowell highlight the values, attitudes, skills and behaviours that underpin excellence in this field and, in doing so, provide a very valuable insight and resource for those training for careers in high-performance sport.

Ken van Someren, PhD, FBASES
Director of Sport Sciences
English Institute of Sport

INDEX

Page numbers that include an f refer to figures or illustrations and those with an n refer to notes.